The United Nations World Water Development Report 2019

LEAVING
NO ONE BEHIND

Published in 2019 by the United Nations Educational, Scientific and Cultural
Organization, 7, Place de Fontenoy, 75352 Paris 07 SP, France

This report is published by UNESCO on behalf of UN-Water. The list of UN-Water
Members and Partners can be found on the following website: www.unwater.org.

ISBN 978-92-3-100309-7

Suggested citation:
WWAP (UNESCO World Water Assessment Programme). 2019. *The United Nations
World Water Development Report 2019: Leaving No One Behind*. Paris, UNESCO.

Original cover design by Phoenix Design Aid

This publication is printed in vegetable inks on FSC Mixed Sources paper, supporting
responsible use of forest reserves, 100% recycled, acid-free and chlorine-free.

Contents

Foreword

by Audrey Azoulay, *Director-General of UNESCO*

Access to water is a human right: it is vital for the dignity of each and every individual.

The 2019 edition of the World Water Development Report focuses on the theme of "Leaving No One Behind". It argues that fulfilling the human rights to safe drinking water and sanitation for all can also significantly contribute to the achievement of the broad set of goals of the 2030 Agenda for Sustainable Development: from food and energy security, to economic development and environmental sustainability. Based on the latest data, this report's findings clearly illustrate the need to make substantial progress towards delivering on the 2030 Agenda promise of reaching the most vulnerable.

The stakes are high: nearly a third of the global population do not use safely managed drinking water services and only two fifths have access to safely managed sanitation services. The intensification of environmental degradation, climate change, population growth and rapid urbanisation — among other factors — also pose considerable challenges to water security. Furthermore, in an increasingly globalised world, the impact of water-related decisions cross borders and affect everyone.

At the current pace of progress, billions of people will remain unable to enjoy their right to access to water and sanitation and the multiple benefits that such access can provide. Yet, this report concludes these objectives are entirely achievable, so long as there is a collective will to do so, entailing new efforts to include those 'left behind' in decision-making processes.

This latest Report, coordinated by UNESCO, is the result of a collaborative effort of the UN-Water Family and was made possible thanks to the long-standing support of the Government of Italy and the Umbria Region, to whom we are extremely grateful.

I am convinced that the 2019 edition will spur action and help support Member States in making informed decisions to build more resilient, more peaceful communities, leaving no one behind.

Audrey Azoulay

Foreword

by Gilbert F. Houngbo, *Chair of UN-Water and President of the International Fund for Agriculture Development*

The 2030 Agenda for Sustainable Development calls on us to transform our world and leave no one behind. The 2019 edition of the United Nations World Water Development Report demonstrates how improving the management of water resources, providing access to safe and affordable drinking water and sanitation for all contribute to the goals that underpin the 2030 Agenda. Water for all is essential for eradicating poverty, building peaceful and prosperous societies and reducing inequality.

The numbers speak for themselves. As the Report shows, if the degradation of the natural environment and the unsustainable pressure on global water resources continue at current rates, 45% of global Gross Domestic Product and 40% of global grain production will be at risk by 2050. Poor and marginalized populations will be disproportionately affected, further exacerbating already rising inequalities.

The 2019 edition looks at different dimensions of inequality linked to food and nutrition, disasters and migration, drawing on data and information from the UN family and others. For example: if women had the same access as men to productive resources – including land and water, they could increase yields on their farms by 20 to 30%, raising total agricultural output in these countries by 2.5 to 4%. This could reduce the number of hungry people in the world by around 12 to 17%. Further, the overall risk of being displaced by disasters has doubled since the 1970s. The depletion of water and other natural resources is increasingly recognized as a driver of displacement that triggers internal and international migration.

The 2019 Report provides evidence of the need to adapt approaches, in both policy and practice, to address the causes of exclusion and inequality. This is key to ensuring the availability and sustainable management of water and sanitation for all.

To build knowledge and inspire people to take action, UN-Water commissions UN-Water publications such as the UN World Water Development Report drawing on the experience and expertise of UN-Water Members and Partners. Thanks are due to all my colleagues, and especially to UNESCO for coordinating the production of this Report that will contribute to greater sustainability and resilience, and to creating a world where no one is left behind.

Gilbert F. Houngbo

Preface

by Stefan Uhlenbrook, *UNESCO WWAP Coordinator*
and Richard Connor, *Editor in Chief*

The 2030 Agenda for Sustainable Development sets a series of ambitious challenges for the global community. These Sustainable Development Goals (SDGs) include targets for access to safe drinking water and sanitation and better water management, as well as goals for addressing inequality and discrimination, including the overarching aims of 'leaving no one behind' and 'reaching the furthest behind first'. These are challenges that, to date, have proven difficult to meet, partly because they are complex, but also due to political inertia. The global context for this agenda may be characterized as 'crisis is the new normal', with political insecurity, social, economic and environmental challenges on a daunting scale. This calls for redoubled efforts and carefully selected approaches towards achieving transformative change.

The issues underlying both water-related goals and leaving no one behind intersect in several ways. Both water supply and sanitation, and issues of equality for all people and for specific disadvantaged groups in particular, are recognized through international human rights instruments and agreements. However, these have not been enough to bring about the necessary changes. To some extent, the issues share both root causes and similar challenges. The same people who are being left behind are those who could benefit most from improved access to water and sanitation. Improved access to water and sanitation, water management and governance, and the multiple benefits they bring, can contribute significantly to positive transformation for marginalized people. Benefits include better health, savings in time and money, dignity, improved access to food and energy, and greater opportunities in terms of education, employment and livelihoods.

These benefits, directly and indirectly, separately and in combination, contribute to improving the lives of all, but can be particularly transformative for people in vulnerable situations. At the same time, engaging with marginalized groups can enhance the achievement and sustainability of water-related goals. This process of engagement can also be transformative in giving a voice to those rarely heard, in turn creating space for vital water-related knowledge and experience that might otherwise be lost.

As the sixth in a series of annual, thematic reports, the 2019 edition of the United Nations World Water Development Report (WWDR) examines how improved water resource management and access to water supply and sanitation services can help address the causes and alleviate the impacts of poverty and social inequity. It provides insights and guidance in helping identify 'who' is being left behind, and describes how existing frameworks and mandates, such as the 2030 Agenda and the SDGs and human rights-based approaches, can help 'reach the furthest first', through improved water management.

The report assesses the issues and offers potential responses from technical, social, institutional and financial perspectives, while taking account of the many different challenges faced in rural and urban settings. With the world witnessing the highest levels of human displacement on record, an entire chapter has been dedicated to the exceptional challenges faced by refugees and forcibly displaced people with respect to water and sanitation.

We have endeavoured to produce a balanced, fact-based and neutral account of the current state of knowledge, covering the most recent developments, and highlighting the challenges and opportunities provided by improved water management in the context of human development. Although primarily targeted at national-level decision-makers and water resources managers, as well as academics and the broader development community, we hope this report will also be well received by those interested in poverty alleviation, humanitarian crises, human rights and the 2030 Agenda.

This latest edition of the WWDR is the result of a concerted effort between the Chapter Lead Agencies, FAO, OHCHR, UNDP, UNESCO-IHP, UN-Habitat, UNHCR, UNU-INWEH, UNU-FLORES, WWAP and the World Bank, with regional perspectives provided by UNECE, UNECLAC, UNESCAP and UNESCWA. The Report also benefited to a great extent from the inputs and contributions of several other UN-Water members and partners, as well as of dozens of scientists, professionals and NGOs, who provided a wide range of relevant material.

On behalf of the WWAP Secretariat, we would like to extend our deepest appreciation to the afore-mentioned agencies, members and partners of UN-Water, and to the writers and other contributors for collectively producing this unique and authoritative report that will, hopefully, have multiple impacts worldwide. Léo Heller, Special Rapporteur on the human rights to safe drinking water and sanitation, deserves specific recognition for having generously shared his knowledge and wisdom in the early critical phases of the report's production process.

We are profoundly grateful to the Italian Government for funding the Programme and to the Regione Umbria for generously hosting the WWAP Secretariat in Villa La Colombella in Perugia. Their contributions have been instrumental to the production of the WWDR.

Our special thanks go to Audrey Azoulay, Director-General of UNESCO, for her vital support to WWAP and the production of the WWDR. The guidance of Gilbert F. Houngbo, President of IFAD, as Chair of UN-Water has made this publication possible.

Last but not least, we extend our most sincere gratitude to all our colleagues at the WWAP Secretariat for their professionalism and dedication, without whom the report would not have been completed.

Stefan Uhlenbrook   Richard Connor

WWDR 2019 Team

Director of the Publication
Stefan Uhlenbrook

Editor in Chief
Richard Connor

Process Coordinator
Engin Koncagül

Publications Assistant
Valentina Abete

Graphic Designer
Marco Tonsini

Copy Editor
Simon Lobach

UNESCO World Water Assessment Programme (WWAP) Secretariat (2018–2019)
Coordinator: Stefan Uhlenbrook

Deputy Coordinator: Michela Miletto

Programmes: Richard Connor, Angela Renata Cordeiro Ortigara, Engin Koncagül, Lucilla Minelli and Natalia Uribe Pando

Publications: Valentina Abete and Marco Tonsini

Communications: Simona Gallese and Laurens Thuy

Administration and support: Barbara Bracaglia, Lucia Chiodini, Arturo Frascani and Lisa Gastaldin

IT and Security: Fabio Bianchi, Michele Brensacchi, Tommaso Brugnami and Francesco Gioffredi

Interns: Daria Boldrin, Francesca Maria Burchi, Tais Policanti, Théo Lecarpentier, Sonia Marcantonio, Charlotte Moutafian, Giulia Scatolini, Andres Valerio Oviedo, Bianca Maria Rizzo, Saunak Sinha Ray and Yani Wang

Acknowledgements

The UNESCO World Water Assessment Programme (WWAP) recognizes the valuable contributions of FAO, OHCHR, UNDP, UNESCO-IHP, UN-Habitat, UNHCR, UNU and the World Bank whose inputs as chapter lead agencies made the content preparation of this report possible. Sincere appreciation goes to the Regional Economic Commissions, UNECE, UNECLAC, UNESCAP and UNESCWA for co-leading Chapter 9 on regional perspectives. We also would like to thank those UN-Water members and partners and all other organizations and individuals who provided useful contributions and comments throughout the production process.

WWAP is grateful for the generous financial contribution from the Italian Government, which allows for the functioning of the WWAP Secretariat and the production of the WWDR series, and for the facilities provided by Regione Umbria.

The Spanish version of the Report is available thanks to the National Association of Water and Sanitation Utilities of Mexico (ANEAS) and its members, and the Inter-American Development Bank (IDB).

We would like to acknowledge the UNESCO Field Offices in Almaty and New Delhi for the translation of the Executive Summary of the WWDR 2019 into Russian and Hindi. Chinese, Arabic and Portuguese editions of the Executive Summary are made possible thanks to the valuable collaboration between China Water and Power Press and UNESCO Office in Beijing, Qatar National Commission for UNESCO and UNESCO Office in Doha and the National Water Agency, the Brazilian Cooperation Agency and the UNESCO Office in Brazil, respectively.

Woman in camp for people displaced by floods in Pakistan

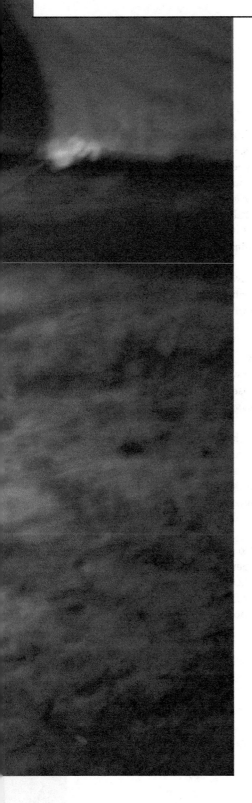

Executive summary

Improvements in water resources management and access to water supply and sanitation services are essential to addressing various social and economic inequities, such that 'no one is left behind' when it comes to enjoying the multiple benefits and opportunities that water provides.

The world's water: An increasingly stressed resource

Water use has been increasing worldwide by about 1% per year since the 1980s, driven by a combination of population growth, socio-economic development and changing consumption patterns. Global water demand is expected to continue increasing at a similar rate until 2050, accounting for an increase of 20 to 30% above the current level of water use, mainly due to rising demand in the industrial and domestic sectors. Over 2 billion people live in countries experiencing high water stress, and about 4 billion people experience severe water scarcity during at least one month of the year. Stress levels will continue to increase as demand for water grows and the effects of climate change intensify.

Access to water supply and sanitation

Three out of ten people do not have access to safe drinking water. Almost half of people drinking water from unprotected sources live in Sub-Saharan Africa. Six out of ten people do not have access to safely managed sanitation services, and one out of nine practice open defecation. However, these global figures mask significant inequities between and within regions, countries, communities and even neighbourhoods.

Global cost–benefit studies have demonstrated that water, sanitation and hygiene (WASH) services provide good social and economic returns when compared with their costs, with a global average benefit–cost ratio of 5.5 for improved sanitation and 2.0 for improved drinking water. It is likely that the benefits of improved WASH services for vulnerable groups would change the balance of any cost–benefit analysis that accounts for changes in these groups' self-perceived social status and dignity.

The human rights to water and sanitation and the 2030 Agenda for Sustainable Development

Safe drinking water and sanitation are recognized as basic human rights, as they are indispensable to sustaining healthy livelihoods and fundamental in maintaining the dignity of all human beings.

International human rights law obliges states to work towards achieving universal access to water and sanitation for all, without discrimination, while prioritizing those most in need. Fulfilment of the human rights to water and sanitation requires that the services be available, physically accessible, equitably affordable, safe and culturally acceptable.

'Leaving no one behind' is at the heart of the commitment of the 2030 Agenda for Sustainable Development, which aims to allow all people in all countries to benefit from socio-economic development and to achieve the full realization of human rights.

Caution must be taken in order to clearly differentiate between 'water rights' and the human rights to water and sanitation. Water rights, which are normally regulated under national laws, are conferred to an individual or organization through property rights or land rights, or through a negotiated agreement between the state and landowner(s). Such rights are often temporary and can potentially be withdrawn. The human rights to water and sanitation are neither temporary nor subject to state approval, and they cannot be withdrawn.

Who are being left behind?
There are multiple prohibitive grounds of discrimination, but poverty usually figures quite prominently.

Women and girls regularly experience discrimination and inequalities in the enjoyment of their human rights to safe drinking water and sanitation in many parts of the world. Ethnic and other minorities, including indigenous peoples, migrants and refugees, and people of certain ancestries (e.g. castes), often experience discrimination, as can religious and linguistic minorities. Disability, age and health status can also be a factor, as persons with physical, mental, intellectual or sensory impairments are disproportionately represented among those who lack access to safe drinking water and sanitation. Differences in property, tenure, residence, and economic and social status can lead to discrimination as well.

These do not necessarily constitute an exhaustive list of such specific disadvantaged groups or individuals in vulnerable situations, and it is important to note that some people may suffer from multiple forms of discrimination (intersectionality).

Delivering water and sanitation services
Water *availability* depends upon the amount of water physically available, and how it is stored, managed and allocated to various users. It includes aspects related to the management of surface water, groundwater, as well as water recycling and reuse.

Water *accessibility* refers to how water is physically delivered or obtained. Piped water is the least costly method to transport water in densely populated areas. Where piped networks are unavailable, people mostly rely on wells or community water supply systems (e.g. water delivery through kiosks and vendors, or water trucks). In the latter case, they often pay prices several times higher for water of lesser quality, further exacerbating inequities between the rich and disadvantaged.

Water *treatment* relates to the processes used to purify, disinfect and protect water against recontamination. The most common methods of water treatment depend upon energy (usually electricity) being available around the clock, which is rarely the case in most developing countries. Low-tech and nature-based solutions also exist but are usually not applied at scale and usually do not guarantee a quality of water that is safe for drinking.

Sanitation generally comprises on- or off-site facilities for the collection, transport, treatment and disposal of wastewater under hygienic conditions. Collection systems usually refer to a toilet system. Transportation in the context of typical grey infrastructure refers to a piped underground sewage system, although in some instances waste is transported by trucks, and treatment — when available — usually involves centralized sewage treatment plants or localized systems (e.g. septic

International human rights law obliges states to work towards achieving universal access to water and sanitation for all, without discrimination, while prioritizing those most in need

tanks). Disposal of end products is usually split into liquid and solid waste that can be disposed of safely into the environment or, if not, collected in hazardous waste facilities to be destroyed in an incinerator.

Water-related natural hazards, such as floods and droughts, can damage water supply and sanitation infrastructure, preventing service to millions of people.

Social dimensions

The social and cultural factors driving exclusion and discrimination need to be taken into account when endeavouring to fulfil the human rights to safe drinking water and sanitation, as well as to implement Sustainable Development Goal (SDG) 6.

Discrimination may happen in various ways and for different reasons. *Direct discrimination* occurs when individuals are discriminated against in laws, policies or practices that intentionally exclude them from service provision or equal treatment. *Indirect discrimination* occurs when laws, regulations, policies or practices seem neutral at face value, but in practice have the effect of exclusion from the provision of basic services.

The basic provision of safe drinking water and sanitation facilities at home and in the workplace enhances workforce health and productivity. Providing similar facilities in schools enhances education outcomes by reducing absenteeism, particularly among adolescent girls.

Comparatively lower levels of access to water and sanitation services can be observed among ethnic minorities and indigenous peoples. Valuing traditional knowledge through the recognition of indigenous peoples' stewardship of land and water supports inclusion and the fulfilment of human rights.

Good governance

Having inclusive institutional structures in place for multi-stakeholder dialogue and cooperation is essential to ensuring equitable access to sustainable water supply and sanitation services.

Government alone cannot always take on the full responsibility for 'providing' water supply and sanitation services to all citizens, especially in low-income settings. When governments' role is geared towards policy setting and regulation, the actual provision of services is carried out by non-state actors or independent departments. Well-functioning accountability mechanisms help institutions with sufficient capacity fulfil their mandates to monitor and enforce the obligations of service providers.

Creating coherence between the various institutional levels is essential to ensure that policies deliver on their objectives. In the current context of multi-level governance, the role of non-governmental organizations (NGOs) in expressing the opinions of civil society and promoting the public's active participation has become increasingly influential in policy formulation. Large corporations can also have a great deal of influence over policy-making as well as policy outcomes.

'Pro-poor' measures are far more common in policy proclamations than in mechanisms for tracking or monitoring service provision. The fulfillment of pro-poor policies can also be hampered by the non-application of financial measures aimed at reducing disparities in water services. Overambitious policies with unrealistic targets can lead to a mismatch between the responsibilities and the resources available to responsible entities. Corruption, excessive regulation and/or rigid conformity to formal rules, which tend to coincide with bureaucratic inertia, can increase transaction costs, discourage investments, and potentially derail or hinder water management reforms.

Having inclusive institutional structures in place for multi-stakeholder dialogue and cooperation is essential to ensuring equitable access to sustainable water supply and sanitation services

The human rights-based approach (HRBA) advocates for the fundamental standards, principles and criteria of human rights frameworks. These include non-discrimination and participation that is active, free and meaningful, as well as representation by and for people in disadvantaged or vulnerable situations. *Good governance* relates to systems that have qualities of accountability, transparency, legitimacy, public participation, justice and efficiency and therefore overlaps with the principles of the HRBA. Good water governance involves measures and mechanisms that promote effective policy implementation along with sanctions against poor performance, illegal acts and abuses of power. Holding decision-makers accountable requires ability, willingness and preparedness among rights-holders (or their representatives) to scrutinize actions and non-actions. This in turn builds on transparency, integrity and access to information.

Economic dimensions

The vulnerable and disadvantaged, who are typically not connected to piped systems, suffer disproportionately from inadequate access to safe drinking water and sanitation services and often pay more for their water supply services than their connected counterparts.

The human rights to water and sanitation place obligations on states and utilities to regulate payments for services and to ensure that all members of the population can afford access to basic services. Ensuring that water is affordable to all requires policy recommendations tailored to specific target groups.

Expenditure on drinking water and sanitation typically includes infrequent, large capital investments, including the cost of infrastructure and connections as well as recurrent spending on operation and maintenance. One way of increasing affordability is to lower the costs of providing the service. Technological innovation and dissemination, the enhancement of management through good governance and increased transparency practices, and the implementation of cost-effective interventions can improve production efficiency and thus lower service costs.

Even with improved efficiency, it is likely that subsidies will continue to be important for achieving universal coverage. Because subsidies are most often linked to capital expenditures and those are most often focused on relatively well-off communities, the non-poor have often been the beneficiaries of subsidy interventions intended to reach the poor. Sanitation services may be more natural candidates for subsidies than water supply services, since willingness to pay for such services is often lower and the wider social benefits are higher. Subsidies that promote greater community participation empower vulnerable groups to allocate resources toward their own priorities.

Setting tariffs — ideally the major funding source of service provision — requires striking a balance between several key objectives: cost recovery, economic efficiency, equity and affordability. Designing tariff structures is challenging precisely because these four objectives conflict, and trade-offs are inevitable. WASH services differ from many other services in that they are considered a basic right and should be provided to people regardless of cost or ability to pay. If, to meet affordability and equity objectives, subsidies are to be delivered through water tariffs, then vouchers or cash distribution might be better than an increasing block tariff (IBT).

Large WASH service providers can use commercial financing and indirectly support vulnerable groups through cross-subsidization. Where this is the case, pricing mechanisms might allow for cross-subsidization between population groups, using a uniform volumetric tariff with a rebate. Ideally, the tariff level paid by the customers who do not receive the rebate should be high enough to repay the principal and interest at commercial terms. In some cases, other funding sources such as domestic tax revenues, grants and private finance may supplement the tariff receipts. Blended finance approaches will require potentially complex combinations of development finance, private finance and government subsidies to ensure that all target groups are being reached.

> **Ensuring that water is affordable to all requires policy recommendations tailored to specific target groups**

Urban settings

Substantial inequality exists between slum and non-slum households in access to water and sanitation facilities. The wealthier often enjoy high levels of service at low cost, whereas the poor pay a much higher price for a service of similar or lesser quality.

Peri-urban areas are often not included in service schemes when residents don't pay taxes or when their housing rental arrangements are part of the informal economy. As a result, many of the world's poorest and most disadvantaged individuals are not recognized or counted as part of the formal system, and most importantly find difficulty in gaining access to basic services, because they have no physical address and thus remain 'hidden' or 'lost' in aggregated statistics.

Traditional approaches to sanitation and wastewater management in urban areas tend to favour large-scale, centralized collection and treatment that allow for economies of scale. The population density in peri-urban areas may be too low to justify the cost of household connections, and not high enough to permit conventionally designed systems. Supplying groups of households (rather than individual households) in peri-urban low-income areas and large villages could reduce investment costs while still allowing a good service level for the poorest.

The provision of urban sanitation infrastructure lags far behind infrastructure for water provision in most urban settings, and the poorest residents of slum areas are the most affected. Moreover, significant improvement in water needs to be matched with a commensurate investment in sanitation. Although water supply systems are sometimes better served with smaller, easily managed networks, the challenges of wastewater and sludge management are often more complex. A main reason is the unwillingness to pay for sanitation services.

There have been numerous attempts to use resource recovery (water, nutrients, metals, biofuel) to offset some of the costs of service provision. Despite the additional recovery efforts, as with all 'waste', when it needs to be transported, the costs thereof often negate the benefits gained. Decentralized wastewater treatment systems (DEWATS) provide an alternative with substantially lower investment and operational costs and can offer more efficient solutions for given circumstances, including in certain peri-urban areas.

Rural poverty

More than 80% of all farms in the world are family farms smaller than 2 hectares. Smallholder family farmers constitute the backbone of national food supplies, contributing more than half of the agricultural production in many countries. Yet, it is in the rural areas that poverty, hunger and food insecurity are most prevalent.

Water infrastructure remains extremely sparse in rural areas, so that millions of women, men and children are not covered by water and sanitation services. Moreover, the institutional capacity, including domestic resource mobilization and budget allocations — both at national and subnational levels — has been insufficient to cater for maintenance needs of the installed water infrastructure.

Water management for smallholder family farmers needs to consider both rainfed and irrigated agriculture. Approximately 80% of the global cropland is rainfed, and 60% of the world's food is produced on rainfed land. Supplemental irrigation in rainfed agricultural systems may not only ensure crop survival, but also double or even triple rainfed yields per hectare for crops such as wheat, sorghum and maize.

Ensuring secure and equal access to water in rural areas, while providing opportunities for future water investments, requires greater recognition of the water-related needs of small-scale irrigators in the context of their contribution to national food security. Water allocations to large-scale users, whether for irrigation or other purposes, must not take place at the expense of small-scale farmers' legitimate needs, irrespective of their ability to demonstrate formally sanctioned water rights.

> The wealthier often enjoy high levels of service at low cost, whereas the poor pay a much higher price for a service of similar or lesser quality

Refugees and forcibly displaced people

The world has been witnessing the highest levels of human displacement on record. Armed conflict, persecution and climate change, in tandem with poverty, inequality, urban population growth, poor land use management and weak governance, are increasing the risk of displacement and its impacts.

Away from home, refugees and internally displaced people (IDPs) are often faced with barriers to access basic water supply and sanitation services. Almost a quarter of these displaced people live in camps, but the overwhelming majority are hosted in cities, towns and villages. These refugees, asylum seekers, IDPs and stateless persons are often not officially recognized by local or national government and are therefore excluded from development agendas.

Mass displacement places strain upon water resources and related services, including sanitation and hygiene, at transition and destination points, creating potential inequalities between existing populations and new arrivals. Host governments often refuse to accept that the displacement situation may become protracted, and insist that refugees/IDPs remain in camps with 'temporary' or 'communal' facilities at a lower level of service than the surrounding host community. The reverse situation may also occur, where refugees receive higher-quality WASH services than what is available for nearby communities.

States have a responsibility to ensure that all refugees/IDPs are granted the rights to adequate sanitation and water, without regard to their legal residence, nationality or other classifications that may serve as hindrances. Like all individuals, refugees/IDPs should have access to information and the opportunity to participate in decision-making processes that affect their rights.

States are encouraged to avoid 'encampment' policies for refugees/IDPs, as these can lead to marginalization (directly linked to legal status and the 'right to work' or 'freedom of movement'), which can exacerbate resource competition with host communities and make it difficult for refugees/IDPs to access labour markets. Instead, states are encouraged to pursue policies for the inclusion of refugees/IDPs within existing urban and rural communities.

Regional perspectives
The Arab region

Water scarcity on a per person basis in the Arab region will continue to increase due to population growth and climate change. The challenge of ensuring access to water services for all under water-scarce conditions is exacerbated in conflict settings where water infrastructure has been damaged, destroyed and targeted for destruction.

A large proportion of refugees tend to remain in protracted situations for decades. Humanitarian assistance has become increasingly intertwined with development work aimed at providing more permanent water supply and sanitation facilities in refugee camps and informal settlements. This has at times caused conflict and tensions with host communities, particularly if the parties do not have equal access to water services. Additional attention has been paid to this problem in recent years with governments, donors and humanitarian agencies recognizing that leaving no one behind means serving refugees and IDPs as well as host communities.

Asia and the Pacific

In 2016, 29 out of 48 countries in the region qualified as water-insecure due to low availability of water and unsustainable groundwater withdrawal. Water scarcity is compounded by the effects of climate change. Natural disasters are becoming more frequent and intense, and disaster risk is outpacing resilience. This has major impacts for the provisioning of WASH services in areas affected by disasters, due to damaged water supply and sanitation infrastructure and water quality issues. It is also a significant challenge to provide adequate services to the areas that receive people who have been displaced from disaster-struck areas.

> **Away from home, refugees and internally displaced people are often faced with barriers to access basic water supply and sanitation services**

Disasters cause disproportionately higher losses to poorer countries and people, as these often lack resilience and the capacity to mitigate the impact of disasters. Disasters are also found to have impacts on gross domestic product (GDP), school enrolment rates, per capita expenditure on health, and can also cause the near poor — those living on between US$1.90 and US$3.10 per day — to fall into extreme poverty.

Europe and North America

Access to safely managed sanitation services remains a challenge in many countries, especially in rural areas. While the situation is particularly severe for a major part of the population in Eastern Europe, the Caucasus and Central Asia, many citizens in Western and Central Europe, as well as in North America, also suffer from the lack of or inequitable access to water and sanitation services. Inequities are frequently related to sociocultural differences, socio-economic factors and the geographical context.

Inequities in access therefore must be fought on three fronts: by reducing geographical disparities, by addressing specific barriers faced by marginalized groups and people living in vulnerable situations, and by reducing affordability concerns.

Latin America and the Caribbean

Millions of people in the region are still without an adequate source of drinking water, while even more suffer the absence of safe and decent facilities for the disposal of excreta. Many people without access to services are concentrated in peri-urban areas, mainly in the poverty belts that exist on the periphery of many of the cities in the region. It has proved difficult to provide these marginal areas with services of acceptable quality.

In many countries, decentralization has left the water supply and sanitation sector with a highly fragmented structure made up of numerous service providers, without real possibilities to achieve economies of scale or economic viability, and under the responsibility of municipalities that lack the necessary resources and incentives to deal effectively with the complexity of the processes involved in providing services. Decentralization has also reduced the size of service areas and made them more homogeneous, thus limiting the possibilities for cross-subsidies and facilitating the 'cream skimming' that marginalizes low-income groups away from service provision.

Sub-Saharan Africa

The lack of water management infrastructure (economic water scarcity), in terms of both storage and supply delivery, as well as for improved drinking water and sanitation services, plays a direct role in the persistence of poverty in Sub-Saharan Africa.

People living in rural areas account for about 60% of the total population of Sub-Saharan Africa, and many of them remain in poverty. In 2015, three out of five of the region's rural residents had access to at least a basic water supply and only one in five had access to at least basic sanitation. About 10% of the population still drank untreated surface water, and many poor people in rural areas, particularly women and girls, spent a considerable amount of time collecting water.

More than half of the population growth expected by 2050 (1.3 out of 2.2 billion globally) will occur in Africa. Providing this growing population with access to WASH services, however, is not the only challenge for Africa, as the demands for energy, food, jobs, healthcare and education will also increase. Population growth especially occurs in urban areas, and without proper planning, this might lead to a dramatic increase of slums. Even if countries have steadily improved living conditions in urban slums between 2000 and 2015, the rate of new home construction lagged far behind the rate of urban population growth.

Strategies and response options

From a *technical perspective*, the potential responses to address the lack of drinking water supply and sanitation services to groups in disadvantaged situations can vary significantly from one place to another. Whereas sizeable high-density urban communities provide opportunities for large-scale centralized WASH infrastructure and

Disasters cause disproportionately higher losses to poorer countries and people

facilities though resource-sharing and economies of scale, less costly decentralized water supply and sanitation systems have been shown to be successful solutions in smaller urban settlements, including refugee camps. For people in low-density rural areas, one main objective is to bring more adequate facilities closer to people's homes. The basic principle behind selecting WASH technologies is therefore not necessarily one of 'best practice', but one of 'best fit'.

Insufficient *funding* and lack of effective *financing* mechanisms have created a barrier to achieving the WASH targets for disadvantaged and marginalized groups. A certain proportion of the investment gap could be overcome through increased system efficiency, which uses already available finances more effectively and can significantly reduce overall costs. However, targeted subsidies for vulnerable groups and equitable tariff structures will remain an important source of funding and cost recovery. The support of the international donor community will remain critical in the developing world but cannot be the main source of funding. Official development assistance (ODA) is particularly helpful in mobilizing investments from other sources, such as commercial and blended finance, including from the private sector. However, it will be incumbent upon national governments to dramatically increase the amounts of public funding made available for the expansion of WASH services.

> **The basic principle behind selecting WASH technologies is not necessarily one of 'best practice', but one of 'best fit'**

However, increasing the amount of funding and investment alone does not necessarily ensure that WASH services will reach all those who are most disadvantaged. Subsidies must therefore be appropriately designed, transparent and targeted, and tariff structures need to be designed and implemented with the objectives of achieving equity, affordability and the appropriate level of service for each targeted group.

Scientific research, development and innovation are essential to support informed decision-making. Although some progress has been made in terms of designing equable tariff structures that benefit — rather than penalize — people in poor and disadvantaged situations, further research and analysis into the economic dimensions of WASH services in support of inclusion is required. The information and capacity-building needs of disadvantaged rural communities are often similar to those described above for the urban poor, but also include knowledge related to water resource allocation and the securing of water rights. Monitoring progress is another important aspect of knowledge and capacity development. Disaggregated data (with respect to gender, age, income groups, ethnicity, geography, etc.) and social inclusion analyses are critical tools in determining which groups are at greatest risk of being 'left behind', and why. Further research in science and engineering is also needed to develop affordable, safe and efficient WASH infrastructure and related devices (e.g. mobile filters, toilets).

Community-based action is critical in addressing the root causes of 'leaving people behind' with respect to water and sanitation. Good governance seeks to move away from hierarchical power structures while embracing concepts of accountability, transparency, legitimacy, public participation, justice and efficiency — principles that are in line with the HRBA. Water resource allocation mechanisms can be established to achieve different socio-economic policy objectives — such as safeguarding food and/or energy security, or for promoting industrial growth — but ensuring that enough water is available (and of suitable quality) to meet everyone's basic human needs (for domestic as well as subsistence purposes) must be a guaranteed priority.

The linkages between water and *migration* have been attracting increasing attention, although they have yet to be fully incorporated into international migration policy. The WASH-related challenges faced by refugees and IDPs require special focused political responsiveness. In the case of service provision in refugee camps, harmonization of service levels with surrounding community/national standards is essential for combatting social discrimination and creating access equality.

All *actors* involved in the realization of the human rights to water and sanitation on a non-discriminatory and equal basis hold specific obligations and responsibilities. Human rights define individuals as rights-holders entitled to water and sanitation, and states as duty-bearers that have to guarantee access to WASH for all, using the maximum of their available resources. Non-state actors also have human rights responsibilities and may be held accountable for the infringement of human rights. NGOs and international organizations can play an important role in service provision and need to ensure substantive equality and accountability in such endeavours. International organizations, such as the United Nations, international trade and financial institutions, and development cooperation partners are called upon to ensure that their assistance is channelled towards the countries or regions that are least able to realize the rights to water and sanitation.

Coda

People from different groups are 'left behind' for different reasons. Discrimination, exclusion, marginalization, entrenched power asymmetries and material inequalities are among the main obstacles to achieving the human rights to safe drinking water and sanitation for all and realizing the water-related goals of the 2030 Agenda. Poorly designed and inadequately implemented policies, inefficient and improper use of financial resources, as well as policy gaps fuel the persistence of inequalities in access to safe drinking water and sanitation. Unless exclusion and inequality are explicitly and responsively addressed in both policy and practice, water interventions will continue to fail to reach those most in need and who are likely to benefit most.

Improving water resources management and providing access to safe and affordable drinking water and sanitation for all is essential for eradicating poverty, building peaceful and prosperous societies, and ensuring that 'no one is left behind' on the road towards sustainable development. These goals are entirely achievable, provided there is a collective will to do so.

Unless exclusion and inequality are explicitly and responsively addressed in both policy and practice, water interventions will continue to fail to reach those most in need and who are likely to benefit most

Prologue

A boy looking at a wooden boat in the middle of a drought

WWAP | Richard Connor, Stefan Uhlenbrook, Tais Policanti, Engin Koncagül and Angela Renata Cordeiro Ortigara

The Prologue provides a general overview of the global status and the main trends on water-related issues, including the state of the world's water resources; the latest figures regarding the global coverage of water supply, sanitation and hygiene services; as well as metrics concerning a broad range of socio-economic development indicators related to the theme of the report: 'Leaving no one behind'.

Introduction

Inequities afflicting the world's poor, disadvantaged and/or marginalized people can be manifested in several different ways. The aim of this report is to highlight how improvements in water resources management and access to water supply and sanitation services are essential to addressing various social and economic inequities, such that 'no one is left behind' when it comes to enjoying the multiple benefits and opportunities that water provides.

As in other recent editions of the World Water Development Report, the Prologue provides a summary overview of latest information — status and trends — regarding global water-related issues and challenges, in terms of both water resources management and water supply and sanitation services. This edition's Prologue also provides a summary overview of a broad range of statistics and trends regarding key socio-economic indicators associated with the theme of the report: 'Leaving no one behind'.

The trends outlined below collectively illustrate that, despite progress made since the turn of the millennium across several sectors, much remains to be done in order to achieve the Sustainable Development Goals (SDGs) and to truly succeed in 'leaving no one behind'. The SDG 6 Synthesis Report clearly demonstrated that, if the current pace of progress remains unchanged, the world will not achieve SDG 6 by 2030 (UN, 2018a).

Several of these trends are already well known and well documented. For example, Sub-Saharan Africa and South Asia clearly stand out as regional 'hotspots', where population growth, urbanization and poverty remain high and access to basic services such as education, electricity and safely managed water supply and sanitation remain grossly inadequate.

It is also clear that women are likely to fare less well than men in nearly all economic indicators, including extreme poverty, land tenure and labour force participation. And with a few exceptions, such as life expectancy, the same applies to social and health-related indicators, including education, food insecurity, disability and even internet access, where women are noticeably at a disadvantage.

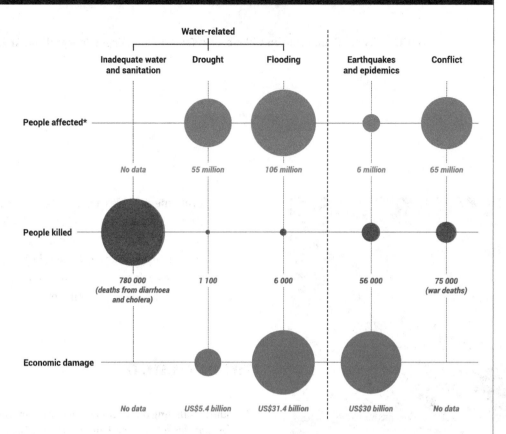

Figure 1 Average annual impact from inadequate drinking water and sanitation services,[1] water-related disasters, epidemics and earthquakes, and conflicts

*People affected are defined as those requiring immediate assistance during a period of emergency; this may include displaced or evacuated people.

Source: Adapted from PBL Netherlands Environmental Assessment Agency (2018, p. 14). Licensed under Creative Commons Attribution 3.0 Unported (CC BY 3.0).

However, global, regional and even country-level trends do not necessarily reflect local realities and discrepancies. For example, the challenges of living in poverty can differ considerably between urban and rural settlements, just like the potential responses and solutions. Improving access to water supply and sanitation services in rural environments will probably require different approaches than addressing the needs of the growing populations of urban centres, where informal settlements (slums) pose a particularly difficult and urgent challenge. In addition, whereas labour market opportunities in rural areas are likely to remain dominated by food and agriculture (a highly water-dependent sector), employment opportunities in urban and peri-urban areas may evolve rapidly as the result of current technological changes and the digitalization of the economy (or 'Industry 4.0').

Another water-related linkage between seemingly different trends is the relationship between rapid urbanization, increased vulnerability to floods and droughts, and the increased risk of displacement (particularly in the case of informal settlements). However, in terms of both the number of people affected and (especially) the number of people killed, the impacts of floods, droughts and conflicts are grossly outweighed by the number of those affected or killed by inadequate drinking water and sanitation services (Figure 1).

These and other trends point to the number of complex and emerging challenges that will require a comprehensive approach based on human rights, involving governments, the private sector, civil society and the international community.

---

[1] In 2015, an estimated 2.1 billion people lacked access to safely managed drinking water services and 4.5 billion lacked access to safely managed sanitation services (WHO/UNICEF, 2017a). However, there are no data available estimating what proportion of these people were 'affected', nor what the resulting overall economic damage would equate to.

Section 1
The state of the world's water resources

i. Water demand and use

Water use has been increasing worldwide by about 1% per year since the 1980s (AQUASTAT, n.d.). This steady rise has principally been led by surging demand in developing countries and emerging economies (although per capita water use in the majority of these countries remains far below water use in developed countries — they are merely catching up). This growth is driven by a combination of population growth, socio-economic development and evolving consumption patterns (WWAP, 2016). Agriculture (including irrigation, livestock and aquaculture) is by far the largest water consumer, accounting for 69% of annual water withdrawals globally. Industry (including power generation) accounts for 19% and households for 12% (AQUASTAT, n.d.).

Global water demand is expected to continue increasing at a similar rate until 2050, accounting for an increase of 20 to 30% above the current level of water use (Burek et al., 2016). Although specific projections can somewhat vary, current analysis suggests much of this growth will be attributed to increases in demand by the industrial and domestic sectors (OECD, 2012; Burek et al., 2016; IEA, 2016). Agriculture's share of total water use is therefore likely to fall in comparison with other sectors, but it will remain the largest user overall over the coming decades, in terms of both water withdrawal and water consumption[2] (Figure 2).

ii. Water availability

Figure 3 provides a global overview of countries experiencing different levels of water stress.

Over 2 billion people live in countries experiencing high water stress. Although the global average water stress is only 11%, 31 countries experience water stress between 25% (which is defined as the minimum threshold of water stress) and 70%, and 22 countries are above 70% and are therefore under serious water stress (UN, 2018a). Growing water stress indicates substantial use of water resources, with greater impacts on resource sustainability, and a rising potential for conflicts among users.

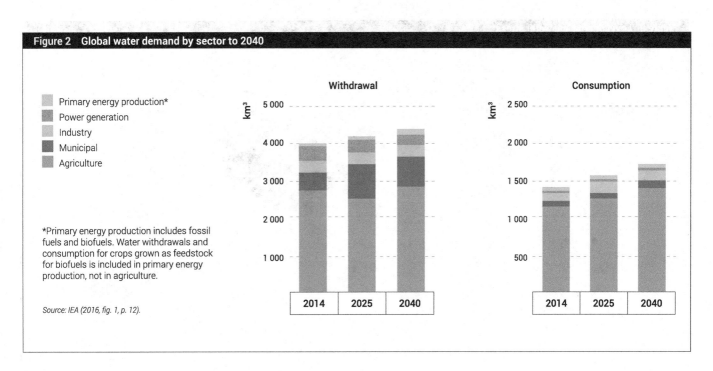

Figure 2 Global water demand by sector to 2040

Withdrawal

Consumption

- Primary energy production*
- Power generation
- Industry
- Municipal
- Agriculture

*Primary energy production includes fossil fuels and biofuels. Water withdrawals and consumption for crops grown as feedstock for biofuels is included in primary energy production, not in agriculture.

Source: IEA (2016, fig. 1, p. 12).

---

[2] **Water withdrawal:** The volume of water removed from a source; by definition withdrawals are always greater than or equal to consumption.
Water consumption: The volume withdrawn that is not returned to the source (i.e. it is evaporated or transported to another location) and by definition is no longer available for other uses locally.

Several other important aspects of water stress need to be highlighted. Firstly, since water availability can be highly variable from season to season, data averaged over the entire year do not show periods of water scarcity. For example, it has been estimated that about 4 billion people, representing nearly two-thirds of the world population, experience severe water scarcity during at least one month of the year (Mekonnen and Hoekstra, 2016). Secondly, such data aggregated at the country level can mask (sometimes enormous) differences in water availability across various river basins within a given country or region. For example, the country-wide low water stress in several countries/regions in Figure 3, such as Australia, South America and Sub-Saharan Africa, should not be misinterpreted, as water stress at the basin or local level can be very significant. Thirdly, physical water stress does not take account of economic water scarcity, where access to water is not limited as a result of the amount of existent water resources themselves, but by a lack of infrastructure to collect, transport and treat water for human purposes. For example, the indicated low water stress in many African countries in Figure 3 does not take the lower status of water resources development into account. Most of these countries have less than 6% of their cultivated area equipped with irrigation systems (AQUASTAT, n.d.) and, therefore, a low withdrawal rate compared to the available freshwater resources at country level/scale, despite potentially severe water stress at local levels.

Levels of physical water stress are likely to increase as populations and their demands for water grow, and the effects of climate change intensify (UN, 2018a). Climate change and increasing climate variability are also likely to vary at the local and basin scales and over different seasons. For the most part, however, dry areas will tend to become drier and wet areas wetter (Figure 4), such that climate change will likely exacerbate water stress in areas that are already the most affected.

Estimates suggest that if the degradation of the natural environment and the unsustainable pressures on global water resources continue, 45% of the global gross domestic product (GDP), 52% of the world's population and 40% of global grain production will be at risk by 2050. Poor and marginalized populations will be disproportionately affected, further exacerbating already rising inequalities (UN, 2018a).

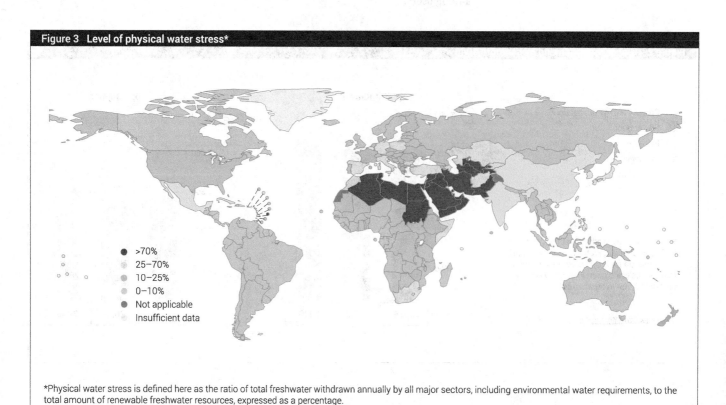

Figure 3   Level of physical water stress*

>70%
25–70%
10–25%
0–10%
Not applicable
Insufficient data

*Physical water stress is defined here as the ratio of total freshwater withdrawn annually by all major sectors, including environmental water requirements, to the total amount of renewable freshwater resources, expressed as a percentage.

Source: UN (2018a, p. 72, based on data from AQUASTAT). © 2018 United Nations. Reprinted with the permission of the United Nations.

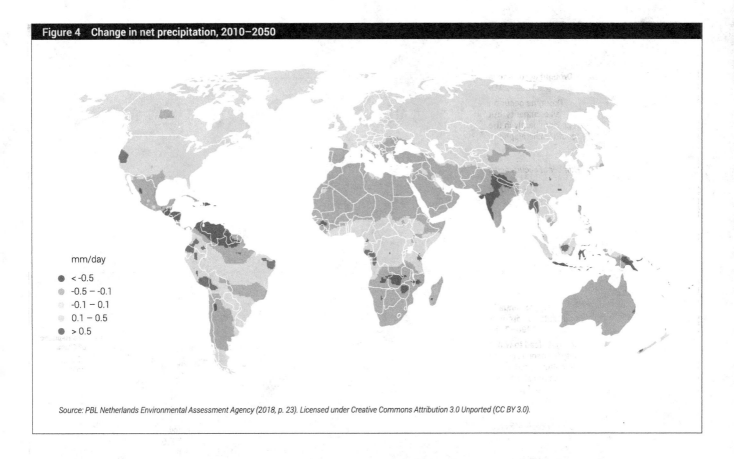

Figure 4 Change in net precipitation, 2010–2050

mm/day
- < -0.5
- -0.5 – -0.1
- -0.1 – 0.1
- 0.1 – 0.5
- > 0.5

iii. Water quality

Water quality problems persist in developed and developing countries alike, and include the loss of pristine-quality water bodies, impacts associated with changes in hydromorphology, the rise in emerging pollutants and the spread of invasive species (UN, 2018a). Poor water quality directly impacts people who rely on these sources as their main supply by further limiting their access to water (i.e. water availability) and increasing water-related health risks (not to mention their overall quality of life).

Several water-related diseases, including cholera and schistosomiasis, remain widespread across many developing countries, where only a very small fraction (in some cases less than 5%) of domestic and urban wastewater is treated prior to its release into the environment (WWAP, 2017).

Nutrient loadings remain one of the most prevalent forms of water pollution and the majority of nutrient emissions originate from agriculture. *"For most regions, nutrient emissions to surface waters are projected to increase, with hotspots in South and East Asia, parts of Africa and Central and Latin America. However, the rapidly growing cities in the developing countries are projected to become major sources of nutrient emissions"* (PBL Netherlands Environmental Assessment Agency, 2018. p. 42), especially where a rapidly growing number of households lack adequate wastewater treatment systems.

iv. Extreme events

About 90% of all natural disasters are water-related. Over the period 1995–2015, floods accounted for 43% of all documented natural disasters, affecting 2.3 billion people, killing 157,000 more and causing US$662 billion in damage. Droughts accounted for 5% of natural disasters, affecting 1.1 billion people, killing 22,000 more, and causing US$100 billion in damage over the same 20-year period. Over the course of one decade, the number of floods rose from an annual average of 127 in 1995 to 171 in 2004 (CRED/UNISDR, 2015). Figure 5 provides a country-level overview of the occurrence of floods and droughts between 1996 and 2015, as well as the number of people affected.

Poor water quality directly impacts people who rely on these sources as their main supply by further limiting their access to water (i.e. water availability) and increasing water-related health risks

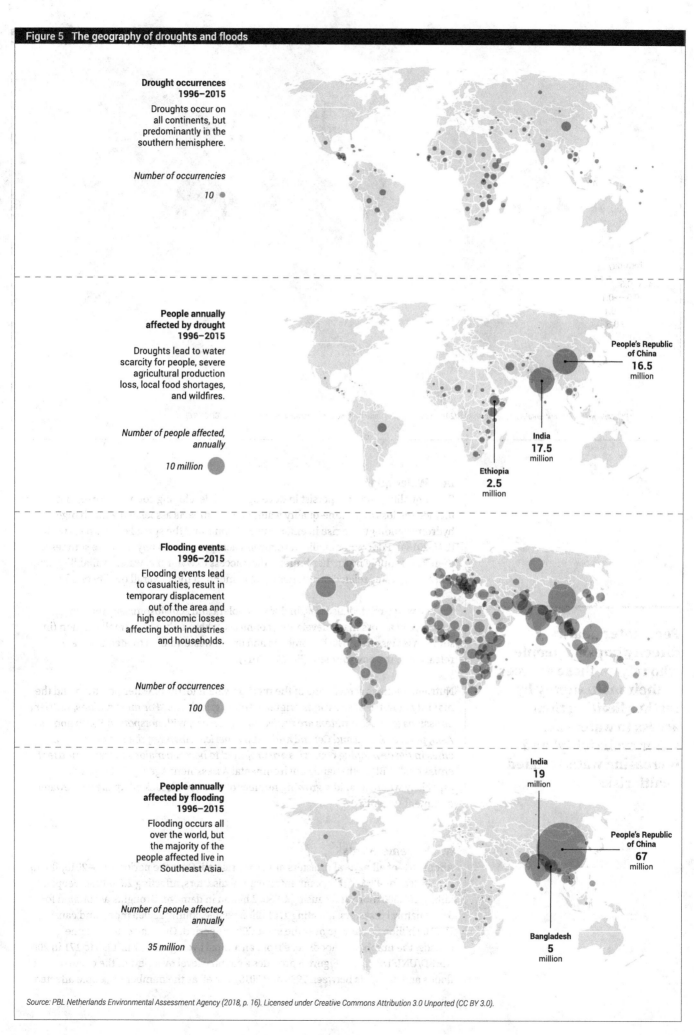

Figure 5 The geography of droughts and floods

Drought occurrences 1996–2015

Droughts occur on all continents, but predominantly in the southern hemisphere.

Number of occurrences

10

People annually affected by drought 1996–2015

Droughts lead to water scarcity for people, severe agricultural production loss, local food shortages, and wildfires.

Number of people affected, annually

10 million

People's Republic of China
16.5 million

India
17.5 million

Ethiopia
2.5 million

Flooding events 1996–2015

Flooding events lead to casualties, result in temporary displacement out of the area and high economic losses affecting both industries and households.

Number of occurrences

100

People annually affected by flooding 1996–2015

Flooding occurs all over the world, but the majority of the people affected live in Southeast Asia.

Number of people affected, annually

35 million

India
19 million

People's Republic of China
67 million

Bangladesh
5 million

The number of people affected and the estimated damage from water-related disasters continue to rise. This increase can be partially explained by the improved reporting and documentation of these disasters and their consequences. Fortunately, the higher number of people affected is not accompanied by a higher number of casualties, although women and children remain disproportionally vulnerable. In fact, the number of people killed by weather-related disasters has decreased over the last decades. This suggests that some areas of disaster risk management, such as improved early warning systems and increased disaster management capacity, are leading to positive results (UNISDR/UNECE, 2018).

Climate change is expected to increase the frequency and magnitude of extreme weather events. The Organisation for Economic Co operation and Development (OECD) *Environmental Outlook* (OECD, 2012) estimates that the number of people and the value of assets at risk from floods will be significantly higher in 2050, compared to today: *"... The number of people at risk from floods is projected to rise from 1.2 billion today to around 1.6 billion in 2050 (nearly 20% of the world's population) and the economic value of assets at risk is expected to be around US$45 trillion by 2050, a growth of over 340% from 2010."* (p. 209).

Urbanization will increase the demand for flood protection and mitigation, raising the issue of the allocation of flood risks across sectors and areas, including agricultural lands (OECD, 2016).

Climate change is expected to increase the frequency and magnitude of extreme weather events

v. Transboundary water resources and water-related conflicts

The concept of 'war over water', where nations engage in military conflict over finite water resources has received considerable attention through the media and other public forums. Given ever rising levels of local water stress (see Prologue, Section 1ii), combined with the fact that there are 286 international rivers and 592 transboundary aquifers shared by 153 countries (UN, 2018a), it could be expected that water-related conflicts have been increasing and/or are likely to increase in the future. However, current evidence does not fully support this hypothesis. Conflicts are often difficult to attribute to a single reason; however, water is often one among several contributing factors.

Water conflicts can arise because of several factors, including territorial disputes, competition over resources, or political strategic advantage. They can also be categorized based on the use, impact, or effect that water had within the conflict. The Pacific Institute's chronological list *Water Conflict Chronology* (Pacific Institute, n.d.) defines three such categories:

- **Trigger**: Water as a trigger or root cause of conflict, where there is a dispute over the control of water or water systems or where economic or physical access to water, or scarcity of water, triggers violence.
- **Weapon**: Water as a weapon of conflict, where water resources, or water systems themselves, are used as a tool or weapon in a violent conflict.
- **Casualty**: Water resources or water systems as a casualty of conflict, where water resources, or water systems, are intentional or incidental casualties or targets of violence.

Items are included in the chronological list when there is violence (injuries or deaths) or threats of violence (including verbal threats, military manoeuvres, and shows of force). During the period 2000–2009, there were 94 registered conflicts where water played a role (49 as a Trigger, 20 as a Weapon and 34 as a Casualty[3]). The period 2010–2018 (up to May 2018) reported 263 registered conflicts (123 with water as a Trigger, 29 as a Weapon, and 133 as a Casualty). Although this might suggest an increasing trend in water-related conflicts overall, these data must be interpreted with caution, as much of the increase could be attributable to greater awareness (and reporting) of such incidents. The eruption of armed conflict in several regions of the world during the period from 2010 to 2018 may also have influenced this apparent trend.

---

[3] The different categories add up to more than the total number, because some conflicts have been listed in more than one category.

Section 2
Water supply, sanitation and hygiene

i. Drinking water

Three out of ten people (2.1 billion people, or 29% of the global population) did not use a safely managed drinking water service[4] in 2015, whereas 844 million people still lacked even a basic drinking water service[5] (Figure 6). Of all the people using safely managed drinking water services, only one out of three (1.9 billion) lived in rural areas (WHO/UNICEF, 2017a).

There has been progress during the implementation phase of the Millennium Development Goals (MDGs). The global population using at least a basic drinking water service increased from 81 to 89% between 2000 and 2015. However, among the countries that had a coverage of less than 95% in 2015, only one in five is on track to achieving universal basic water services by 2030 (UN, 2018a).

Coverage of safely managed water services varies considerably across regions (from only 24% in Sub-Saharan Africa to 94% in Europe and Northern America). There can also be significant variability within countries between rural and urban areas, wealth quintiles and subnational regions, as exemplified by the stark contrast between the provinces of Luanda and Uige (Angola) (Figure 7) (WHO/UNICEF, 2017a).

By 2015, 181 countries had achieved a coverage of over 75% for at least basic drinking water services (Figure 8). Of the 159 million people still collecting untreated (and often contaminated) drinking water directly from surface water sources, 58% lived in Sub-Saharan Africa (WHO/UNICEF, 2017a).

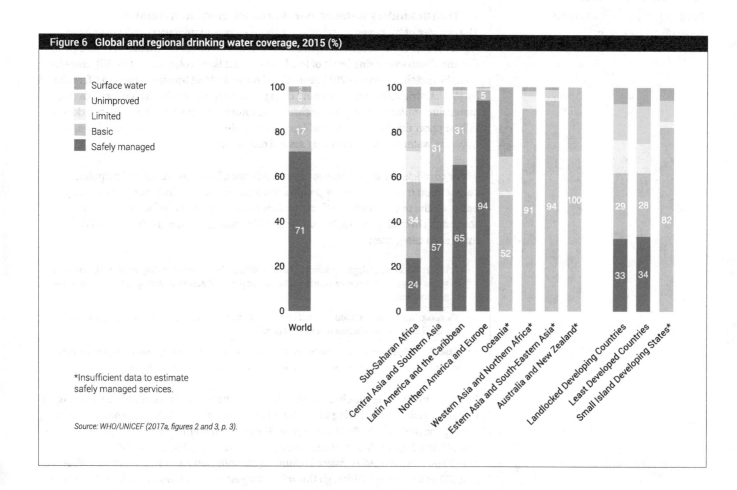

Figure 6   Global and regional drinking water coverage, 2015 (%)

Legend: Surface water, Unimproved, Limited, Basic, Safely managed

*Insufficient data to estimate safely managed services.

Source: WHO/UNICEF (2017a, figures 2 and 3, p. 3).

---

[4] Drinking water from an improved water source that is located on premises, available when needed and free from faecal and priority chemical contamination ('improved' sources include: piped water, boreholes or tube wells, protected dug wells, protected springs, rainwater, and packaged or delivered water).
[5] Drinking water from an improved source, provided collection time is not more than 30 minutes for a round trip, including queuing.

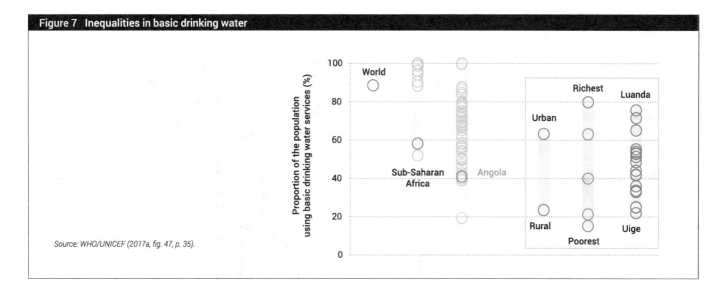

Figure 7   Inequalities in basic drinking water

Source: WHO/UNICEF (2017a, fig. 47, p. 35).

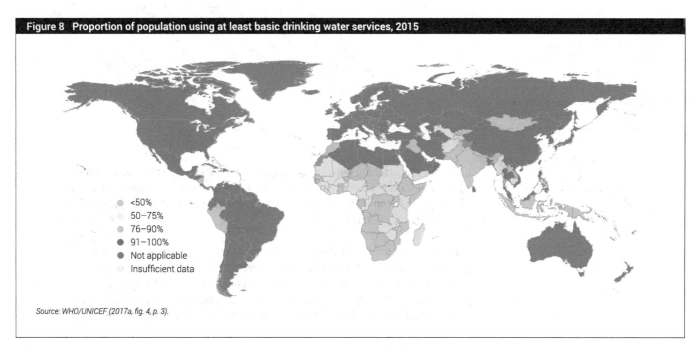

Figure 8   Proportion of population using at least basic drinking water services, 2015

- <50%
- 50–75%
- 76–90%
- 91–100%
- Not applicable
- Insufficient data

Source: WHO/UNICEF (2017a, fig. 4, p. 3).

ii. Sanitation

Worldwide, only 2.9 billion people (or 39% of the global population) used safely managed sanitation services[6] in 2015 (Figure 9). Two out of five of these people (1.2 billion) lived in rural areas. Another 2.1 billion people had access to 'basic' sanitation services.[7] The remaining 2.3 billion (one out of every three people) lacked even a basic sanitation service, of which 892 million people still practiced open defecation (WHO/UNICEF, 2017a).

Progress was also achieved in sanitation coverage during the implementation phase of the MDGs, but it still lags behind compared to the progress in drinking water supply. By 2015, 154 countries had achieved a coverage of over 75% for at least basic sanitation services. The global population using at least a basic sanitation service increased from 59 to 68% between 2000 and 2015. However, among the countries with a coverage of less than 95% in 2015, only one out of ten is on track to achieving universal basic sanitation by 2030 (UN, 2018a).

---

[6] Use of improved facilities that are not shared with other households and where excreta are safely disposed of in situ or transported and treated off-site ('improved' facilities include flush/pour flush to piped sewer systems, septic tanks or pit latrines; ventilated improved pit latrines, composting toilets or pit latrines with slabs).

[7] Use of improved facilities that are not shared with other households.

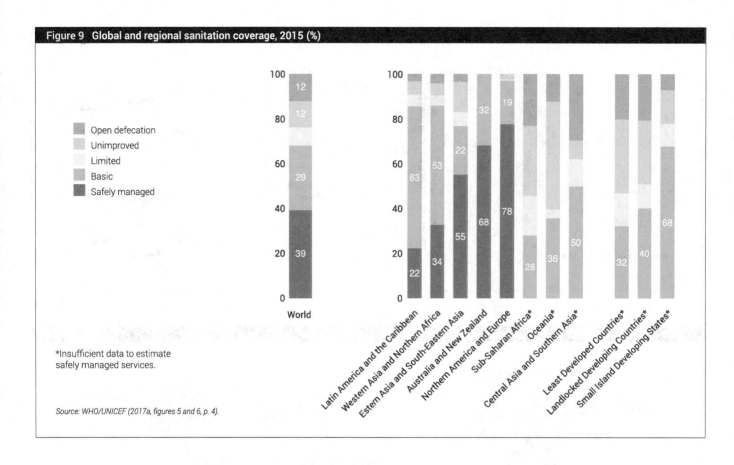

Figure 9   Global and regional sanitation coverage, 2015 (%)

Legend:
- Open defecation
- Unimproved
- Limited
- Basic
- Safely managed

*Insufficient data to estimate safely managed services.

Source: WHO/UNICEF (2017a, figures 5 and 6, p. 4).

Similarly to drinking water, a very large level of variability can be observed in terms of access to basic sanitation within countries, as exemplified by the stark contrast between the provinces of Panamá and Guna Yala (Panamá) (Figure 10) (WHO/UNICEF, 2017a).

By 2015, 154 countries had achieved over 75% coverage with at least basic sanitation services (Figure 11). Overall coverage is generally lower for basic sanitation than for basic water, and no SDG region (with the exception of Australia and New Zealand, where coverage is already nearly universal) is on track to achieving universal basic sanitation by 2030 (WHO/UNICEF, 2017a).

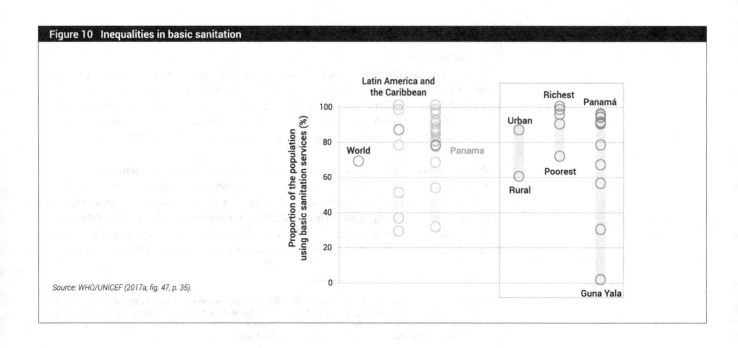

Figure 10   Inequalities in basic sanitation

Source: WHO/UNICEF (2017a, fig. 47, p. 35).

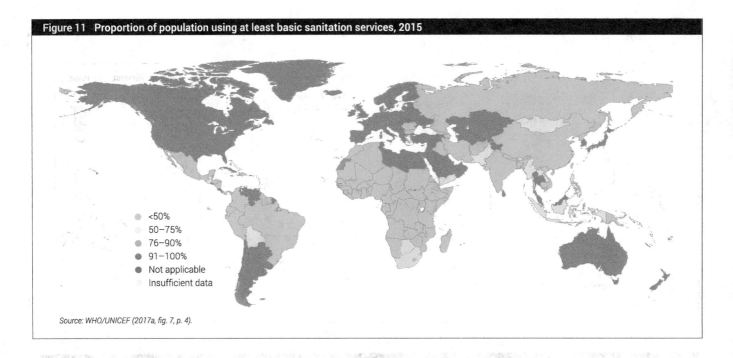

Figure 11 Proportion of population using at least basic sanitation services, 2015

- <50%
- 50–75%
- 76–90%
- 91–100%
- Not applicable
- Insufficient data

Source: WHO/UNICEF (2017a, fig. 7, p. 4).

iii. Hygiene

Coverage of basic handwashing facilities with soap and water varied (on a regional average) from 15% in Sub-Saharan Africa to 76% in Western Asia and Northern Africa (Figure 12). However, data available for 2015 (representing only 30% of the global population) were insufficient to produce a global estimate, or estimates for other SDG regions. As with water supply and sanitation, there can be significant inequalities within countries, as shown by the example of Tunisia (Figure 13) (WHO/UNICEF, 2017a).

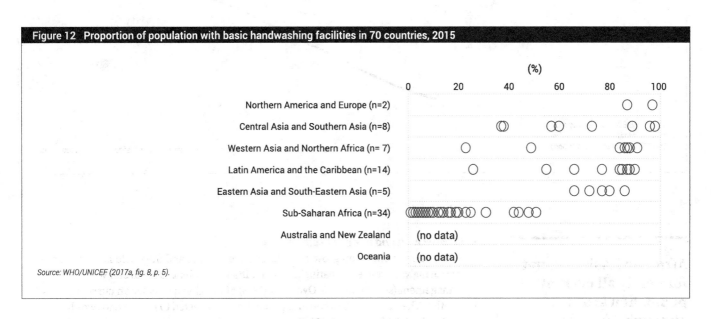

Figure 12 Proportion of population with basic handwashing facilities in 70 countries, 2015

Source: WHO/UNICEF (2017a, fig. 8, p. 5).

Section 3
Socio-economic development indicators

i. Demographics
Global population growth

Population growth is a significant driver of increasing water demand, both directly (e.g. for drinking water, sanitation, hygiene and household uses) and indirectly (e.g. through growing demands for water-intensive goods and services, including food and energy).

The global population reached 7.6 billion people as of June 2017. It is expected to reach about 8.6 billion by 2030 and further increase to 9.8 billion by 2050 (Figure 14) (UNDESA, 2017a).

Africa and Asia account for nearly all current population growth, although Africa is expected to be the main contributor beyond 2050 (Figure 15) (UNDESA, 2017a).

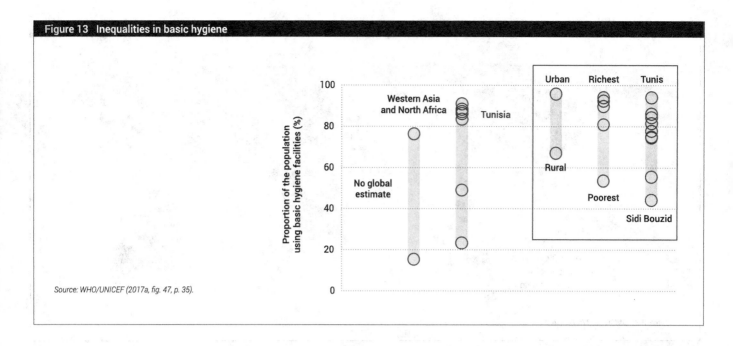

Figure 13 Inequalities in basic hygiene

Source: WHO/UNICEF (2017a, fig. 47, p. 35).

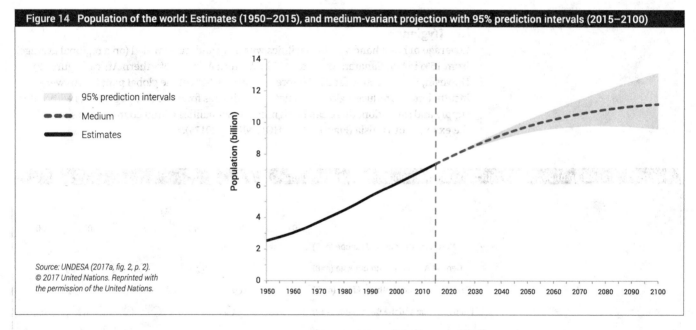

Figure 14 Population of the world: Estimates (1950–2015), and medium-variant projection with 95% prediction intervals (2015–2100)

Source: UNDESA (2017a, fig. 2, p. 2).
© 2017 United Nations. Reprinted with
the permission of the United Nations.

Africa and Asia account for nearly all current population growth, although Africa is expected to be the main contributor beyond 2050

Urbanization and informal settlements

Nearly all net population growth is taking place in cities and the world is becoming increasingly urbanized, creating new and difficult challenges for urban water management (see Chapter 6). Over half (54%) of the global population currently lives in cities. The ratio of urban-to-rural population is expected to increase to two-thirds (66.4%) by 2050 (UNICEF, 2017). Sustainable development challenges will therefore be increasingly acute in cities, particularly in the lower and middle-income countries where population growth and the pace of urbanization are greatest (Figure 16). However, people in rural areas, who account for the vast majority of the extreme poor (see Chapter 7), must also not be 'left behind' in terms of development policy.

Although the overall proportion of the urban population living in slums worldwide fell from 28% in 2000 to 23% in 2014, in absolute terms, the number of urban residents living in slums rose from 792 million to an estimated 880 million over the same period. In Least Developed Countries, nearly two-thirds (62%) of urban dwellers live in slum conditions (Figure 17). Slums remain most pervasive in Sub-Saharan Africa (UN, 2017).

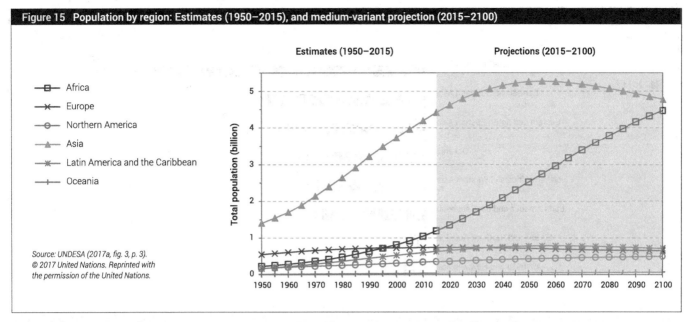

Figure 15 Population by region: Estimates (1950−2015), and medium-variant projection (2015−2100)

Estimates (1950−2015)   Projections (2015−2100)

Legend:
- Africa
- Europe
- Northern America
- Asia
- Latin America and the Caribbean
- Oceania

Source: UNDESA (2017a, fig. 3, p. 3).
© 2017 United Nations. Reprinted with the permission of the United Nations.

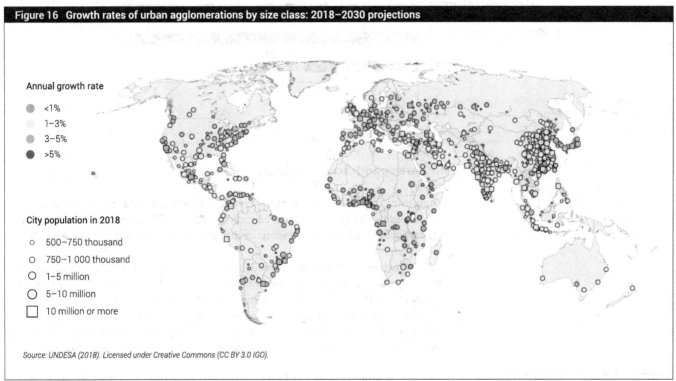

Figure 16 Growth rates of urban agglomerations by size class: 2018−2030 projections

Annual growth rate
- <1%
- 1–3%
- 3–5%
- >5%

City population in 2018
- 500–750 thousand
- 750–1 000 thousand
- 1–5 million
- 5–10 million
- 10 million or more

Source: UNDESA (2018). Licensed under Creative Commons (CC BY 3.0 IGO).

Age distribution

Life expectancy, which has risen by five years globally between 2000 and 2015 (WHO, 2016a), has become a significant driver of population growth. Life expectancy for both sexes combined is projected to rise from 71 years in 2010–2015 to 77 years in 2045–2050, with women living on average four years longer than men. With the exception of Africa, all regions of the world will have nearly a quarter or more of their populations at ages 60 and above by 2050 (UNDESA, 2017a).

There are also more young people in the world than ever before — about 1.8 billion between the ages of 10 and 25 (UNFPA, 2014). Nearly 80% of the world's 2.3 billion young people (aged 15 to 34) live in low- and middle-income countries, and they constitute a large share of the population in countries experiencing rapid economic growth (Kwame, 2018), although they do not all necessarily directly benefit from such growth.

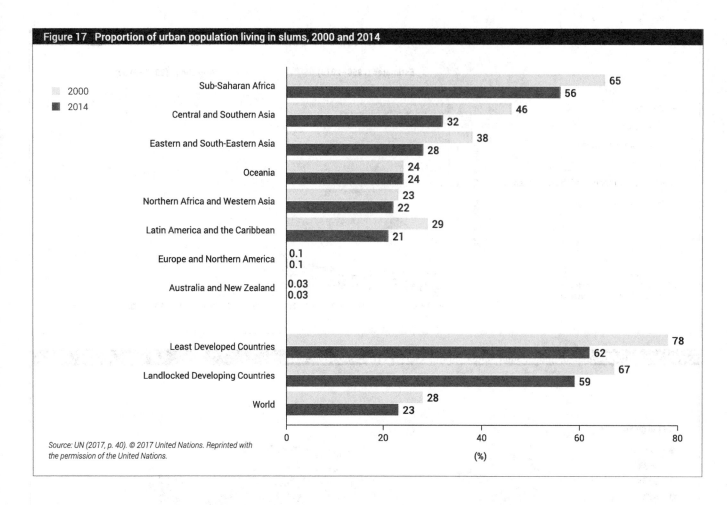

Figure 17 Proportion of urban population living in slums, 2000 and 2014

2000
2014

Region	2000	2014
Sub-Saharan Africa	65	56
Central and Southern Asia	46	32
Eastern and South-Eastern Asia	38	28
Oceania	24	24
Northern Africa and Western Asia	23	22
Latin America and the Caribbean	29	21
Europe and Northern America	0.1	0.1
Australia and New Zealand	0.03	0.03
Least Developed Countries	78	62
Landlocked Developing Countries	67	59
World	28	23

(%)

Source: UN (2017, p. 40). © 2017 United Nations. Reprinted with the permission of the United Nations.

ii. Poverty and income disparity

Poverty

People living in poverty struggle every day to fulfil their most basic needs, including access to water and sanitation, healthcare, education, and a reliable source of energy. They are also particularly vulnerable to impacts of climate change (Castaneda Aguilar et al., 2016).

In 2013 (the most recent estimates available), 767 million people (more than 10% of the global population) were living below the international extreme poverty line of US$1.90 per day (2011 PPP)[8], and 2.1 billion people (about 30% of the global population) were living on less than US$3.10 a day (2011 PPP). Nearly 80% of the extreme poor lived in rural areas. The overwhelming majority of people living below the international extreme poverty line lived in Southern Asia and Sub-Saharan Africa (World Bank, 2016a).

The absolute number of people living in extreme poverty fell from 1.85 billion in 1990 to 0.76 billion in 2013. Sub-Saharan Africa is the only region that between 1990 and 2013 registered an increase in the absolute number of people living in extreme poverty, although the overall share of people in extreme poverty in the region dropped from 54% to 41% over that period (Figure 18) (World Bank, n.d.).

Children account for 44% of the extreme poor worldwide and poverty rates are highest among children (Figure 19). As girls and boys grow older, the gender gap widens between the ages of 20 and 35, with 122 women living in poor households for every 100 men of the same age group (Munoz Boudet et al., 2018).

Sex disparities in poverty rates for adults aged 20 to 40 are closely linked to marital and parenthood status. One of the contributing factors to poverty for working-age women in some countries is the increasing proportion of non-partnered women with children (UNDESA, 2015).

> **In 2013, nearly 80% of the extreme poor lived in rural areas**

[8] '2011 PPP' stands for 2011 purchasing power parity. The international poverty line for extreme poverty is US$1.90 a day 2011 PPP and the 'median' poverty line is US$3.10 a day 2011 PPP.

The United Nations World Water Development Report 2019

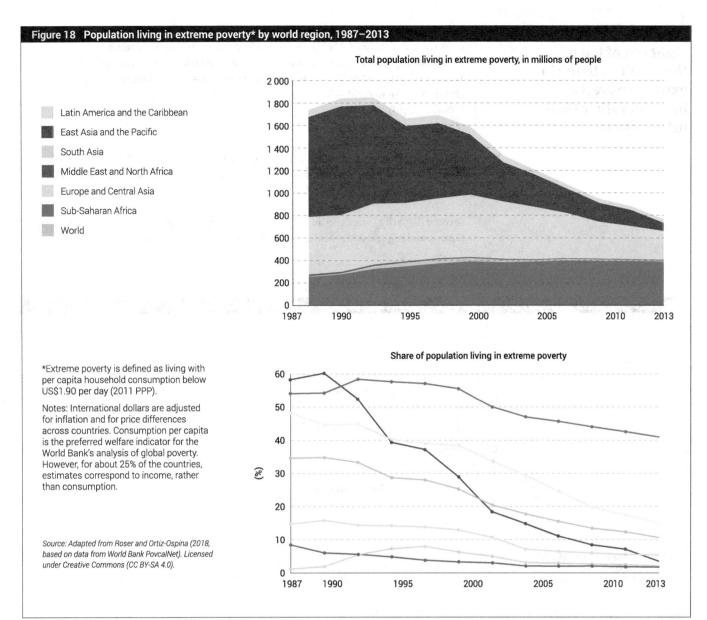

Total population living in extreme poverty, in millions of people

Latin America and the Caribbean
East Asia and the Pacific
South Asia
Middle East and North Africa
Europe and Central Asia
Sub-Saharan Africa
World

*Extreme poverty is defined as living with per capita household consumption below US$1.90 per day (2011 PPP).

Notes: International dollars are adjusted for inflation and for price differences across countries. Consumption per capita is the preferred welfare indicator for the World Bank's analysis of global poverty. However, for about 25% of the countries, estimates correspond to income, rather than consumption.

Source: Adapted from Roser and Ortiz-Ospina (2018, based on data from World Bank PovcalNet). Licensed under Creative Commons (CC BY-SA 4.0).

Share of population living in extreme poverty

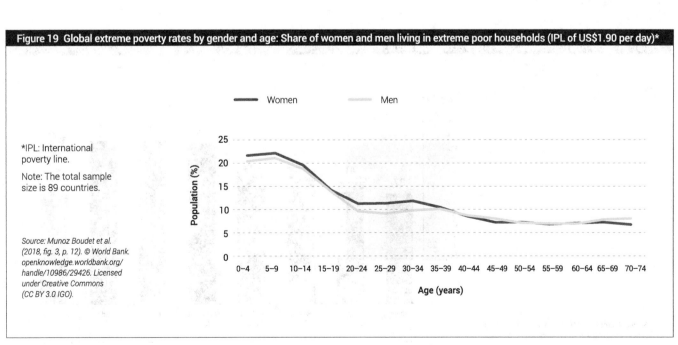

*IPL: International poverty line.

Note: The total sample size is 89 countries.

Source: Munoz Boudet et al. (2018, fig. 3, p. 12). © World Bank. openknowledge.worldbank.org/handle/10986/29426. Licensed under Creative Commons (CC BY 3.0 IGO).

Eight out of ten of the children living in extreme poverty live in rural, rather than urban, areas

Eight out of ten of the children living in extreme poverty live in rural, rather than urban, areas. Over 25% of children living in rural areas live in extreme poverty, compared to just over 9% of children in urban areas (UNICEF/World Bank, 2016). Poverty is by no means limited to developing countries. An estimated 30 million children — one in eight — living in the world's richest countries are growing up poor (UNICEF, 2014).

Income disparity

While the global income share of the bottom 50% earners has oscillated around 9% since 1980, the global top 1% income share rose from 16% in 1980 to around 20% by 2015 (Figure 20).

Income disparity varies considerably across different regions. It is generally lowest in Europe and highest in the Middle East (Figure 21) (Alvaredo et al., 2018).

Figure 20   The rise of the global top 1% versus the stagnation of the global bottom 50%, 1980–2016

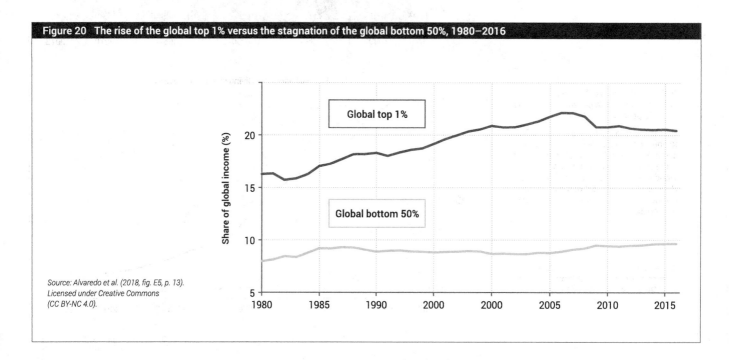

Source: Alvaredo et al. (2018, fig. E5, p. 13). Licensed under Creative Commons (CC BY-NC 4.0).

Figure 21   Top 10% national income share across the world, 2016

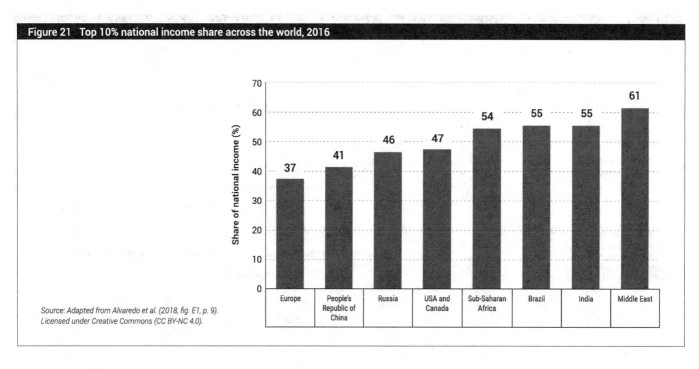

Source: Adapted from Alvaredo et al. (2018, fig. E1, p. 9). Licensed under Creative Commons (CC BY-NC 4.0).

According to the World Inequality Report 2018, *"Economic inequality is largely driven by the unequal ownership of capital, which can be either privately or public owned. We show that since 1980, very large transfers of public to private wealth occurred in nearly all countries, whether rich or emerging. While national wealth has substantially increased, public wealth is now negative or close to zero in rich countries. Arguably this limits the ability of governments to tackle inequality; certainly, it has important implications for wealth inequality among individuals."* (Alvaredo et al., 2018, p. 14).

iii. Health and nutrition
Burden of disease
According to global estimates of cause-specific disability-adjusted life years[9] (DALYs), the number of DALYs per 100,000 population dropped from 45,000 in 2000 to 36,300 in 2015, suggesting an improvement in the overall disease burden over that 15-year period. There was a drop in DALYs related to nearly all nutritional deficiencies and communicable diseases, including diarrhoeal diseases, which fell over 50% from 2,530 to 1,160 DALYs per 100,000 population. The rate of the decline in diarrhoeal diseases DALYs was similar across all income groups. However, waterborne diseases remain a significant disease burden among vulnerable and disadvantaged groups worldwide, especially among low-income economies where 4% of the population (an estimated 25.5 million people, 1 in 25) suffered from diarrhoea in 2015, among whom 60% were children under the age of five (WHO, 2016b).

Disabilities
People with disabilities can often face difficulties in accessing water access points and sanitation facilities, often not designed to account for their particular needs. About 1 billion people (15% of the world's population) experience some form of disability. Of this number, between 110 million and 190 million adults experience significant difficulties in functioning. It is estimated that some 93 million children — or 1 in 20 of those under 15 years of age — live with a moderate or severe disability (WHO, 2015). Global prevalence is greater for women than men, standing at 19% and 12%, respectively. In low and middle-income countries, women are estimated to comprise up to three-quarters of persons with disabilities (UN Women, 2017).

People with disabilities are more likely to experience adverse socio-economic outcomes than people without disabilities. These outcomes include lower education levels, poorer health, inferior levels of employment, and higher rates of poverty (WHO, 2011).

The number of people who experience disability will continue to increase as populations age, aligned with a global increase in chronic health conditions (WHO, 2015).

According to the World Health Organisation (WHO): *"Disability disproportionately affects women, older people, and poor people. Children from poorer households, indigenous populations and those in ethnic minority groups are also at significantly higher risk of experiencing disability … [and] face particular challenges in accessing services."* (WHO, 2015, pp. 2–3).

Nutrition and food insecurity
The number of chronically undernourished people on the planet increased from 777 million in 2015 to 815 million in 2016 (even if it is still less than the 900 million in 2000). Deteriorations in food security have particularly been observed in situations of conflict, especially when combined with droughts or floods. The situation has worsened in particular in parts of Sub-Saharan Africa, South-Eastern Asia and Western Asia. Women are slightly more likely to be food insecure than men in every region of the world (Figure 22) (FAO/IFAD/UNICEF/WFP/WHO, 2017). At the same time, obesity has nearly tripled worldwide since 1975. In 2016, more than 1.9 billion adults (older than 18 years) were overweight and more than one-third of these (over 650 million) were obese (WHO, 2018).

Globally, 155 million children under five years of age suffer from stunted growth, although the prevalence of stunting fell from 29.5% to 22.9% between 2005 and 2016. In 2016, 41 million children under five years of age were overweight (FAO/IFAD/UNICEF/WFP/WHO, 2017). Lack of access to safe water, sanitation and hygiene (WASH) contributes to

Deteriorations in food security have particularly been observed in situations of conflict, especially when combined with droughts or floods

---

[9] DALYs are years of healthy life lost to premature death and disability.

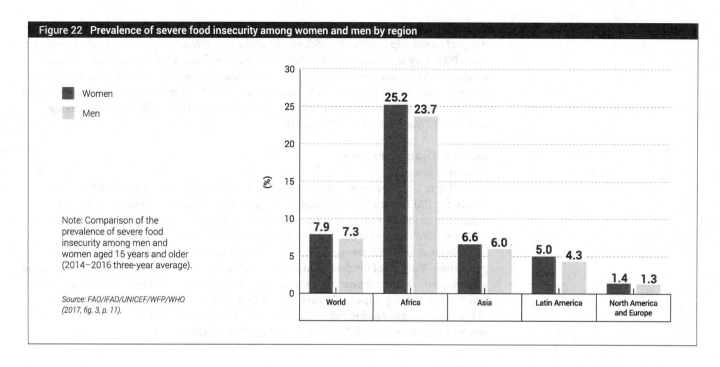

Figure 22 Prevalence of severe food insecurity among women and men by region

Note: Comparison of the prevalence of severe food insecurity among men and women aged 15 years and older (2014–2016 three-year average).

Source: FAO/IFAD/UNICEF/WFP/WHO (2017, fig. 3, p. 11).

undernutrition by transmitting pathogens, while infections inhibit nutritional uptake (World Bank, 2017a). These factors are related to retarded growth among children (UN, 2018a).

iv. Education and literacy
Education
Water and sanitation facilities in schools are fundamental for promoting good hygienic behaviour and children's health and well-being. Lack of latrines and safe water for drinking and hygiene, and otherwise inappropriate and inadequate sanitary facilities, contribute to absenteeism and high drop-out rates, especially among girls.

In 2016, an estimated 58 out of the 92 countries surveyed had over 75% coverage of drinking water in schools (Figure 23). Nearly half of schools in Sub-Saharan Africa, and over a third of schools in Small Island Developing States had no drinking water service (WHO/UNICEF, 2018a).

Furthermore, in 2016, 67 out of 101 countries had over 75% coverage of improved single-sex sanitation facilities classified as providing a basic sanitation service (Figure 24). An estimated 23% of schools had no sanitation service, (defined as an unimproved facility or no facility at all), and over 620 million children worldwide lacked a basic sanitation service at their school (WHO/UNICEF, 2018a).

Early childhood education opportunities are often distributed in a highly unequal fashion. In low and middle-income countries, just over two 3- to 4-year-olds from the poorest quintile of households attended an organized learning programme, for every ten children from the richest quintile. In Serbia and Nigeria, the attendance rate was over 80% for the richest children and no more than 10% for the poorest (UNESCO, 2017a).

Literacy
Literacy can be a major catalyst for eradicating poverty and improving hygiene and family health. Fifty years ago, almost one-quarter of youth lacked basic literacy skills compared to less than 10% in 2016. However, 750 million adults — two-thirds of whom are women — remain illiterate. 102 million of the illiterate population are between 15 and 24 years old. The global adult literacy rate was 86% in 2016, while the youth literacy rate was 91%. The adult and youth literacy rates are estimated to have grown by only 4% each over the 2000–2015 period. The lowest literacy rates are observed in Sub-Saharan Africa and in Southern Asia (Figure 25) (UNESCO, 2017b).

> **Water and sanitation facilities in schools are fundamental for promoting good hygienic behaviour and children's health and well-being**

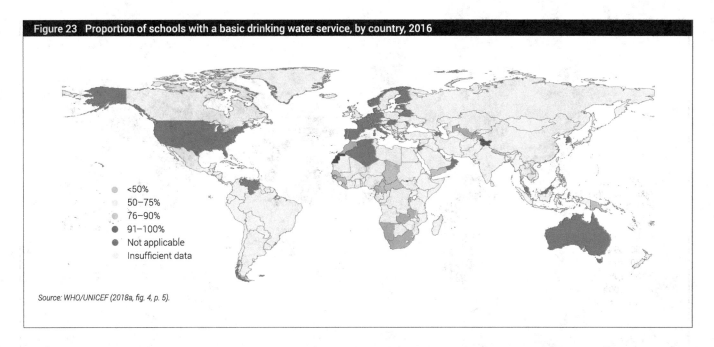

Figure 23 Proportion of schools with a basic drinking water service, by country, 2016

- <50%
- 50–75%
- 76–90%
- 91–100%
- Not applicable
- Insufficient data

Source: WHO/UNICEF (2018a, fig. 4, p. 5).

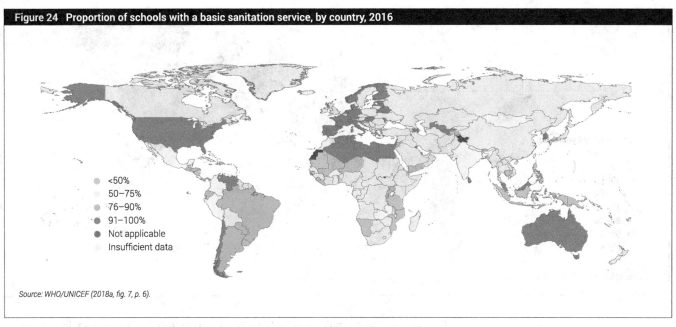

Figure 24 Proportion of schools with a basic sanitation service, by country, 2016

- <50%
- 50–75%
- 76–90%
- 91–100%
- Not applicable
- Insufficient data

Source: WHO/UNICEF (2018a, fig. 7, p. 6).

v. Labour and employment

Labour force participation

An estimated four out of five jobs are water-dependent. Examples of sectors with heavily water-dependent jobs include agriculture, forestry, inland fisheries and aquaculture, mining and resource extraction, power generation, and manufacturing and transformation industries (WWAP, 2016).

The global labour force participation of the world's working-age population has been on a downward trend since 1990, and this trend is projected to continue until at least 2030, driven mainly by a steady decline in Asia and the Pacific. Africa is the only region where the labour force participation rate is expected to increase in the coming decades (ILO, 2017a).

The lack of access to adequate sanitation facilities in the workplace can dissuade women from seeking employment in establishments and institutions that do not provide adequate facilities (e.g. different washroom areas for women and men). This contributes to the already lower participation rates of women and girls in national employment figures (UNESCWA, 2013).

Figure 25 Adult and youth literacy rates by country, 2016

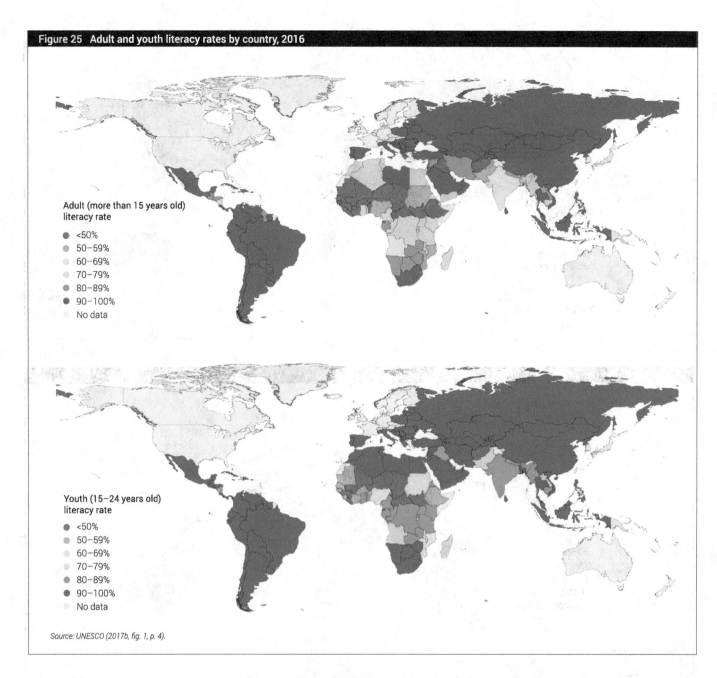

Source: UNESCO (2017b, fig. 1, p. 4).

On average, women make up about 43% of the agricultural labour force in developing countries. Evidence indicates that if women had the same access to productive resources — including land and water — as men, they could increase yields on their farms by 20 to 30%, raising total agricultural output in these countries by 2.5 to 4%. This could reduce the number of hungry people in the world by around 12 to 17% (FAO/IFAD/WFP, 2012).

Agriculture is the largest employer of the youth labour force, particularly in rural areas in low- and middle-income countries (Yeboah, 2018). These jobs are particularly vulnerable to the impacts of extreme events such as droughts and floods.

Digitalization and Industry 4.0

Service sector jobs tend to be less water-dependent than those in agriculture and industry (WWAP, 2016). The digitalization of the economy (or Industry 4.0) will likely have significant consequences for job creation/destruction. However, the extent to which broader application of information and communication technology (ICT) and new digital technologies (including artificial intelligence, utilization of big data, etc.) will cause change, eliminate existing jobs, and create new activities and jobs remains the subject of some debate. Globalization, economic developments and the changing preferences of consumers and producers will also change labour demand and supply (EESC, 2017).

Current technological changes have created huge productivity gains. However, some evidence indicates that the current technological changes may further segment the labour market and widen wage inequality (ILO, 2015).

vi. Ethnicity and culture
Racial, ethnic, religious and other minorities are often more at risk of being 'left behind' in terms of water than others.

Minorities
There is often discrimination against migrants and ethnic minorities with respect to access to safe drinking water and sanitation. This can occur in response to tensions arising from international migration and the increasing salience of religious tensions, and persistent discrimination against the elderly in many countries and regions. There are substantial non-ascriptive minorities who also face persistent discrimination. In Sub-Saharan Africa, for example, sufferers of HIV-AIDS are liable to mistreatment and exclusion (Foa, 2015).

Indigenous peoples
Indigenous peoples number about 370 million, accounting for about 5% of the global population. They are over-represented among the poor (15% of the total and one-third of the world's 900 million extremely poor rural people),[10] the illiterate and the unemployed. Even in developed countries, indigenous peoples consistently lag behind the non-indigenous populations in terms of most indicators of well-being, including access to water supply and sanitation services.

Many indigenous women and men find employment in the informal economy and engage in a range of activities such as casual and seasonal wage work on farms, plantations, construction sites in informal enterprises, street vending or as domestic workers. Indigenous peoples tend to have relatively higher rates of unemployment than non-indigenous peoples in urban areas (ILO, 2017b).

vii. Migration[11]
Migrants can face exceptional difficulties and challenges in accessing safe and reliable water supply and sanitation services in transit and destination areas. Migration occurs as a result of a complex interplay of social, economic and environmental factors acting at different levels (individual, household, external).

International migration
By December 2017, there were an estimated 258 million people living in a country other than their country of birth — an increase of 49% since 2000. Over 60% of all international migrants live in Asia (80 million) or Europe (78 million). Northern America hosted the third largest number of international migrants (58 million), followed by Africa (25 million), Latin America and the Caribbean (10 million) and Oceania (8 million) (UNDESA, 2017b).

In 2017, 48.4% of international migrants were women. Female migrants outnumbered males in all regions except Africa and Asia (UNDESA, 2017b).

According to a report from the Population Division of the United Nations Department of Economic and Social Affairs (UNDESA), *"Large and persistent economic and demographic asymmetries between countries are likely to remain key drivers of international migration for the foreseeable future. Between 2015 and 2050, the top net receivers of international migrants (more than 100,000 annually) are projected to be the United States of America,*

Migrants can face exceptional difficulties and challenges in accessing safe and reliable water supply and sanitation services

---

[10] Although these figures are frequently cited in several recent reports by United Nations agencies (among others), including ILO (2017b) as cited in this report, these estimates are based on reports published as far back as 2003 (i.e. World Bank, 2003).

[11] Migrants are defined here — and elsewhere in the report — as people who have chosen to move from one place to another mainly to improve their lives (e.g. finding work, seeking better education, reuniting with family), not because of a direct threat or persecution. It is critical to distinguish between people who are forcibly displaced and those who leave for other reasons. Detailed metrics and information on refugees, asylum seekers and internally displaced people (IDPs) are provided in Chapter 8.

Germany, Canada, the United Kingdom, Australia and the Russian Federation. The countries projected to be net senders of more than 100,000 migrants annually include India, Bangladesh, China, Pakistan, and Indonesia." (UNDESA, 2017a, p. 10).

However, evidence shows that migration flows between developing countries are larger than those from developing to developed countries. In 2015, the number of people that moved between developing countries represented 38% of the total number of international migrants, compared to 35% of those who moved from south to north (FAO, 2018a). Similarly, in Sub-Saharan Africa people tend to move mostly to neighbouring countries or within the region (Mercandalli and Losch, 2017).

Internal migration

The vast majority of migrants do not cross borders but remain within their own country. Data concerning this type of migration are sparse, although the total number of internal migrants was 'conservatively' estimated at 740 million in 2009 (UNDP, 2009). The current number is likely to be significantly higher. Internal migration patterns are prevalently rural-rural and rural-urban (Mercandalli and Losch, 2017).

viii. Access to resources (land, energy and ICT)

Land tenure

Access to water resources is often related to land tenure, particularly in rural settings. Less than 20% of the world's landholders are women. In Sub-Saharan Africa, women make up an average of 15% of all agricultural land owners (Figure 26), while in North Africa and Western Asia they represent fewer less 5% (FAO/IFAD/WFP, 2012).

Land tenure security is closely linked to poverty reduction. According to the International Fund for Agricultural Development (IFAD), *"In rural societies, the poorest people often have weak or unprotected tenure rights. They therefore risk losing land they depend on to more powerful neighbours, to private companies — domestic or foreign — and even to members of their own family. [...] Women are particularly vulnerable because their land rights may be obtained through kinship relationships with men or marriage. [...] Lack of secure land tenure exacerbates poverty and has contributed to social instability and conflict in many parts of the world."* (IFAD, 2015, p. 1).

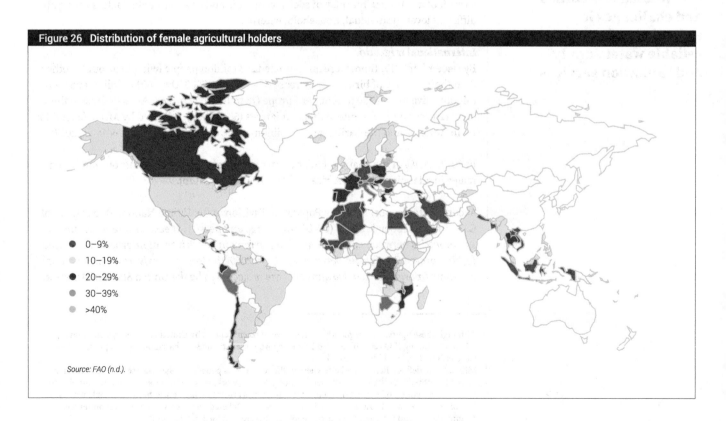

Figure 26   Distribution of female agricultural holders

- 0–9%
- 10–19%
- 20–29%
- 30–39%
- \>40%

Source: FAO (n.d.).

Energy

Water and energy are closely linked. Whereas energy is required for the pumping and distribution of water (including for irrigation), water supply, wastewater treatment and water desalination, the energy sector also requires water to cool thermal power plants, generate hydropower and grow biofuels (WWAP, 2014).

The number of people without access to electricity fell from 1.7 billion in 2000 to 1.1 billion in 2016. However, despite progress in the last few years, the electrification rate in Sub-Saharan Africa remains below 45% (IEA, 2017). Of those gaining access to electricity worldwide since 2010, the vast majority (80%) are in urban settlements (UNSD, n.d.).

Digitalization

As of January 2018, over 4 billion people around the world have internet access (We are Social and Hootsuite, 2018). However, despite the rapid rise in the number of people online, there are still significant differences between the richest countries and the rest of the world (Figure 27).

About 80% of the population in developed countries is online, compared to 40% in developing regions and 15% in the Least Developed Countries. In 2016, the global rate of internet user penetration was 12% lower for women than for men. The gender gap remains even larger in the Least Developed Countries, at 31%. Fixed-broadband services remain largely unaffordable and unavailable throughout large segments of the developing world (UNESCO, 2017a).

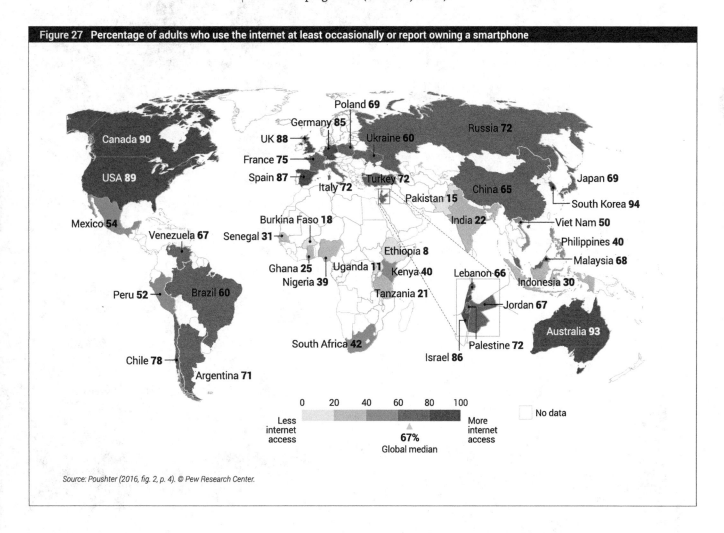

Figure 27   Percentage of adults who use the internet at least occasionally or report owning a smartphone

Source: Poushter (2016, fig. 2, p. 4). © Pew Research Center.

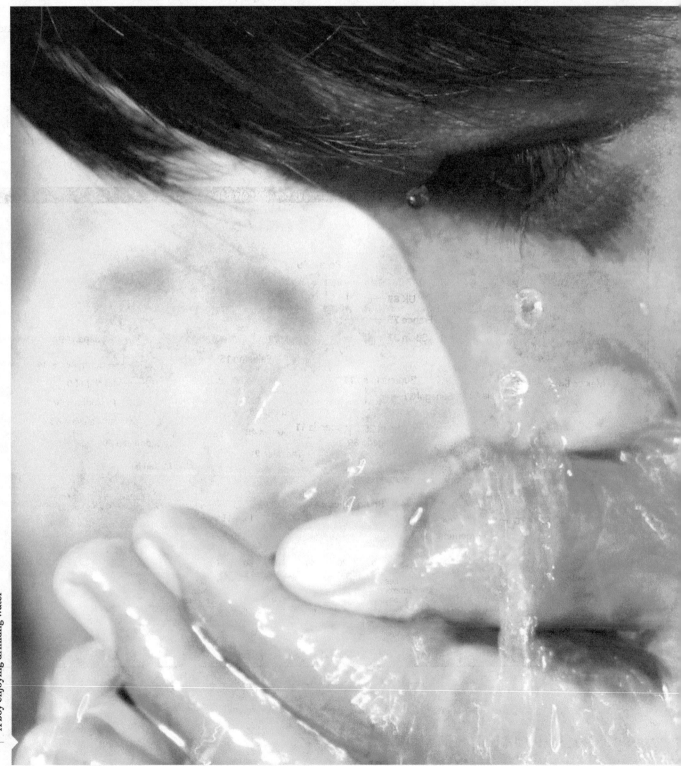

CHAPTER 1

The human rights to water and sanitation and the 2030 Agenda for Sustainable Development

A boy enjoying drinking water

OHCHR | Rio Hada

WWAP | Lucilla Minelli, Richard Connor, Engin Koncagül and Stefan Uhlenbrook

With contributions from: Léo Heller (Special Rapporteur on the human rights to safe drinking water and sanitation); Marianne Kjellén (UNDP); Ileana Sinziana Puscas and Daria Mokhnacheva (IOM); Maria Teresa Gutierrez and Carlos Carrion-Crespo (ILO); Solène Le Doze (UNESCAP); Ryan Schweizer (UNHCR); Andrei Jouravlev (UNECLAC); and Jenny Grönwall (UNDP-SIWI Water Governance Facility)

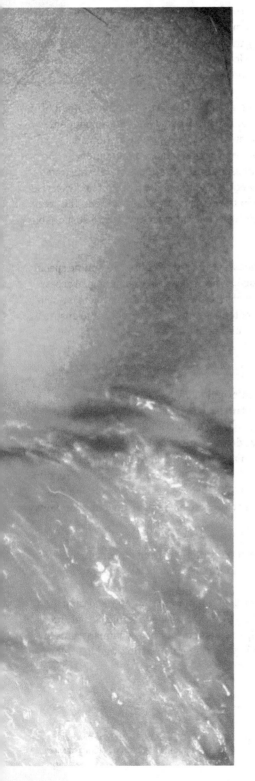

This introductory chapter frames the report by describing the main concepts related to the human rights to safe drinking water and sanitation, with an empahsis on targeting disadvantaged groups and people in vulnerable situations.

"As we embark on this great collective journey, we pledge that no one will be left behind. Recognizing that the dignity of the human person is fundamental, we wish to see the goals and targets met for all nations and peoples and for all segments of society. And we will endeavour to reach the furthest behind first."
Transforming our world: The 2030 Agenda for Sustainable Development (UNGA, 2015a, para. 4)

1.1
Introduction

Water is the essence of life. Safe drinking water and sanitation are recognized as basic human rights, as they are indispensable to sustaining healthy livelihoods and fundamental in maintaining the dignity of all human beings. People-centred policies to provide water and sanitation services, and sound and sustainable management of water resources and of our ecosystems as a whole, are therefore integral to sustainable development and to the full enjoyment of the human rights to water and sanitation, as well as a wide range of other human rights, including the rights to life, health and food.

Since 2000, billions of people have gained access to basic water and sanitation services, thanks to concerted global efforts under the Millennium Development Goals (MDGs). Yet globally, 2.1 billion people lack access to safe, readily available water at home, and 4.5 billion people lack safely managed sanitation in 2015. Huge inequalities exist between and within countries, and between the richest and the poorest (WHO/UNICEF, 2017a).

Almost half of people drinking water from unprotected sources live in Sub-Saharan Africa (WHO/UNICEF, 2017a), where the burden of collecting water lies mainly on women and girls, many of whom spend more than 30 minutes on each trip to collect water (UNICEF, 2016). Without safe, accessible water and sanitation, these people are likely to face multiple challenges, including poor health and living conditions, malnutrition, and lack of opportunities for education and employment. Water stress, including insufficient access to water and sanitation services, has been associated with social unrest, conflict and even violence, and ultimately with increasing trends in human displacement and migration (Miletto et al., 2017).

'Leaving no one behind' is at the heart of the commitment of the 2030 Agenda for Sustainable Development, which aims to allow all people in all countries to benefit from socio-economic development and to achieve the full realization of human rights, without discrimination on the basis of gender, age, race, language, religion, political (or other) opinions, national or social origin, property, disability, residency status (including citizenship, residency, immigration, refugee, statelessness, etc.) or any other social, economic or political status. Achieving the 2030 Agenda and its promise of 'leaving no one behind' requires a people-centred focus grounded in international human rights and an integrated approach among the social, economic and environmental dimensions of sustainable development in partnership with all stakeholders.

The 17 Sustainable Development Goals (SDGs) with their 169 targets respond to this vision and were designed to be comprehensive and indivisible (UNGA, 2015a). More often than not, the SDGs are not isolated objectives, but prerequisites to achieve all the others. The SDG 6 on clean water and sanitation is considered to be one of these central SDGs, because of its vital functions related to human health, dignity, environmental integrity and prosperity, and the very survival of the planet (UN, 2018a). Achieving the targets of SDG 6, and particularly those that specifically address water and sanitation services, will require improvements in the levels of planning, capacity, governance and funding at both national and local levels.

The human rights to water and sanitation are inextricably linked to the management of water resources and the environment as a whole. The interlinked and interdependent nature of human rights and the call to 'leave no one behind' require more holistic, integrated and people-centred approaches to water resource management and environmental policy-making, a challenge addressed through the concept of 'integrated water resources management' (IWRM). When people are able to learn about and exercise their rights, and are empowered to participate in the decisions that affect them, they can help to ensure that those decisions respect their need for water security and a sustainable environment.

The human rights-based approach (HRBA) provides a critical perspective to examine specific groups that are lagging or are being left behind due to discrimination or an unequal access to resources and opportunities to participate in decision-making processes. It can also help identify legal obligations and standards to guide potential actions and responses to ensure that the human rights to water and sanitation are fulfilled.

> **International human rights law obliges states to work towards achieving universal access to water and sanitation for all, without any discrimination, while prioritizing those most in need**

1.2
The human rights to water and sanitation

Access to safe drinking water and sanitation are internationally recognized human rights, derived from the right to an adequate standard of living under Article 11(1) of the International Covenant on Economic, Social and Cultural Rights (ICESCR, 1967). On 28 July 2010, the United Nations (UN) General Assembly adopted a historical resolution recognizing *"the right to safe and clean drinking water and sanitation as a human right that is essential for the full enjoyment of life and all human rights"* (UNGA, 2010, para. 1). Furthermore, since 2015, the General Assembly and the Human Rights Council have recognized both the right to safe drinking water and the right to sanitation as closely related but distinct human rights (UNGA, 2015b; HRC, 2016a).[12]

International human rights law obliges states to work towards achieving universal access to water and sanitation for all, without any discrimination, while prioritizing those most in need.

The following sections describe the key content of the human rights to water and sanitation as elaborated in the General Comment No. 15 of the Committee on Economic, Social and Cultural Rights (CESCR, 2002a), the work of the Special Rapporteur on the human rights to water and sanitation, and the resolutions adopted by the General Assembly and the Human Rights Council (OHCHR, n.d.).

---

[12] Given this recognition by the United Nations in 2015, this Report refers to the human rights to water and sanitation in the plural, except when directly quoting from the language contained in United Nations official documents prior to 2015.

1.2.1 Availability of water and sanitation

Availability of water means that the water supply is sufficient and continuous for personal and domestic uses, including drinking, personal sanitation, washing clothes, food preparation, and personal and household hygiene (CESCR, 2002a, para. 12). According to the World Health Organization (WHO, 2017a), approximately 50 litres of water per person per day are needed to ensure that most basic needs are met while keeping public health risks at a low level. However, these amounts are indicative as they might depend on particular contexts and some individuals and groups may also require additional water due to health, climate and working conditions (CESCR, 2002a).

With respect to the availability of sanitation, there must be a sufficient number of sanitation facilities within or in the immediate vicinity of each household, and all health or educational institutions, workplaces and other public places to ensure that all the needs of each person are met. Moreover, they should be available continuously and in a sufficient number to avoid overcrowding and unreasonable waiting times (HRC, 2009, para. 70).

1.2.2 Physical accessibility of water and sanitation

Water supply and sanitation infrastructure must be located and built in such a way that it is genuinely accessible, with consideration given to people who face specific barriers, such as women, children, elderly people, people with disabilities and chronically ill people (De Albuquerque, 2014). Some aspects are particularly important: the design of the facilities; the time and distance to collect water or to reach a sanitation facility; and physical security.

Providing access to safely managed water, the agreed objective of SDG 6, is defined by WHO/UNICEF (2017a, p. 8) as *"drinking water from an improved water source that is located on premises, available when needed and free from faecal and priority chemical contamination"*. While there is no international legal standard for the physical accessibility of water, the criteria for a basic drinking water service established by the Joint Monitoring Programme (JMP) states a maximum of 30 minutes per round trip (including queuing time) to collect water from an improved source located off-premises (WHO/UNICEF, 2017a). There are no similar criteria established in the context of the SDGs (in terms of disctance or time) for sanitation facilities, as basic sanitation services require improved facilities that are not shared with other households (and are thus located on-site).

1.2.3 Affordability

Everyone must be able to afford water and sanitation services in a way that does not limit one's capacity to acquire other basic goods and services (such as food, health and education) that are essential for the realization of other human rights. *"While human rights laws do not require services to be provided free of charge, States have an obligation to provide free services or put adequate subsidy mechanisms in place to ensure that services always remain affordable for the poor"* (De Albuquerque, 2014, p. 35). Moreover, disconnection of water services because of failure to pay due to a lack of means may constitute a violation of human rights (HRC, 2014).

As the affordability of water supply and sanitation services is highly contextual (see Section 5.3), states should determine such standards at the national and/or local level, together with standards about the adequate quantity and quality as well as other key elements of human rights to water and sanitation (see HRC, 2015). A number of countries[13] have defined national standards, and international organizations[14] have developed recommendations in this regard.

> **Disconnection of water services because of failure to pay due to a lack of means may constitute a violation of human rights**

---

[13] For instance, the regulatory authorities of the United Kingdom (UK) define any expenditure on water above 3% of the household spending as an indicator of hardship (UNDP, 2006, p. 51).

[14] For instance, the Water Supply and Sanitation Collaborative Council recommends that the costs for water and sanitation services should not exceed 5% of a household's income (UN-Water DPAC/WSSCC, n.d.).

1.2.4 Quality and safety

The human rights framework specifies that the water required for each personal or domestic use must be safe and free from micro-organisms, chemical substances and radiological hazards that constitute a threat to a person's health. Furthermore, water should be of an acceptable colour, odour and taste for each personal or domestic use (CESCR, 2002a, para. 12b). Sanitation facilities must be hygienically safe to use, meaning that the infrastructure must effectively prevent human, animal and insect contact with human excreta; ensure access to safe water for hand washing and menstrual hygiene; be designed in a way that takes the needs of persons with disabilities and children into account; and be regularly cleaned and maintained.

1.2.5 Acceptability

All water facilities and services must be culturally acceptable and appropriate, and sensitive to gender, life-cycle and privacy requirements (CESCR, 2002a, para. 12c). Cultural values and different perspectives must be taken into account regarding design, positioning and conditions for use of sanitation facilities. In most cultures, acceptability will require separate facilities for women and men in public places, and for girls and boys in schools (HRC, 2009, para. 80). Toilets for women and girls should take needs for menstruation hygiene management into consideration, particularly with respect to ensuring privacy and safety (HRC, 2018a, para. 78; UNGA, 2016, para. 44). Facilities need to allow for culturally acceptable hygiene practices, such as hand washing and anal and genital cleansing.

1.3
Groups and individuals 'left behind' in terms of access to water and sanitation

The human rights to safe drinking water and sanitation, as any other human right, are deeply rooted in the indivisible principles of non-discrimination and equality (Box 1.1). A better understanding of these concepts contributes to identifying specific groups that currently are or at risk of being 'left behind' in terms of access to water and sanitations services; at the same time, it also helps to highlight roles and responsibilities in ensuring that everybody is treated fairly with equal access to resources and opportunities. *"In order to reach equality of water and sanitation service provision, States must work towards eliminating existing inequalities. This requires knowledge of disparities in access, which typically exist not only between and within groups with different incomes, but also between and within rural and urban populations. There are further disparities based on gender and the exclusion of disadvantaged individuals or groups."* (De Albuquerque, 2014, p. 30)

Box 1.1   The indivisible principles of non-discrimination and equality

While human rights to water and sanitation, like other economic, social and cultural rights, are to be progressively realized over time, there are certain obligations that are of an immediate nature. An important part of such immediate obligations is the elimination of discrimination. Discrimination in international human rights law is defined as *"any distinction, exclusion or restriction which has the purpose or the effect of impairing or nullifying the recognition, enjoyment or exercise, on an equal basis with others, of human rights and fundamental freedoms in the political, economic, social, cultural, civil or any other field"* (CEDAW, 1979, article 1). Moreover, Article 2 of the Universal Declaration of Human Rights sets out the basic principle of equality and non-discrimination as regards the enjoyment of human rights and fundamental freedoms, forbidding *"distinction of any kind, such as race, colour, sex, language, religion, political or other opinion, national or social origin, property, birth or other status ..."* (UNGA, 1948).

The principles of non-discrimination and equality recognize that people face different barriers and have different needs, whether because of inherent characteristics or as a result of discriminatory practices, and therefore require differentiated support or treatment. As further clarified by the Human Rights Committee, the equal enjoyment of rights does not mean identical treatment in every instance (HRI, 1994).

The international human rights legal framework contains international instruments to combat specific forms of discrimination; however, it is important to note that grounds of discrimination may change over time, and that no list of prohibited grounds can be considered exhaustive.

Box 1.2 Intersectionality and multiple forms of discrimination

"Although women — at every economic level, all over the world — may suffer disproportionate disadvantages and discrimination, they cannot be seen as a homogeneous group. Different women are situated differently and face different challenges and barriers in relationship to water, sanitation and hygiene. Gender-based inequalities are exacerbated when they are coupled with other grounds for discrimination and disadvantages. Examples include when women and girls lack adequate access to water and sanitation and at the same time suffer from poverty, live with a disability, suffer from incontinence, live in remote areas, lack security of tenure, are imprisoned or are homeless. In these cases, they will be more likely to lack access to adequate facilities, to face exclusion or to experience vulnerability and additional health risks. The effects of social factors such as caste, age, marital status, profession, sexual orientation and gender identity are compounded when they intersect with other grounds for discrimination."

Source: HRC (2016b, para. 12).

1.3.1 Grounds for discrimination

There are multiple prohibitive grounds of discrimination that may have an impact on access to water and sanitation services. These include, for example, political (or other) opinion and marital/family status (CESCR, 2002a, para. 20). An analysis prepared by UN-Water and the Office of the High Commissioner for Human Rights (OHCHR) in 2015, *Eliminating discrimination and inequalities in access to water and sanitation* (UN-Water, 2015), put a spotlight on the possible grounds for discrimination that cause certain groups and individuals to be particularly disadvantaged in terms of access to water, sanitation and hygiene. The following does not necessarily constitute an exhaustive overview of such specific groups or individuals, and it is important to note that some people may suffer from multiple forms of discrimination (intersectionality).

Sex and gender

In many parts of the world, women and girls experience discrimination and inequalities in the enjoyment of their human rights to water and santiation (see UN-Water, 2015 and HRC, 2016b). However, women and girls should not be regarded as a homogeneous group (Box 1.2). Based on assigned gender roles, women and girls often bear the primary responsibility for domestic tasks such as fetching, managing and safeguarding water, which are largely unpaid and unrecognized (WWAP, 2016). As a result, girls are in effect obliged to drop out of school, forfeiting their right to education and other opportunities. The absence of sanitation and menstrual hygiene facilities at schools and in workplaces contribute to high rates of female absenteeism, which in turn leads to further discrimination against women in the labour market. Pregnant women are more vulnerable to consequences of water- and sanitation-related diseases. Women and girls are also at risk of abuse (physical, mental and sexual) when they have to travel long distances to fetch water, to visit public toilets or to go out at night for open defecation. The taboo and stigma surrounding menstruation contributes to ignore women's specific sanitation needs, forcing girls and women to use unhygienic sanitary methods and use toilets only after dark, thus risking their safety. The lack of sex-disaggregated data is a major obstacle to the production of scientific evidence on gender inequalities related to water and to the formulation of evidence-based policies (WWAP, 2015).

Indigenous peoples, migrants, and ethnic and other minorities

In some countries, indigenous peoples living on reserves, nomadic/traveling populations (such as Roma in many European countries) or people of certain ancestries (e.g. castes) experience discrimination in access to water or sanitation services. Religious and linguistic minorities also face inequalities in many countries.

In addition, even though accordingly with the General Comment No. 20 to the International Covenant on Economic, Social and Cultural Rights *"The Covenant rights apply to everyone, including non-nationals, such as refugees, asylum-seekers, stateless persons, migrant workers and victims of international trafficking, regardless of legal status and documentation"* (CESCR, 2009, item I, para. 30), asylum seekers and other migrants often struggle to access water and sanitation facilities in receiving countries, as do internally displaced people (see Chapter 8).

The rights to water and sanitation must be ensured throughout the migration cycle, especially in situations of displacement. Migration, internally or across borders, often results from unemployment, social unrest, food insecurity, disasters and the adverse effects of climate change, including drought, among other factors. It is important to note that water scarcity and exclusion from access to safe water and sanitation in countries of origin could exacerbate these drivers. However, migration can also serve as a strategy of adaptation to new climate and environmental conditions and have positive outcomes, including increased access to water (FAO, 2017a). Moreover, *"in the context of water scarcity, vulnerability will depend on the incidence of climatic variability as well as on a person's or community's resilience and adaptive capacity to this stressor, as adaptive capacity is intrinsically linked to social structures, such as gender, class, caste and ethnicity"* (Miletto et al., 2017, p. 15).

Disability, age and health status

Human rights law provides strong protections for persons with disabilities, in particular through the Convention on the Rights of Persons with Disabilities (CRPD, 2006). Nevertheless, persons with some kind of physical, mental, intellectual or sensory impairment are disproportionately represented among those who lack access to safe drinking water and sanitation (HRC, 2010). Water and sanitation facilities may not be designed to meet the needs of persons with disabilities. A case study in Ethiopia revealed that the entrances to toilets are often too narrow for wheelchairs, forcing individuals to crawl or drag themselves on the floor to reach the toilets (Wilbur, 2010). Accessibility problems also apply to children, (chronically) ill and older people as facilities may not be within easy and safe reach. Some illnesses can generate stigmatization (such as HIV/AIDS) and people affected may suffer from exclusion and be denied access to facilities.

Property, tenure, residence, economic and social status

Global monitoring shows a stark discrepancy between persons living in rural and urban areas. In 2015, two out of five people in rural areas had access to piped water supplies (a form of 'improved' supply, but not necessarily a 'safely managed' supply), whereas four out of five people in urban areas had piped supplies. Sewer connections dominate in urban areas, where they are used by 63% of the population, compared to only 9% in rural areas (WHO/UNICEF, 2017a). However, rapid urbanization does not always keep pace with the extension of public services to the poorest, and there is a huge discrepancy in service provision between formal and informal areas in cities. Causes include reluctance of governments to formalize informal settlements by extending service provision in these areas as well as fear from people living in these settlements to claim access to clean water and sanitation facilities (see Chapter 6). Such inactions by authorities are not in line with the state obligations under international human rights law. More accurate data on the actual situation in these settlements are needed to reveal existing inequalities.

> **There is a huge discrepancy in service provision between formal and informal areas in cities**

1.3.2 Disadvantaged groups and people in vulnerable situations

There can be many different disadvantaged groups in a country, and a subset of people living in vulnerable situations in the same country may face different challenges based on their location, history, local culture and other factors (as noted above). People in vulnerable situations or those who rely exclusively on amenities provided by the state, for example people placed in institutions such as prisons, refugee camps, hospitals, care centres and schools, must be given special attention (CHR, 2005). Box 1.3 provides a non-exhaustive list of groups that are particularly vulnerable to being 'left behind' in terms of access to Water, Sanitation and Hygiene (WASH) services (see Table 5.1).

Box 1.3 Examples of groups and inviduals who live in vulnerable situations or are disadvantaged in terms of accessing water, sanitation and hygiene (WASH) services

- **People living in poverty** face higher proportional costs to access WASH services than the better-off, while generally having access to a lower level of service.

- **Slum dwellers** tend to receive WASH services from informal providers and at very high prices, while higher service levels are often either inaccessible or the initial capital investment in infrastructure is unaffordable.

- Population groups living in **remote and isolated places** tend to pay higher prices, as the unit costs of service provision usually increase with distance.

- Many **indigenous peoples** and **ethnic groups** tend to live in remote and isolated places (which can increase the costs of service provision).

- **Single-headed households**, especially those headed by single women, are likely to have lower incomes than households with two or more adults and may therefore not be able to afford WASH services.

- **Children** may face a lower service level since customs might prioritize the adults' use of a household toilet, and schools may provide poor WASH services. Access may also diminish in a large family with many dependents.

- The **elderly, the sick and physically disabled** often require the support of technologies with specific features, which may come at a high cost. At the same time, their financial resources may be limited since they often do not earn income (and safety nets or pensions barely exist in many nations).

- Limited WASH options are available to **people faced with emergencies** (such as natural disasters), especially when they are situated far away from population centres.

- **Refugees** in the developing world are usually provided temporary solutions for their WASH needs, and their degree of access to WASH services is left largely at the mercy of donors and non-governmental organizations (NGOs).

- **Prisoners** are often subject to poor WASH access, which leads to indignities and suffering.

Contributed by the World Bank.

1.4
Human rights-based approach to integrated water resources management (IWRM)

Since water is multidimensional and essential for human well-being, economic and social activities, energy and food production, and the maintenance of ecosystems, a multitude of institutions are involved in its management. As pressures on the world's freshwater resources increase, organizations and all stakeholders dealing with IWRM face increasing challenges.

IWRM covers both the 'hard' (e.g. infrastructure) and 'soft' (e.g. governance) aspects of water resources management. In 2000, the Global Water Partnership formulated a widely used definition of IWRM: *"IWRM is a process which promotes the co-ordinated development and management of water, land and related resources, in order to maximize the resultant economic and social welfare in an equitable manner without compromising the sustainability of vital ecosystems."* (GWP, 2000, p. 22).

SDG Target 6.5 aims to *"by 2030, implement integrated water resources management at all levels, including through transboundary cooperation as appropriate"*. This commitment of states to IWRM and transboundary water cooperation has been a significant step in the 2030 Agenda. Putting IWRM to practice is arguably the most comprehensive step that states have made towards achieving SDG 6. The United Nations (UN, 2018a) shows that the global average degree of implementation of IWRM is considered medium-low (ca. 48%) and that there are significant variations among countries and regions. Only 25% of the countries in the three lower human development index (HDI) groups reached the medium-low classification. The global progress over the past 10–12 years has been classified as modest. However, most states will not meet the target by 2030 at their current speed of implementing IWRM, including the transboundary component (UN, 2018a).

The human rights framework establishes water for human consumption as the priority water use. The many competing — and sometimes conflicting — demands on water resources will give rise to questions of justice, such as the question what would be considered to be a 'balanced' allocation of water for different uses (Cap-Net/WaterLex/UNDP-SIWI WGF/Redica, 2017). Taking account of disadvantaged individuals and groups, which may in some cases also include the environment as a legal persona, is particularly important but also challenging, and is usually framed under a human rights-based approach (HRBA). Figure 1.1 shows how the concepts of HRBA and IWRM may overlap and differ in their elements. The HRBA can provide a helpful 'perspective' to understanding and implementing IWRM with emphasis on its accountability, participation and non-discrimination principles.

Caution must be taken in order to clearly differentiate between water resources management (including water rights) and the human rights to water and sanitation (Box 1.4). The types of approaches that move water towards equity include: treating water as a common good, not an economic resource; making WASH decision-making transparent and participatory; adopting water policies that recognize and address political and economic imbalances; and ensuring that water is available for future as well as present uses (Wilder and Ingram, 2018).

Figure 1.1	Relationship of a human rights-based approach to water and sanitation in relation to the elements of integrated water resource management

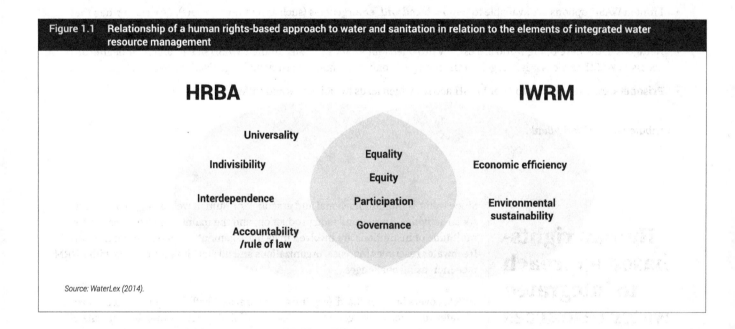

Source: WaterLex (2014).

Box 1.4 Distinguishing water rights from the human rights to water and sanitation

"The human right to water is held by every individual, regardless of who he or she is, or where he or she lives, and safeguards his or her access to water for personal and domestic use. Water rights, on the other hand, are generally conferred to an individual or company through property rights or land rights, and are rights to access or use a water resource. These are generally gained through land ownership or through an agreement with the State or landowner, and are granted for a variety of water uses, including for industry or agriculture." (De Albuquerque, 2014, p. 39).

People availing themselves of their water rights may be violating other people's human rights to water and sanitation, for example, in cases of over-extraction or pollution. A water right is a temporary right that can be provided to an individual and, importantly, that can be withdrawn from that individual. The human right to water is not temporary, it is not subject to state approval, and it cannot be withdrawn (Cap-Net/WaterLex/UNDP-SIWI WGF/Redica, 2017).

1.5

Links between the human rights to water and sanitation and other human rights

The human rights to water and sanitation do not exist in isolation from other human rights. Good water management and governance are fundamental to and have an impact on the realization of a range of human rights, including the right to life, the right to health, the right to food and the human rights related to a healthy environment.

Priority should be given to the supply of water for domestic and personal use, as well as to the requirements of the other Covenant rights; for example, water for substistence farming and for health interventions that protect people from disease (CESCR, 2002a). Water and sanitation are indispensable to human dignity as their lack can be linked to the human right to life (UNGA, 1948, article 3; ICCPR, 1966, article 6(1)) and jeopardize the right to health (UNGA, 1948, article 25; ICESCR, 1967, article 12). For the realization of the right to adequate housing, access to essential services such as water and sanitation is indispensable (OHCHR/UN-Habitat/WHO, 2010). Privacy and physical security (ICCPR, 1966, article 9) are also at risk in situations where women and children use shared latrines or open spaces to defecate, as such a situation makes them particularly vulnerable to harassment, attacks, violence or rape (OHCHR/UN-Habitat/WHO, 2010). Moreover, the right to education (UNGA, 1948, article 26; ICESCR, 1967, articles 13 and 14) cannot be guaranteed if water is not available at school and sanitary facilities are not separated by sex, because often girls will not attend school during their menstrual periods if sanitation is inadequate. Access to water is essential for subsistence farming and therefore to the realization of the right to adequate food (ICESCR, 1967, articles 11(1)(2)). Water access and availability can have an impact on the right to freedom of movement as well, as water access and availability can determine whether people can stay in their homes and communities or are forced to move temporarily or even permanently in search of water sources and green pastures for themselves, their families and their livelihoods (Mach, 2017). The right to work can be negatively affected if there is a lack of access to water and sanitation at the workplace, particularly for women during menstruation and pregnancy (HRC, 2009). Human rights and the environment are interdependent, and there are human rights obligations related to the enjoyment of a safe, clean, healthy and sustainable environment (HRC, 2018b). Finite resources must be protected from overexploitation and pollution (HRC, 2013), and facilities and services dealing with excreta and wastewater should ensure a clean and healthy living environment (Razzaque, 2002; UNGA, 2013). The prohibition of discrimination and the right to equality, including gender equality, and the rights to information and to free, full and meaningful participation are also essential for the realization of the human rights to water and sanitation, with realization of each right having an impact on the others (OHCHR/UN-Habitat/WHO, 2010).

CHAPTER 2

Physical and environmental dimensions

Rossens Dam in Switzerland

UNU-INWEH | Nidhi Nagabhatla

UNU-FLORES | Tamara Avellán

With contributions from: Panthea Pouramin, Manzoor Qadir and Pream Mehta (UNU-INWEH); John Payne (UNIDO Department of Environment, Industrial Resource Efficiency Division); Catalin Stefan (TUD); Stephan Hülsmann (UNU-FLORES); Tommaso Abrate and Giacomo Teruggi (WMO); Frederik Pischke (GWP); Robert Oakes (UNU-EHS); Serena Ceola and Christophe Cudennec (IAHS); and Ignacio Deregibus and Stephanie Kuisma (IWRA)

This chapter examines the physical and environmental dimensions of water provisioning and sanitation services, with a particular focus on addressing the specific needs of disadvantaged groups, viz. slum-dwellers, displaced people, women and girls, and communities living in vulnerable situations.

2.1
Water-provisioning systems

Three out of ten people worldwide did not have access to safely managed water supply services in 2015 (WHO/UNICEF, 2017a; see Prologue, Section 2.i). To ensure water-provisioning services, such as drinking water for all, a set of preconditions are: i) water needs to be *available*; ii) water needs to be *accessible*; and iii) water needs to be sufficiently *treated*. Water availability depends upon the amount of water physically available, and how it is stored, managed and allocated to various users.[15] Water accessibility refers to how water is delivered (or obtained) across different socioeconomic groups and demographics, including women, children and communities in vulnerable situations. Water treatment relates to the importance of safe water, free of bacterial contamination, free of heavy metals, free of foul odour, and possessing little to no turbidity.

2.1.1 Water availability
Surface water
The most commonly known options for collecting and storing surface water (and thus enhancing supply) include dams, reservoirs and other storage structures. Larger structures usually operate at community to regional scales, but there are also smaller-scale options suitable for individual or household needs (e.g. wells, ponds and ditches).

Dams and river systems have long served to cope with seasonal changes in water availability and provide water for various sectoral users when most needed. Overall, dams have served human population growth and development by enhancing capabilities of managing water resources, and thus helped sustain food and energy security (Chen et al., 2016). The size and type of built

---

[15] Groups and communities living in vulnerable situations include but are not limited to people living in poverty (in rural and urban areas), people with disabilities, displaced people, people living with HIV, and the elderly. This applies wherever the term is used in this chapter.

dams and reservoirs can vary enormously, depending on their purpose and site-specific conditions, ranging from sand dams in seasonal rivers to mega-projects such as the Three Gorges Dam in the People's Republic of China (see Box 2.1 in WWAP/UN-Water, 2018).

In rural communities and smaller villages, locally suited fit-for-purpose dams and reservoirs hold potential to provide water to disadvantaged groups that traditionally encounter particular challenges in obtaining and securing water supplies. Emerging innovative solutions similar to small-scale infrastructure (e.g. sand dams) are typically local-scale interventions and are noted to have profound positive impacts on local communities, especially in water-scarce areas as in Kenya (Ryan and Elsner, 2016).

Large-scale dam projects principally require large direct investments and can come with high environmental as well as socio-economic costs. The sociocultural and financial consequences of building dams could adversely impact communities and people living in vulnerable areas, particularly women and girls, who may be burdened by displacement during the construction of canals, irrigation schemes, roads, power lines and accompanying developments (Ronayne, 2005). Such arguments are made in the case of the Sardar-Sarovar Dam and Tehri Dam projects in India (Banerjee et al., 2005).

The International Commission on Large Dams database (ICOLD, n.d.) shows that approximately 74% of all registered dams[16] are single-purpose, with roughly 13% of them being used for water supply and 50% for irrigation. However, multi-purpose facilities are becoming more popular, especially in the case of rehabilitating old dams (Bonnet et al., 2015; Branche, 2015). Small-scale, local and fit-to-purpose dams and reservoirs can contribute to water security and flood protection, as well as provide renewable energy for local populations.

Appropriately designed nature-based solutions (NBS), which provide water management services that can replace, augment or work in parallel with those delivered by grey infrastructure (WWAP/UN-Water, 2018), can improve surface water retention. This in turn can enhance infiltration to groundwater and thus provide increased storage (WWAP/UN-Water, 2018). Natural and constructed wetlands can also help improve water quality (WWAP/UN-Water, 2018; Nagabhatla and Metcalfe, 2018) but do not usually guarantee a quality of water that is safe for drinking.

Groundwater
Sub-surface water storage can complement surface water availability, especially during periods of water scarcity. In addition to potentially being accessed directly (via wells, for instance), aquifers can also augment surface water availability via lateral groundwater flows into natural waterways.

Managed aquifer recharge (MAR) provides natural storage for groundwater by intentionally recharging an aquifer with surface water for later use or to provide environmental benefits (Dillon, 2005). Medium- and long-term benefits in both rural and urban areas include: the securing and enhancing of seasonal water availability; the improvement of land value and biodiversity; mitigation of flood-related risks; protection against aquifer salinization; freshening of coastal aquifers affected by saltwater intrusion; maintenance and augmentation of environmental flows and groundwater-dependent ecosystems; and improvements in water quality through soil-aquifer treatment (Dillon et al., 2009). MAR has been successfully tested in various parts of the world for the restoration of affected groundwater-dependent ecosystem services, as detailed in Box 2.1.

Unconventional water resources
Unconventional water resources are a by-product of specific processes or can result from specialized technology to collect/access water. These resources often need proper pre-use treatment, and when used for irrigation, they require appropriate on-farm management (Qadir et al., 2007). Key examples of unconventional water resources include groundwater confined in deep geological formations; atmospheric moisture harvested through cloud seeding and fog collection (Box 2.2); physical transportation of water through icebergs;

> **Appropriately designed nature-based solutions (NBS), which provide water management services that can replace, augment or work in parallel with those delivered by grey infrastructure, can improve surface water retention**

---

[16] There are about 59,100 registered dams (ICOLD, n.d.).

Box 2.1 Using check dams to increase water availability in Rajasthan, India

Mosaic irrigation[1] with groundwater provides the primary source of income for most farming villages in southern Rajasthan. The relatively low monsoon rainfall (600mm) lasts an average of only 30 days in the wet season, and most rain quickly runs off the hard rock upland catchments. The monsoon is followed by a 9-month period with only negligible rainfall, characterized by high evaporation rates. As a coping mechanism, thousands of check dams[2] are built on streams to reduce the streamflow of the water and to increase groundwater recharge (Dashora et al., 2017). The MARVI (Managing Aquifer Recharge and Groundwater Use through Village-Level Intervention) project (Maheshwari et al., 2014) trained farmers to measure groundwater levels in order to assess the resource and to plan their planting schedules accordingly. It also trained them to monitor check dam water levels to determine their effectiveness and the need for silt-scraping in the dry season to maintain recharge rates. Four monitored check dams near Dharta are responsible for on average 200,000 m³/year each, securing approximately 16% of dry-season crops in adjacent villages (Dashora et al., 2017).

[1] Mosaic irrigation is an alternative to large irrigated systems and includes "*number of small, localised irrigated areas dispersed as a mosaic across the landscape.*" (Paydar et al., 2010, p. 455).

[2] A check dam is a small, sometimes temporary, dam in a small watercourse, built to reduce streamflow, minimize erosion and/or divert water.

Box 2.2 Fog water collection in Morocco: Aït Baamrane

The biggest fog water collection system is at Mount Boutmezguida, Aït Baamrane, Morocco. This project combines technology and research to achieve community development by enhancing access to clean water and sanitation in rural Berber communities. The fog collectors installed have an estimated daily water production of 6,300 litres, providing water to a total of 500 people in the community during fog events. Women and children perceived the major positive impacts in the community, which address health, culture and educational challenges. Multiple stakeholders, including local communities, rural community authorities and international researchers, participate in the initiative, and multiple partners (e.g. the United States Agency for International Development (USAID), Munich Re Foundation and other public and private parties) provide financial support for technology improvements and comprehensive community development.

Source: Dodson and Bargach (2015).

micro-scale capture of rainwater where it otherwise evaporates; desalinated water; and residual water from urban areas and agriculture (Figure 2.1).

Upscaling unconventional methods can balance the amount of water currently extracted from surface and groundwater sources while minimizing environmental degradation and conflicting/competing usages.

Water reuse offers opportunities for enhancing conventional water supplies, especially in cities relying on more distant sources of water

Water reuse offers opportunities for enhancing conventional water supplies, especially in cities relying on more distant sources of water. Treating wastewater to a quality standard that is safe and susceptible to a user (i.e. 'fit-for-purpose' treatment) not only improves its overall appeal, but also makes water reuse more economically feasible (WWAP, 2017). Furthermore, some states and communities plan to implement the vision of zero discharge and 100% recycling of wastewater in industrial settings through processes such as stream separation, material and energy recovery, as well as various wastewater management tools (WWAP, 2006, 2017).

Despite multiple benefits, the potential of most unconventional water resources — and especially water reuse and recycling — is still highly under-explored and under-exploited (WWAP, 2017; Qadir et al., 2018). While both the technologies and the knowledge for the development of unconventional resources are emerging along with an increasing number of applications, there are financial, technological and policy barriers to exploiting their full potential. Most unconventional water resources are not part of national water policies and budgets, even in countries with high potential.

Figure 2.1 Examples of unconventional water resources

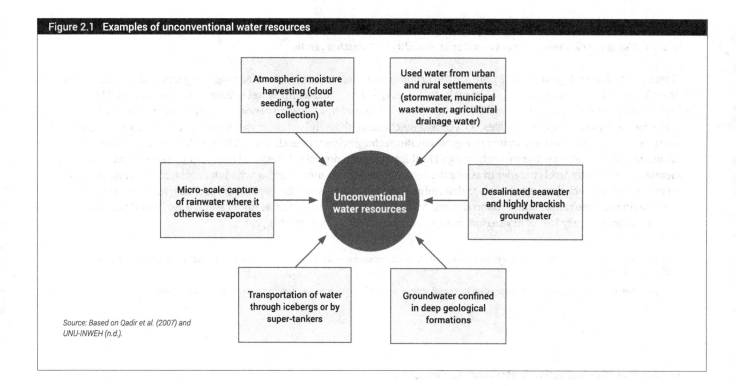

Source: Based on Qadir et al. (2007) and UNU-INWEH (n.d.).

Two additional examples of alternatives for managing water availability include rainwater harvesting and inter-basin transfers (IBTs). Managing water availability using rainwater harvesting is mostly done at small or local scales and involves collecting, storing and using rainwater when it falls for industrial and domestic uses, thereby helping to meet the high demand of water. Rainwater harvesting is advantageous as it is cost-effective, and water is provided near the household, decreasing the burden of travelling long distances for collection, particularly for women and children (Helmreich and Horn, 2009; Ojwang et al., 2017). IBTs have been utilized for millennia and still represent a very common means of enhancing water availability through transfer of water from one river basin to a geographically different one, or from one river system to another. At the turn of the millennium, they accounted for 540 km³ or 14% of the global water withdrawals (ICID, 2005) and this ratio was predicted to rise over the near future (Gupta and Van der Zaag, 2008).

The local institutions supporting specific water resources such as micro-scale rainwater harvesting and safely managed wastewater use are often still limited or lacking capacity for scalability. However, solutions exist in the form of indoor water conservation technologies, for example low-volume toilets, water-saving devices for faucets (Hejazi et al., 2013) or outdoor conservation technologies, such as xeriscaping[17] or roof-top rainwater harvesting.

2.1.2 Water accessibility

The vast majority of the 5.2 billion people with access to safely managed drinking water services (see Prologue, Section 2.i) rely on piped networks, along with other conventional, centralized and decentralized water supply and treatment systems. Most urban dwellers have access to safely managed drinking water services, and a source of water located on their premises, available when needed and free from contamination.

Piped water is the least costly method to transport water. However, it is far too often unavailable to the poor, thus aggravating inequality, especially in urban slums and in remote and rural areas. Where water supply via piped networks is unavailable, people mostly rely on wells or community water supply systems (e.g. water delivery through kiosks and vendors, trucking water) to access water. In the latter case, they generally pay prices several times higher per litre of water compared to individuals or communities serviced by water pipe systems (see Chapters 5 and 6), further exacerbating inequities between the rich

---

[17] Xeriscaping can be referred to as smart landscaping whereby native plants with low water demands are used in arid regions (Vickers, 2006).

and disadvantaged. For example, WaterAid (2016) reported that poor people in low- and middle-income countries (LMICs) can typically spend 5–25% of their income on water to meet their basic needs (about 50 litres per person per day), and in certain parts of Madagascar and Papua New Guinea, some people spend over half of their income to buy water from vendors. The point being, in many (if not most) cases, the poor pay more to receive less water, and it is often of lower quality.

Of the 844 million people currently lacking basic drinking water services, 263 million people (4% of the population) spend over 30 minutes in round trips collecting water from an improved source, while 159 million people collect drinking water directly from surface water sources. Nearly 60% of the latter group lives in Sub-Saharan Africa (WHO/UNICEF, 2017a).

In many rural environments, local streams, ponds or lakes are sources for water collection. Small reservoirs can also play a pivotal role in facilitating accessibility of water resources, making water available and in some cases, physically accessible.

The burden of collecting water in these settings falls disproportionately on women and girls (Figure 2.2) as *"women and girls are responsible for water collection in 8 out of 10 households with water off premises, so reducing the population with limited drinking water services will have a strong gender impact."* (WHO/UNICEF, 2017a, p. 11). Consequently, the lack of WASH leads to physical and psychosocial stress, increasing the risk of mortality (i.e. preterm birth and low infant birth weight causing maternal and child mortality) (Baker et al., 2018). Fetching water over long distances poses several challenges for communities, groups and people living in disadvantaged and vulnerable situations, including risks to physical safety when collecting water, lost time for education and other income-generating activities, as well as adverse health outcomes. Carrying a heavy load over long distances can also take a physical toll, often leading to increased musculoskeletal injuries. A study from Limpopo Province in South Africa illustrates how women experience spinal pain potentially associated with carrying water for domestic purposes (Geere et al., 2010).

Innovations like WaterWheels (Patwardhan, 2017) and the 'Hippo Water Roller' (see photo), a container that can be rolled along the ground with a capacity of up to 90 litres of water, have been developed to reduce the burden of travelling long distances for obtaining water. The advantage is that transporting water is less strenuous for the elderly and children and allows transportation of a larger quantity of water, thereby reducing the number of trips needed. These innovations have somewhat assisted those with basic drinking water needs, but the lack of access to safely managed drinking water is still a persisting problem.

Piped water is the least costly method to transport water

Women pushing Hippo Water Rollers

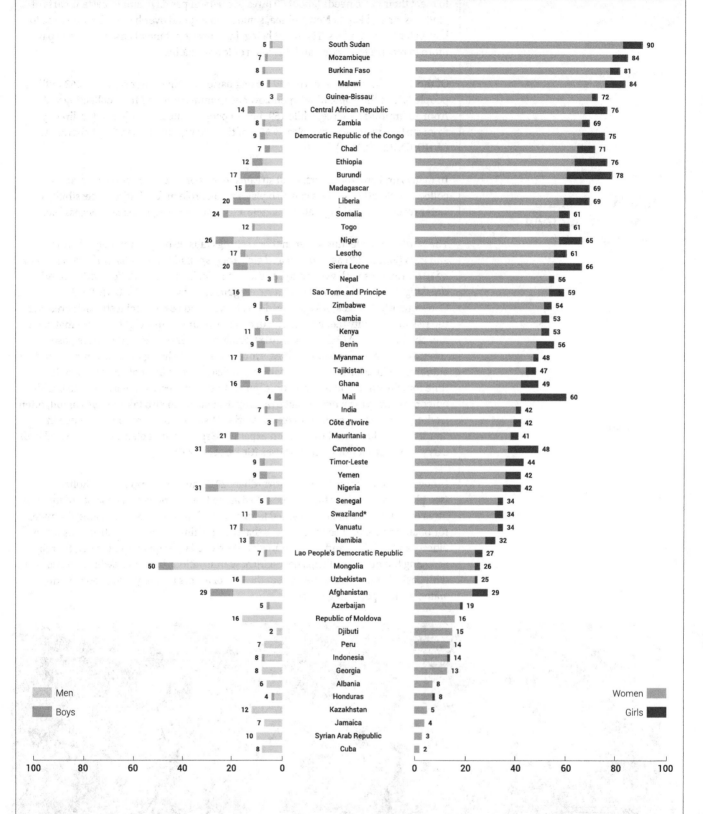

	Men		Women
5	South Sudan	90	
7	Mozambique	84	
8	Burkina Faso	81	
6	Malawi	84	
3	Guinea-Bissau	72	
14	Central African Republic	76	
8	Zambia	69	
9	Democratic Republic of the Congo	75	
7	Chad	71	
12	Ethiopia	76	
17	Burundi	78	
15	Madagascar	69	
20	Liberia	69	
24	Somalia	61	
12	Togo	61	
26	Niger	65	
17	Lesotho	61	
20	Sierra Leone	66	
3	Nepal	56	
16	Sao Tome and Principe	59	
9	Zimbabwe	54	
5	Gambia	53	
11	Kenya	53	
9	Benin	56	
17	Myanmar	48	
8	Tajikistan	47	
16	Ghana	49	
4	Mali	60	
7	India	42	
3	Côte d'Ivoire	42	
21	Mauritania	41	
31	Cameroon	48	
9	Timor-Leste	44	
9	Yemen	42	
31	Nigeria	42	
5	Senegal	34	
11	Swaziland*	34	
17	Vanuatu	34	
13	Namibia	32	
7	Lao People's Democratic Republic	27	
50	Mongolia	26	
16	Uzbekistan	25	
29	Afghanistan	29	
5	Azerbaijan	19	
16	Republic of Moldova	16	
2	Djibouti	15	
7	Peru	14	
8	Indonesia	14	
8	Georgia	13	
6	Albania	8	
4	Honduras	8	
12	Kazakhstan	5	
7	Jamaica	4	
10	Syrian Arab Republic	3	
8	Cuba	2	

Men   Boys   Women   Girls

*The country name was changed to Eswatini from the former name of Swaziland as of 19 April 2018.
See www.un.org/en/member-states/.

Source: WHO/UNICEF (2017b, fig. 20, p. 31).

Water kiosks provide an alternative and potentially affordable solution to accessibility challenges, and are a prominent feature in areas where water supply is otherwise limited or unavailable, including urban slums (Contzen and Marks, 2018). In Kenya (Box 2.3), water kiosks make up approximately 23% of water vendors and provide the most affordable option for those living in slums (US$0.03 for 20 litre jerry can units from kiosks vs. an average of US$0.15 for 20 litre jerry can units across pushcart vendors) (UNDP, 2011a). Water kiosks can also help lower disease burdens, as reported in Haiti during the cholera epidemic (UN News, 2016). In Mombasa (Kenya), where 50% of the population were only receiving water 2 to 3 days per week, water kiosks or vendors have helped improve access to drinking water (Economic and Social Rights Centre, 2016). In high-income countries (HICs), residential use rates in 2014 ranged from 200 litres to as much as 600 litres per person per day (IWA, 2014).

Another method of providing access to water includes water tinkering (or water trucking), which also serves as a rapid way to transport water during emergencies (WHO/WEDC, 2011). However, trucking is an expensive alternative and can be time-consuming to administer. Water trucking is not limited to developing countries. In Canada, for example, over 13% of homes on native reserves are dependent on water tankers as the primary source of potable water supply (WaterCanada, 2017). Water tankers also provide a solution for disadvantaged groups, including people living in refugee camps (e.g. the Zaatari refugee camp in Jordan) (see Box 9.1) where water supply and wastewater disposal are constant concerns (EcoWatch, 2018).

Future efforts to improve global accessibility of clean water require innovative solutions at the local level. Scaling locally adopted methods of managing availability and accessibility need to account for local geography, culture and level of technical capacity (Carter et al., 2010). Context-specific, place-based and fit-for-purpose solutions for water delivery and access need to be selected based on their cost and payment structures or mechanisms to ensure that groups are not denied access due to cost and/or distance (see Chapter 5) (Fonseca and Pories, 2017).

Other issues need to be addressed besides considering costs and payment structures associated with purely conventional water supply methods. For instance, without a comprehensive analysis, the costs of producing unconventional water resources can be perceived to be high. However, with conventional storage and distribution systems, women and girls spend hours fetching water over long distances and are exposed to waterborne diseases. These risks are reduced with unconventional water resources, such as fog water collection or trucking, which should be accounted for when assessing their overall monetary cost. Furthermore, the potential to use the increased water and time availability for other income-generating activities, thereby enhancing opportunities for women to partake in other tasks and for girls to remain in school, should also be taken into consideration.

Water kiosks provide an alternative and potentially affordable solution to accessibility challenges

---

Box 2.3 Delegated Management Model for improving water quality and affordability – the case of slum dwellers in Kisumu, Kenya

While addressing some problems of non-revenue water[1] and to better serve Kisumu's large informal settlements, Kisumu Water and Sewerage Company (KIWASCO) installed meter chambers at various points on their bulk water supply network and appointed Master Operators (MOs) to run the water supply from those chambers. The MOs are registered groups coming from the community to be served, with the intention of improving the water-provisioning services and facilitating greater stakeholder participation in decision-making. Over time, the intervention created a generally positive impact on the extent as well as quality of services received by residents. In 2012, the project was serving around 64,000 people through 366 kiosks and 590 individual household connections. Prices for water were lowered from US$0.20 to US$0.03 per 20 litres and the quantity of non-revenue water recorded a 6.5% reduction. Fewer water shortages were recorded. Women and children travelled shorter distances and noted less time for water collection. Residents were also empowered to influence decisions at the utility, while also serving as master operators.

Source: UN-Habitat (n.d.).

---

[1] Non-revenue water is the difference between the volume of water put into a water distribution system and the volume that is billed to customers.

The most common methods of water purification depend upon electricity/energy being available around the clock – which is certainly not a reality everywhere

2.1.3 Water treatment

In 2012, the Global Burden of Disease Study found that unimproved water and sanitation continue to contribute to the disease burden, particularly in childhood communicable diseases (Lim et al., 2012). These health impacts disproportionately affect groups/people living in vulnerable situations within LMICs, such as women and girls during different reproductive life stages, particularly in rural areas (Baker et al., 2017). Providing safe drinking water to individuals in disadvantaged situations is a challenge even in HICs (Box 2.4).

In many LMICs, women are not only mainly responsible for collecting and storing water, but also for disposing of wastewater that contains contaminants including chemicals or microbes, further increasing their disease burden. Collecting water from untreated surface water sources (e.g. rivers, streams) and washing clothes in contaminated water expose them to waterborne diseases (e.g. typhoid, cholera, dysentery, diarrhoea). One study has demonstrated that, under such conditions, pregnant women are at increased risk of infection from Hepatitis E (Navaneethan et al., 2008).

For treating water to drinking level quality, centralized water management employs pipe network systems, while decentralized supply systems involve three critical categories: point-of-use system (POU), point-of-entry system (POE), and small-scale system (SSS). These categories are classified based on the quantity of treated water that they can supply (Peter-Varbanets et al., 2009), as illustrated in Figure 2.3.

The most common methods of water purification depend upon electricity/energy being available around the clock, which is certainly not a reality everywhere. POU and POE systems use purification methods consisting of three main categories (Peter-Varbanets et al., 2009):

- Heat or radiation
- Chemical treatment
- Physical removal processes

Heat or radiation can effectively destroy pathogens (e.g. techniques include boiling, solar radiation, etc.). Even if these methods kill the pathogens, they do not offer protection against recontamination. Chemicals are widely used to purify, disinfect and protect against recontamination. Physical removal helps reduce microbial and chemical contaminants, by separating pollutants from the water, using sedimentation or filtration techniques. The technologies utilised by SSS are generally the same as in POU and POE systems. The difference is that they are scaled up, providing drinking water for communities in quantities of 1,000–10,000 litres per day, and can include technologies applied on a large scale. SSS is also most often employed to provide emergency water supply.

Source water can be naturally contaminated (with arsenic, for instance), or it can be contaminated from industrial, domestic/municipal, or agricultural sources. A number of emerging pollutants, such as pharmaceutical substances, may be posing increasing health risks (WWAP, 2017). Phytoremediation, which uses plants to degrade (by removing or transforming) toxic chemicals in soils, groundwater, surface water and the atmosphere, can be an effective technology for cleaning polluted areas (WWAP/UN-Water, 2018). Furthermore, groundwater bioremediation has been practiced for years, particularly in industrial settings (existing and legacy sites) for cleaning up organic contamination (experiments have been conducted by Gross et al., 1995 and Jewett et al., 1999). While biological processes are energy-efficient, the remediation cycle is often long and the toxic plant material requires safe disposal. Thus, the development of innovative, high-performance and low-cost remediation techniques could be valuable for marginalized communities residing in or alongside contaminated sites (Nagabhatla and Metcalfe, 2018).

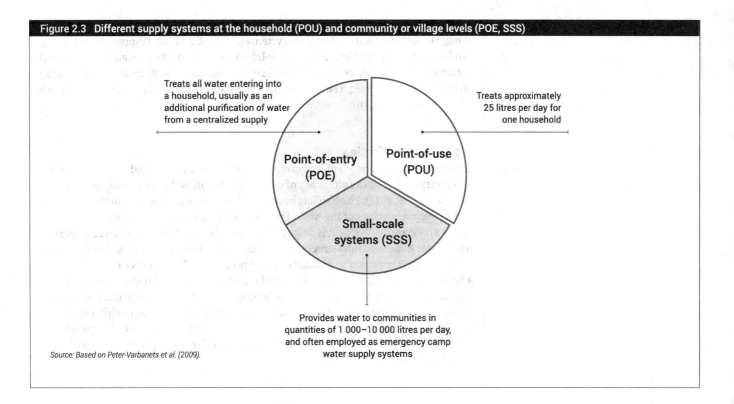

Figure 2.3 Different supply systems at the household (POU) and community or village levels (POE, SSS)

Treats all water entering into a household, usually as an additional purification of water from a centralized supply

Treats approximately 25 litres per day for one household

Point-of-entry (POE)

Point-of-use (POU)

Small-scale systems (SSS)

Provides water to communities in quantities of 1 000–10 000 litres per day, and often employed as emergency camp water supply systems

Source: Based on Peter-Varbanets et al. (2009).

2.2
Sanitation

Only two of out five people worldwide had access to safely managed sanitation services in 2015 (WHO/UNICEF, 2017a; see Prologue, Section 2.ii). Menstrual health management (MHM) is rarely considered in a traditional sanitation context, and, as a result, women's reproductive and sexual health needs are not being fully met in many countries (see Box 2.5), with direct impacts on the well-being of women and girls.

Generally, sanitation comprises on- or off-site facilities for the collection, transport, treatment and disposal of waste under hygienic conditions. Collection systems usually refer to a toilet system. Transportation in the context of typical grey infrastructure refers to a piped underground sewage system, although in some instances waste is

---

Box 2.5 WASH in the context of menstrual health management (MHM)

WASH is pivotal to improve women and girls' reproductive and sexual health, and thereby for allowing women to be productive members of society. Meeting MHM[1] goals are central to the health and well-being of women and girls. However, this dimension is often lacking or insufficiently addressed in many low- or middle-income countries (LMICs). A key consequence of this oversight includes women and girls using unsanitary materials, thereby increasing incidences of infection and the disease burden, augmenting, for instance, the risk of urinary tract infections (UTIs). UTIs are a public health problem globally and are pervasive within LMICs (Sumpter and Torondel, 2013). In case of school-going girls, often low attendance or drop-out from education is attributed to lack of MHM facilities. The spill-over effect of this situation is lack of future employment opportunities, and women becoming less productive (see Box 14.1 in WWAP, 2016).

Furthermore, UTIs are associated with an increased risk of Human Immunodeficiency Virus (HIV) infection (Atashili et al., 2008). The state of women's reproductive health is concerning, especially within LMICs, where women are at higher risk of developing infections during birth due to facilities lacking WASH provisions. Approximately 38% of healthcare facilities in 54 countries do not have access to basic water sources and around 20% do not have access to primary sanitation infrastructure (WHO/UNICEF, 2015a). Impoverished conditions exist in Sub-Saharan Africa where, among 39 of 46 countries analysed, less than 15% of women who delivered at home had access to WASH infrastructure (Gon et al., 2016).

[1] MHM is defined as: *"Women and adolescent girls using a clean menstrual management material to absorb or collect blood that can be changed in privacy as necessary for the duration of the menstruation period, using soap and water for washing the body as required, and having access to facilities to dispose of used menstrual management materials."* (Budhathoki et al., 2018, p. 2).

transported by trucks, and treatment, when available, usually involves centralized sewage treatment plants or localized systems (e.g. septic tanks). Disposal of end products is usually split into liquid and solid waste that can be disposed of safely into the environment or, if not, can be collected in hazardous waste facilities to be destroyed in an incinerator. However, a large amount of variation exists within each of these steps to address various types of situations.

2.2.1 Waste collection

Even though the collection of wastewater has little effect on the final quality of water that is disposed of or the efficiency of treatment, it is often the most costly part of the system (WWAP, 2017). Flush toilets have provided safe sanitation systems in developed and developing regions of the world for a very long time. While this has solved issues of pathogen exposure on site, it is only useful in the context of the advanced sewage and wastewater treatment infrastructure, for which many LMICs are lacking the facilities, financing and capacity. The amount of water needed for flush toilets can also create a burden on available water resources and thereby increase water stress in densely populated areas. Also, the available nutrients and organic matter contained in human faecal waste becomes diluted and mixed, making their recovery more difficult. Box 2.6 provides an example of communities in Haiti solving the problem of lacking wastewater infrastructure by using dry toilets and community-led transport to produce fertilizer from human waste.

Box 2.6 Using waste to fertilize soils in Haiti

Communities in Haiti have been benefiting from dry toilets as well as community-driven transported composting of human waste to produce resources such as fertilizer. The group called Sustainable Organic Integrated Livelihoods (SOIL) empowers people within a community to transform their waste into a resource. This is done through using EkoLakay household dry toilets whereby SOIL workers weekly collect human waste to transform into compost through a waste treatment facility. This promotes development by creating new jobs and providing sustainable sanitation options.

The social business model works because customers rent a toilet that is built by local contractors using local materials for approximately US$5 per month. This fee also includes carbon cover material (used for covering up waste material to avoid smell) and weekly waste collection, which SOIL then transports to compost sites. Through a carefully monitored process, the waste is transformed into nutrient-rich compost. The compost is sold for use in agriculture and reforestation projects, providing an environmentally friendly alternative to chemical fertilizers while simultaneously generating revenue to support the provision of sanitation services.

Figure | Ecological Sanitation Method

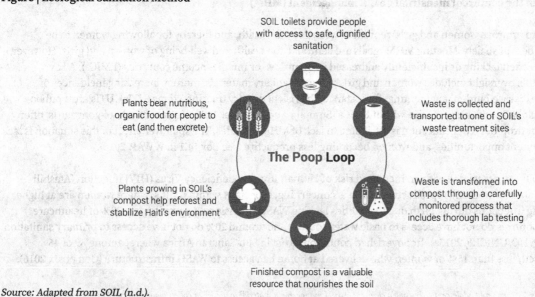

Source: Adapted from SOIL (n.d.).

2.2.2 Treatment

The centralized approach of wastewater treatment has a long history of use, especially in HICs. It includes the collection and disposal of wastewater at centralized points (Massoud et al., 2009). Another approach is decentralized wastewater treatment, whereby wastewater is treated close to the place of origin and, in most cases, reused or disposed of near or at the site of its generation (see Chapter 6). The strengths and weaknesses for both systems are summarized in Table 2.1.

2.2.3 Waste disposal

Disposal of treated wastewater and solid waste (e.g. garbage, greases and oils, sludge, etc.) needs to be carried out in an environmentally sound manner to reduce contamination and disease risk. Worldwide, over 80% of all wastewater returns to the environment without being treated (WWAP, 2017). Treated wastewater is generally released into surface water bodies, while sludge and other solid waste are sent to landfills. The need for innovative technologies and fit-for-purpose and cost-effective solutions remains pertinent to ensure the safe collection, transport, treatment and disposal of waste. Valorizing sludge as a resource for other purposes, such as biogas production, co-incineration or as fertilizer in landscaping and agriculture, can provide additional revenue for communities. Solutions should also be locally adapted and implemented in a collaborative and inclusive manner, involving all key stakeholers, beneficiaries and leaving no one behind (WWAP, 2017).

Table 2.1 Advantages and disadvantages of centralized and decentralized systems, with limitations or benefits

Centralized sewage system		Decentralized sewage system	
Advantage	Disadvantage	Advantage	Disadvantage
Does not require the participation and information of the population, at least not to a degree that is necessary for the decentralized approach (Barnard et al., 2013).	Collection of wastewater is expensive, and can pose a serious threat to environment and public health (e.g. leaks, flooding or destruction of treatment sites) (Gikas and Tchobanoglous, 2009).	Collection of wastewater from various sites is not necessary (Massoud et al., 2009).	Maintenance of treatment facilities is time-consuming and if faulty or broken can pose dangerous threats to the environment and population (Massoud et al., 2009).
Wastewater treatment is controllable and provides power to the local authorities and governments to effectively implement their goals and measures; processes can be monitored by trained personnel (Oakley et al., 2010).	The costs of wastewater collection are even greater for remote locations or densely populated areas, because sewer systems need to reach isolated places and cover greater distances.	Wastewater composition and variability in quantity and quality can be better estimated (Almeida et al., 1999; Anh et al., 2002). Predictability of composition allows for specialized treatment methods that can be optimized (Gillot et al., 1999).	Wastewater treatment is less controllable as more stakeholders can be involved. Insufficient oversight can cause serious problems and endanger the success of the project (Lienert and Larsen, 2006; Libralato et al., 2012).
Methods have been optimized for decades, providing a large amount of experience in maximizing the potential (and addressing the limitations) of centralized wastewater treatment (Anh et al. 2002).	Mixture of different flows of wastewater makes wastewater difficult to control (Anh et al. 2002). Municipal wastewater generation varies depending on the time of the day, holidays, population growth, or in- or defluxes in the long term.	New opportunities for optimized treatment effort; growing potential for reclaimed wastewater use. Specialized treatment methods can reduce treatment time and costs, and raise the potential of reuse in the surrounding area (Asano and Levine, 1996).	
Limitations or benefits of centralized sewage systems		Limitations or benefits of decentralized sewage systems	
Requires sufficient funding (from government or other sources) to manage the systems in a sustainable manner.		Information about the area of implementation are very difficult to obtain (Tsagarakis et al., 2001), especially in regions that can profit the most (rural or isolated, poor, sparsely populated).	
Requires adequate technical and human capacity to manage, operate and monitor treatment of wastewater.		Can provide a multitude of benefits for certain regions under the right conditions (Massoud, et al., 2009).	
		Adaptability of such systems, as they are often built modularized and can be expanded or reduced to meet the current needs (Otterpohl et al., 2004), especially for refugee camps or other temporary shelters.	

Source: UNU-FLORES.

2.3
Disaster risk reduction

Valorizing sludge as a resource for other purposes, such as biogas production, co-incineration or as fertilizer in landscaping and agriculture, can provide additional revenue for communities

Water-related natural hazards, such as floods and droughts, can affect water supply and sanitation infrastructure, leading to significant economic and social losses and impacts (see Prologue, Section 1.iv). Such hazards are projected to increase in frequency and intensity as a result of climate change. The short and long-term impacts of water-related extreme events include loss of life, spread of communicable diseases, interruptions in water and food-provisioning systems, damage to financial assets and social disruption (Mata-Lima et al., 2013).

The impact of disasters in LMICs is often exacerbated due to a combination of poor infrastructure and weak governance. Further investigation is needed to create a climate- and hazard-resilient water supply and sanitation infrastructure, and to increase the transferability of knowledge and technologies.

To mitigate the impacts caused by climate change and disasters, a paradigm shift from post-disaster response to proactive risk reduction is needed. This approach requires hydrological data and information to support science-based risk management decisions, as well as investments in early warning systems (EWS) that provide lead time and integrate forecasting. EWS combined with public awareness, education and preparedness can allow people to quickly respond to hazard information, thereby increasing human safety while reducing potential human losses. The myth of absolute control over natural disasters and absolute safety from them should also be abandoned, in favour of solutions that promote mitigation and adaptation strategies. Furthermore, an integrated approach to water management needs to be applied, abandoning measures with a narrow sectoral focus and adopting a holistic approach that encompasses land management, environmental protection, and social and economic aspects. Women and girls often bear the burden of adverse impacts, due to their gendered role, particularly

Aerial view of Neretva River valley, Croatia

in water-related crisis scenarios. For instance, when analysing disaster mortality, it has been established that in less developed countries, women have higher mortality rates resulting from floods and tropical cyclones than men (Cutter, 2017).

2.4
Conclusions

For millions of individuals, including women and girls in vulnerable situations, access to acceptable and affordable drinking water is a persisting problem. Similarly, access to sanitation services is another major development challenge, mostly in LMICs and for groups/people living in poverty and disadvantaged situations. Place-based, fit-for-purpose solutions are required to provide for the safe collection, transport, treatment and disposal of human waste at multiple scales and in multiple geographies.

Low-technology solutions similar to Hippo Water Rollers, community-managed small-scale reservoirs etc. demonstrate potential for increasing the availability, accessibility and quality of water, even in water-scarce areas. However, the scalability of these solutions in LMICs and among groups, communities and people in vulnerable and disadvantaged situations requires focused efforts and investments. While innovative solutions are increasingly reported within regions and communities, offering potential to enhance water availability, quality and access, barriers to scalability include financing and social acceptance. Another crucial paradigm is managing the demand–supply dynamics. In water management scenarios worldwide, the water supply cannot always meet water demand, but adopting a demand-driven approach can help to overcome this challenge to a fair extent. It is widely argued that various, innovative and geographically fitting solutions to managing water availability, acessibility and quality, including options explained as nature-based solutions, can potentially assist in overcoming the challenge of mitigating water stress, and achieving water security.

CHAPTER 3

Social dimensions

Terraced rice fields in Yuanyang county, Yunnan, People's Republic of China

UNESCO-IHP | Alexander Otte

With contributions from: Marianne Kjellén (UNDP); Indika Gunawardana (Cap-Net UNDP); Julia Heiss, Jyoti Hosagrahar, Akane Nakamura, Christine Delsol, Nada Al Hassan, Susanna Kari, Laicia Gagnier, Nina Schlager, Nicole Webley and Giuseppe Arduino (UNESCO); Maria Teresa Gutierrez and Rishabh Kumar Dhir (ILO); Lesha Witmer (WfWP); Rio Hada (OHCHR); and Andrei Jouravlev (UNECLAC)

This chapter describes the key mechanisms of exclusion and the drivers behind social inequality and discrimination over access to water supply and sanitation services, with a focus on specific groups in potentially vulnerable situations.

3.1
Introduction

The human rights to water and sanitation entitle everyone, without discrimination, to sufficient, safe, acceptable, physically accessible and affordable water for personal and domestic use. This includes water for drinking, personal sanitation, washing of clothes, food preparation, and personal and household hygiene (see Chapters 1 and 4). The Member States of the United Nations have explicitly acknowledged that access to clean drinking water and sanitation are fundamental to the realization of all human rights, underlining the importance of water and sanitation for a dignified life, livelihoods and peaceful development, especially for populations in the most vulnerable situations (UNGA, 2010; UN-Water, 2015).

The resolution recognizing the human right to safe drinking water and sanitation and other relevant agreements and declarations (see Chapters 1 and 4) underline particular social challenges that need to be overcome to ensure respect for human rights and the implementation of the Sustainable Development Goals (SDGs). These challenges are not limited to SDG 6, as the cross-cutting nature of water and sanitation affects the implementation of most other SDGs. The transversal role of water across all segments of societies contributes to the complexity of ensuring respect for the related human rights for all, leaving no one behind.

The *United Nations Human Development Report 2016* highlights that groups living in poverty or in marginalized and disadvantaged situations are also those requiring most attention to ensure they benefit from the implementation of the SDGs. This includes indigenous peoples, ethnic minorities, refugees (see Chapter 8) and migrants. Women also often are disadvantaged in terms of their enjoyment of human rights across several societies worldwide. Key barriers and mechanisms of exclusion (Figure 3.1), which have come into existence either intentionally or unintentionally, deprive certain groups of people from the possibility to realize their full potential (UNDP, 2016).

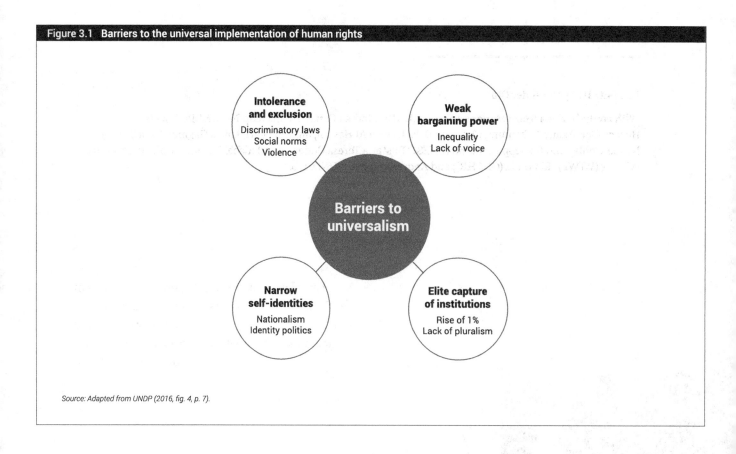

Figure 3.1 Barriers to the universal implementation of human rights

Intolerance and exclusion
Discriminatory laws
Social norms
Violence

Weak bargaining power
Inequality
Lack of voice

Barriers to universalism

Narrow self-identities
Nationalism
Identity politics

Elite capture of institutions
Rise of 1%
Lack of pluralism

Source: Adapted from UNDP (2016, fig. 4, p. 7).

3.2

Impediments to implementing the rights to water and sanitation

3.2.1 Social and cultural drivers of inequality and discrimination

The social and cultural reasons behind the difficulties in implementing the rights to safe drinking water and sanitation for everyone are complex and intertwined. They closely relate to political and institutional factors (see Chapters 1 and 4) and to the socio-economic status of disadvantaged and marginalized groups (see Chapters 5 and 6, and Section 9.4). The normative cultural settings and resulting mindsets are sometimes also reflected in development approaches. The implementation of the human rights, which the United Nations (UN) Member States recognize as indispensable for equitable human development, is hampered by inequalities that relate to gender, age, poverty, ethnicity, sexual orientation, disabilities, religion, socio-economic class and geographic location, among other factors (see Chapter 1). Overlapping combinations of these factors can aggravate discrimination and exclusion (HRC, 2016b).

The social and cultural factors that are driving exclusion and discrimination with regard to access to water and sanitation services often depend on complex and diverse historical developments, socioeconomic settings and cultural patterns, each varying among and within countries, communities and social groups. They contribute to shaping mindsets, attitudes, behaviours and policies (Hassan, 2011). This social complexity should be taken into account when attempting to fulfil the human rights to safe drinking water and sanitation, as well as to implement SDG 6.

To sustainably change such patterns can be a long process, especially when they are anchored in traditions or belief systems that determine values and social norms for coexistence in society and shape the perception of the individuals that constitute them. Social norms can hinder the prospect of certain groups to enjoy their human rights. Groups outside the normative frame of the mainstream society, for instance belonging to a certain ancestry (e.g. castes), a low socio-economic status or an alternative sexual orientation can be discriminated against in terms of access to water supply and sanitation services. Gender can also be a determining factor, as social norms in many countries reduce the choices and opportunities for women and girls as well as for people with alternative gender identities.

The water governance principles, laid out by the Organisation for Economic Co-operation and Development (OECD), recognize the importance of promoting *"stakeholder engagement for informed and outcome-oriented contributions to water policy design and implementation"*, and notes that special attention should be paid *"to under-represented categories (youth, the poor, women, indigenous people, domestic users)"* (OECD, 2015, p.12).

Even among UN Member States that have recognized the human rights to safe drinking water and sanitation, sometimes no effective implementation mechanisms are in place and equality before the law is not guaranteed. The groups concerned may also lack information about their rights and the options to ensure their realization, for instance due to language and educational barriers, or geographical isolation. Enabling the access to this information constitutes an important basis for human rights implementation (Cap-Net/WaterLex/UNDP-SIWI WGF/Redica, 2017). Persons with disabilities may have particularly limited access to public information, due to reduced mobility and lack of adapted information material, e.g. for blind people (House et al., 2017).

Discrimination may happen in various ways (see Section 1.3.1) and for different reasons (Box 3.1).

> *"**Direct discrimination** occurs when individuals are discriminated against in laws, policies or practices that intentionally exclude people from service provision or equal treatment. Direct discrimination takes place when an individual or group is treated less favourably compared to others in a similar situation for reasons related to a prohibited ground as described above.*
>
> *"Discrimination, however, is also manifest in more indirect ways. Discrimination in practice — **indirect discrimination** — occurs when laws, regulations, policies or practices seem neutral at face value, but in practice have the effect of exclusion from the provision of basic services. For instance, requiring a municipal registration certificate to subscribe to the local water provider may seem neutral, but may in fact discriminate against persons that live in informal settlements"* (UN-Water, 2015, p. 8).

The supply and demand of water and the perception of scarcity can be considered as a relative construct of, inter alia, cultural and economic value systems that affect water use and distribution. Johnson et al. (2012) underline that *"scarcity might reflect a person's economic ability to pay for water, or the customs, social conditions, and relationships that privilege access for one person or group while withholding from others"* (p. 266).

The *United Nations Human Development Report 2016* recalls that *"inequalities in income influence inequalities in other dimensions of well-being, and vice versa"* (UNDP, 2016, p. 7). Many groups are excluded from social progress and their position is weak when it comes to initiating positive change in institutions. Excluded groups *"lack agency and voice and so have little political leverage to influence policy and legislation"*, especially through traditional institutional means (UNDP, 2016, p. 7), which, in turn, also makes them more vulnerable in the face of direct and indirect discrimination.

Box 3.1 Drivers of and against discrimination

Mechanisms/drivers of discrimination:
- sex and gender
- race, ethnicity, religion, national origin, birth, caste, language and nationality
- disability and health status
- property, tenure, residence, economic and social status
- multiple discriminations
- limited access to justice

Mechanisms/drivers against discrimination:
- substantive equality
- legislation and policies
- active participation
- service provision
- monitoring
- access to justice

Source: UN-Water (2015).

This may also be the case in developed countries, as exemplified through the drinking water pollution crisis in Flint, Michigan, the United States of America (USA), where the city's water users, including thousands of children, were exposed to unsafe levels of lead and other toxins through the municipal drinking water system, leading to systematic blood lead level monitoring documenting the contamination (Flint Water Advisory Task Force, 2016; MDHHS, 2018). People in poor neighbourhoods and of low socio-economic status were particularly exposed (MCRC, n.d.). Switzer and Teodoro (2017) describe how socio-economic status constitutes a major variable for citizen participation in the political process, which, in turn, impacts environmental equity, as well as access to safe drinking water. Accommodation with below-standard water and sanitation infrastructure is highlighted as one of the factors that generate particular vulnerability in poor and predominantly non-white communities (MCRC, n.d.).

3.2.2 Water, sanitation and education

The basic provision of a safe, affordable and reliable water supply for human consumption, including sanitation facilities at home and in the workplace, enhances workforce health and productivity and can thus contribute to economic growth (WWAP, 2016). Evidence suggests that people with less access to water and sanitation are more prone to also having other basic needs unmet, a situation that exacerbates their economic condition and deprivation of human development, prolonging the cycle of poverty. The education, health and income of parents can play an important role with regard to the opportunities their children may have to move out of poverty. In this way, poverty of one generation can be handed down to the following (UNDP, 2016; World Bank, 2017a).

> **Many societies deny women the access to productive assets, such as the right to land, often linked to access to water**

The Global Education Monitoring (GEM) Report by the United Nations Educational, Scientific and Cultural Organization (UNESCO) suggests that students from poorer households have far lower chances of attending a school with adequate water and sanitation facilities than those of households with higher socio-economic status (UNESCO, 2017a). Inadequate water and sanitation facilities in schools are long known to negatively impact education, especially of girls, and to hamper social progress (UNDESA, 2004). Figures show that three in ten primary schools lacked an adequate water supply in 2013 (UNESCO, 2016). In Latin America, *"more than four in five grade 3 students from the richest quarter of households in participating countries attended schools with adequate water and sanitation facilities, compared to one in three from the poorest quarter* (Figure 3.2) *(Duarte et al., 2017). In Mexico, only 19% of the poorest grade 3 students attended schools with adequate water and sanitation facilities, compared to 84% of the richest students."* (UNESCO, 2017a, p. 228). *"Improving water, sanitation and hygiene facilities in education institutions can have significant positive effects on health and education outcomes. Improved facilities, coupled with hygiene education, can also reduce absenteeism and increase demand for education, particularly among adolescent girls, who may drop out due to a lack of girls-only toilet facilities."* (UNESCO, 2016, p. 308).

3.2.3 Gender inequalities

Gender inequalities in access to water supply and sanitation are large and persistent in many countries. According to the Human Development Index (HDI), women worldwide have a lower HDI value, on average, compared to men (up to 20%, in South Asia), which hints at the widespread impact of the inequalities affecting women. Among the multifaceted and dynamic reasons are social norms. Some social norms are important for harmonizing community life in societies, while others can lead to discrimination and exclusion, reducing choices and opportunities for girls and women (UNDP, 2016).

Inequalities are especially striking when it comes to the collection of water (see Section 2.1.2). According to the United Nations Children's Fund (UNICEF), three-quarters of households without access to drinking water on their premises task women and girls with the primary responsibility to collect it (UNICEF, 2016). Although water collection routines vary in different parts of the world in terms of frequency, a study of time and water poverty in 25 Sub-Saharan African countries estimated that women spend at least 16 million hours a day collecting drinking water, while men spend 6 million hours, and children 4 million hours on the task (WHO/UNICEF, 2012).

Source: UNESCO (2017a, fig. 16.4, p. 229).

"Women across different regions, socio-economic classes and cultures spend an important part of their day on meeting the expectations of their domestic and reproductive roles." (Ferrant et al., 2014, p. 1). On average, *"women devote one to three hours more a day to housework than men; two to ten times the amount of time a day to care (for children, elderly, and sick), and one to four hours less a day on market activities."* (World Bank, 2012, p. 80). This is in addition to their paid activities, thus creating the "double burden" of work for women (Ferrant et al., 2014).

When paid and unpaid work (such as fetching water and providing domestic care) are combined, women in developing countries work more than men, with less time for education, leisure, political participation and self-care. At the same time, many societies deny women the access to productive assets, such as the right to land, often linked to access to water (see Prologue, Section 3.viii). *"Only 10-20% of landholders in developing countries are women"* (UNDP, 2016, p. 5).

How society and policy-makers address issues concerning unpaid care work has important implications for the achievement of gender equality and equal access to water resources and services: they can either expand the capabilities and choices of women and men, or confine women to traditional roles associated with femininity and motherhood.

3.2.4 Discrimination against indigenous peoples

Comparatively lower levels of access to water and sanitation services can be observed among ethnic minorities and indigenous peoples (Clementine et al., 2016). Indigenous peoples may have different or unique perceptions, modes of participation, and recognition of rights towards access to water and sanitation (Boelens and Zwarteveen, 2005). An understanding of the term 'indigenous' is provided in Box 3.2. The patterns of how indigenous peoples are deprived of access to water supply and and sanitation services often combine characteristics and intersectionalities affecting an array of disadvantaged groups.

Indigenous peoples account for about 5% of the world's population, with an estimated number of over 370 million persons (UNPFII, n.d.) in 70 countries. Yet, they constitute approximately 15% of the world's poor, and are often among the poorest (ILO, 2017b).[18] The rights of indigenous peoples are recognized under international law, including human rights law and other specific international instruments, such as the ILO Indigenous and Tribal Peoples Conventions No. 107 and No. 169, (ILO, 1957; ILO, 1989) and the United Nations Declaration on the Rights of Indigenous Peoples (UN, 2008). However, they *"face discrimination and exclusion in the legal framework, in access to education in their own language and in access to land, water, forests and intellectual property rights"* (UNDP, 2016, p. 5).

Indigenous peoples can be important actors in sustainable development and climate action. A significant proportion of their livelihood practices, for instance small-scale food production (which can be shared with other, often equally disadvantaged groups), are arguably examples of sustainability and therefore warrant special consideration within the text and the implementation of the SDGs (UNGA, 2015a). Indigenous peoples are custodians of biologically and culturally diverse environments; their lands contain some 80% of the world's biodiversity (Sobrevila, 2008; ILO, 2017b; WWAP/UN-Water, 2018) and they possess invaluable knowledge of their water resources regarding resilience to climate change (Denevan, 1995; Solón, 2007; Altieri and Nicholls, 2008). In many cases, indigenous peoples' knowledge systems and traditions have maintained a sustainable balance with their living environment, including its water, for thousands of years. Their value expands well beyond the cultural sphere that brought them to life (UNESCO, 2018a).

The continuity of indigenous peoples' cultural and geographical existence across periods and throughout colonization often places them in antagonistic situations with dominant political and economic actors and the mainstream of society and politics, which have interests in disposing of land and water in ancestral indigenous territories, as resources. This historically developed situation can generate direct and indirect discrimination, and inequalities that can lead to exclusion. Indigenous peoples are often ignored in decision-making on water, unequally treated in conventional water management systems, and disproportionately affected by water conflicts (Barber and Jackson, 2014), many of which are driven by conflicting water uses. These range from mining and industrial agriculture to hydropower dams and large-scale infrastructure (Jiménez et al., 2015), as well as other uses such as conservation and tourism. Such conflicts are a threat to many indigenous peoples' fundamental rights and well-being, and can directly affect the development and operation of water projects. They exemplify contradictions in terms of lifestyles, concepts and means of development, with implications for human rights and sustainable development.

> **In many cases, indigenous peoples' knowledge systems and traditions have maintained a sustainable balance with their living environment, including its water, for thousands of years**

[18] Although these figures are frequently cited in several recent reports by United Nations agencies (among others), these estimates are based on reports published as far back as 2003 (i.e. World Bank, 2003).

Indigenous peoples, to some extent representative of many poor and disadvantaged groups, often share strong cultural ties with their ecosystems and depend on renewable natural resources for their economic activities and livelihoods, endangered by climate variability and extremes. With high levels of exposure and vulnerability to climate change, many indigenous peoples may be also forced to migrate, which could exacerbate social and economic vulnerabilities, potentially forcing many into informal settlements with inadequate access to water (ILO, 2017b).

The limited involvement in decision-making processes, combined with a lack of recognition and institutional support, hampers access of many indigenous communities to remedies, increases their vulnerability to climate change, undermines their ability to mitigate and adapt to the changing environment, and consequently also poses a threat to the advances made in securing their rights. Indigenous women, in particular, face intersectional discrimination from both within and outside their communities, with distinct implications for their access to water and sanitation (ILO, 2017b).

To highlight and ultimately alleviate another key factor limiting indigenous peoples' bargaining power and enjoyment of rights, UNESCO, with the support of the United Nations Department of Economic and Social Affairs (UNDESA), facilitates 2019's International Year of Indigenous Languages.[19]

Indigenous peoples' concerns receive increasing visibility worldwide (APF/OHCHR, 2013), as well as greater international recognition for their distinct rights, interests and cultures. Their participation in the global consultation process for the 2030 Agenda helped *"designing a framework that makes explicit references to Indigenous peoples' rights and development concerns, [...] founded on principles of universality, human rights, equality and environmental sustainability"*, as stated by the UN Permanent Forum for Indigenous Issues (UNPFII, 2016).

3.3
Inequalities related to finance, infrastructure and beyond

Especially in developing countries, it is necessary to invest in infrastructure for water, sanitation and hygiene (WASH) services to overcome inequalities of socioeconomic and discriminatory nature and accomplish SDG Targets 6.1 and 6.2, which call for *"universal and equitable access to safe and affordable drinking water"* and *"access to adequate and equitable sanitation and hygiene for all"*, respectively (UNGA, 2015a).

While the scope of the infrastructure needs may vary and must be adapted to the dynamic context and capacities of each country or community, a large financing gap remains one of the main common barriers (see Chapter 5). A study by Hutton and Varughese (2016) concludes that current levels of funding towards WASH services are mainly below the capital costs required to meet basic WASH services by 2030 (see Figure 3.3). Furthermore, these requirements fall far behind the investment needs for achieving safe WASH services (SDG Target 6.1. and 6.2). To that end, a threefold increase in current annual investment levels (to US$114 billion) would be required. It is noteworthy that the estimated resource needs do not include operation and maintenance costs, thus, the actual funding requirements are even higher.

Results of UN-Water's *Global Analysis and Assessment of Sanitation and Drinking-Water (GLAAS) 2017* study (WHO, 2017b) suggest that the insufficiency of financial resources is a major constraint to achieving higher investment levels in most countries. Although government WASH budgets are increasing at an annual average real rate of 4.9%, over 80% of monitored countries report having insufficient financing to attain their national drinking water, sanitation and water quality objectives in urban areas, while this share increases to 90% when referring to rural areas. The level of sufficiency of financial resources allocated to meet national targets for sanitation (in 71 countries) is presented in Figure 3.4.

---

[19] For further information, please see en.iyil2019.org/.

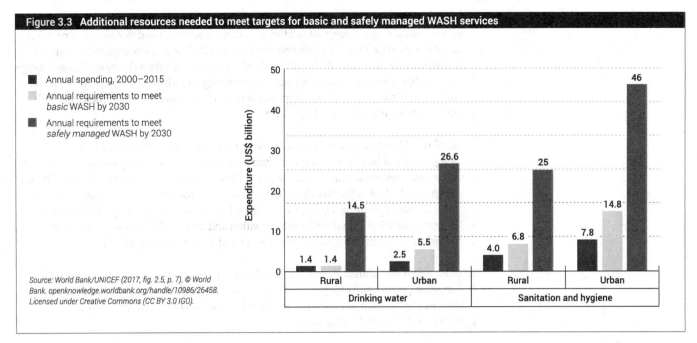

Figure 3.3 Additional resources needed to meet targets for basic and safely managed WASH services

■ Annual spending, 2000–2015

▨ Annual requirements to meet *basic* WASH by 2030

■ Annual requirements to meet *safely managed* WASH by 2030

Drinking water:
- Rural: 1.4, 1.4, 14.5
- Urban: 2.5, 5.5, 26.6

Sanitation and hygiene:
- Rural: 4.0, 6.8, 25
- Urban: 7.8, 14.8, 46

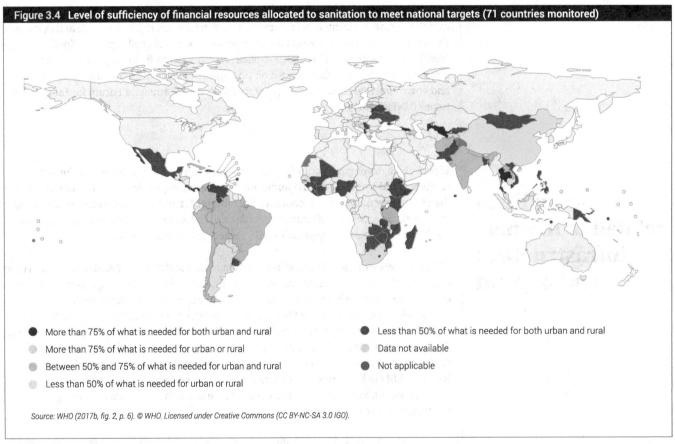

Figure 3.4 Level of sufficiency of financial resources allocated to sanitation to meet national targets (71 countries monitored)

● More than 75% of what is needed for both urban and rural

● More than 75% of what is needed for urban or rural

● Between 50% and 75% of what is needed for urban and rural

● Less than 50% of what is needed for urban or rural

● Less than 50% of what is needed for both urban and rural

● Data not available

● Not applicable

These funding needs will be amplified as countries start to incorporate SDG targets into their national plans, given the targets' relatively high ambitions. Furthermore, achieving financial sustainability in operations and maintenance (O&M) services constitutes an equally relevant challenge, as these are key in avoiding deterioration of assets and minimizing failure rates. In many cases, those disproportionally affect disadvantaged populations.

In regions and countries where the infrastructure access gap is large and public budgets are restricted, accounting for the different aspects of the decision-making process becomes particularly relevant (Andrés et al., 2014). Governments need to define targets for the water, sanitation and/or hygiene sector, including social priorities and desirable service levels and standards. They also need to identify which reforms, including legal, regulatory, organizational and institutional aspects, are required to improve the enabling environment (of which equity, non-discrimination and the mitigation of social conflicts are integral parts), and to implement the necessary policies to those ends (World Bank/ UNICEF, 2017).

Also in countries where the water and sanitation infrastructure is largely in place, finance and infrastructure measures, including maintenance, must go together with institutional change, capacity development and participation to end inequalities, exclusion and intersectional discrimination (see Chapter 4). In the United States of America (USA), Switzer and Teodoro (2017, p. 11) find that *"members of racial and ethnic minorities face greater risk of unsafe drinking water"* and that *"the significance of race is most pronounced in the very poorest communities"*. In response to the Flint water crisis (mentioned above in Section 3.2.1.), the Michigan Civil Rights Commission recommended a series of measures centred around institutional and human capacity development to build *"a deeper understanding of the roles of structural racialization and implicit bias and how they affect decision-making throughout all branches"* of government in a given context (MCRC, 2018, p. 7).

Finally, it is important for managers of water supply and sanitation projects to understand and respect the different belief systems and related habits. A set of recommendations (developed by the UNDP-SIWI Water Governance Facility) (Jiménez et al., 2014) on how to work with indigenous peoples in rural water and sanitation projects emphasizes the importance of continuous dialogue to generate mutual trust and maintain long-term supportive relations. The sensitization of project managers and stakeholders regarding equality and non-discrimination in community-led total sanitation programmes for poor communities in developing countries is also at the core of the approach used by the Water Supply and Sanitation Collaborative Council (WSSCC) (House et al., 2017), which pays particular attention to vulnerabilities related to age, disabilities, gender and diversity.

> It is important for managers of water supply and sanitation projects to understand and respect the different belief systems and related habits

3.4
Supporting the implementation of the human rights to water and sanitation

Equality and non-discrimination, with a particular focus on gender, go together with empowerment and participation of those whose right to safe drinking water and sanitation has yet to be realized. However, the groups that must not be left behind are highly diverse, and solutions for inequality and discrimination must be adapted and tailored to the respective contexts to strengthen opportunities and capacities. This applies to the integration of local and indigenous knowledge through methods of integrated water resources management (IWRM), to infrastructure development, as well as to education. A guiding principle for empowering change is the adage *Nothing about us, without us.*

3.4.1 Valuing local, traditional and indigenous knowledge
Taking into account local and traditional knowledge and customary water arrangements (where these exist) can be an effective means to enhance sustainable development in a river basin. The IWRM approach (see Sections 1.4 and 4.2.3) provides a possible means of addressing the lack of participation of marginalized groups, as it seeks to enhance dialogue between different stakeholders and favours decision-making at the lowest appropriate institutional level. Good water governance (see Chapter 4) allows and encourages decision-making processes that are inclusive of all stakeholders and water practices without discrimination, integrating, for example, customary water arrangements of indigenous peoples, tribes, rural communities and other groups. In this endeavour, tools like Cap-Net's manual for a human rights-based approach to integrated water resources management (Cap-Net/WaterLex/UNDP-SIWI WGF/Redica, 2017) or the UNDP Training Package on Indigenous Peoples and Integrated Water Resources Management (Cap-Net, n.d.) can be of substantial help (Box 3.3).

Valuing traditional knowledge through the recognition of indigenous peoples' stewardship of land and water supports inclusion and access to human rights.

Box 3.3 Training package on indigenous peoples and integrated water resources management

Bringing the hidden indigenous and traditional knowledge into light, Cap-Net, UNDP-SIWI Water Governance Facility, WaterLex, International Rivers, Nile IWRM Net and Justicia Hídrica jointly developed a training package on *Indigenous Peoples and Integrated Water Resources Management (IWRM).* The package provides ways for integrating indigenous peoples into water management, including their specific knowledge for sustainable planning and resource management. It also addresses the role of water in the fulfilment of indigenous rights and, in light of the many conflicts over resource uses, provides guidance on conflict management.

Water use conflicts further increase indigenous peoples' vulnerability. It is also important to note that traditional knowledge can play a significant role in climate change mitigation and adaptation, for which its effective use is critical.

For instance, the Indigenous Peoples and IWRM training package discusses how an intercultural approach that recognizes and integrates indigenous peoples' rights, knowledge, perspectives and interests in any planned action can be used to create spaces for the meaningful participation and continuous dialogue between all parties. Integrating the understandings and perspectives of a specific group of people into decision-making promotes their fair treatment and inclusion.

Source: (Cap-Net, n.d.).

The creation of UNESCO's International Indigenous Peoples Forum on World Heritage recognizes that the nationally proposed, internationally highly visible World Heritage sites must respect human rights, as well as land, resource and tenure rights at the interface of culture and nature, and the capacity of indigenous peoples to act as custodians, owners and decision-makers (IIPFWH, n.d.).

Water heritage reflects human ingenuity, tireless efforts and trial-and-errors to achieve optimal use of water in often challenging natural environments. Social organization that evolved along with this heritage has enabled people to manage water in a cooperative and inclusive manner, often expressed in customary water arrangements. Lessons can be learned from how people have organized themselves around water (Box 3.4).

> **Water heritage reflects human ingenuity, tireless efforts and trial-and-errors to achieve optimal use of water in often challenging natural environments**

3.4.2 Inclusive infrastructure programmes

The Employment Intensive Investment Programme of the International Labour Organization (ILO), promotes employment-intensive approaches and local resource-based technologies in delivering public investments, in particular for local infrastructure, as a technical solution to creating and maintaining assets, as well as decent jobs and income. Combining local participation and the use of locally available skilled and unskilled labour with local materials, knowledge and appropriate technologies has proven to be an effective and economically viable approach to infrastructure works and job creation in many local settings. Community contracting provides a mechanism to empower communities by promoting capacity development and providing experience in negotiating, organizing and contracting (ILO, 2018a).

Community-led total sanitation programmes evolve and pay increasing attention to age, gender and disabilities. The Equality and Non-Discrimination in Community-Led Total Sanitation Programme of the WSSCC chartered options for supporting the most disadvantaged groups (Figure 3.5). The study by House et al. (2017) underlines the importance of time scale for behavioural change programmes. Even if effective in the short term (e.g. providing freshwater and menstrual hygiene facilities in schools or significantly reducing open defecation in communities), change can only be lasting and sustainable if good practices are not only executed upon initiation, but learned, adapted, integrated, maintained and transmitted, thus empowering current and future generations. Water education plays a crucial role in this regard.

Within the household
Extended family
(including from the diaspora)

Support from family

Local masons
Diaspora
Religious institutions
Neighbours
Local groups
(savings-related; women's;
widows; youth)
Village leadership
(development and WASH
committees)
Community-based
organizations and unions
Youth

Local NGOs
Disabled persons'
organizations
Local businesses

Support from NGOs, private sector, others

Support for people who may be disadvantaged

Support from community

Support from government

Financial alternatives

Village
District
National

Support options for people who may be disadvantaged

From within the community

- Solidarity groups
- Free labour

From outside the community

- Provision of local materials
- Reduced price (subsidised) materials
- Provision of purchased materials
- Paid for skilled labour (masons)
- Paid for physical labour
- Revolving funds
- Savings groups

From either within or outside the community

- Vouchers
- Direct provision of finance
- Subsidized low-interest loans
- Community rewards

Source: Adapted from House et al. (2017, fig. 4, p. 29).

3.4.3 Water education for sustainable development

Technical solutions alone have failed to lead to the lasting and sustainable realization of the human rights to water and sanitation, or to water security. In the array of transformative means, education and capacity development can provide the values, knowledge and skills that are essential components of any meaningful strategy towards implementing the SDGs.

Box 3.4 Putting traditional knowledge into practice

Recovery of the ancestral water system of Los Paltas, Ecuador

The recovery of the ancestral water system of Los Paltas to supply water to the city of Catacocha in southern Ecuador exemplifies the benefits that traditional knowledge can have in improving access to water. The San Pedro Mártir micro-basin provides 70% of the water of the city of Catacocha. In colonial times, the Spanish colons and mestizos transformed the basin's pre-Columbian hydrological system, based on lentic wetlands and dykes, to recharge the aquifers and to use the lands for livestock and agriculture. This greatly diminished the vegetation cover and water availability in the ecosystem. The rediscovery of ancestral local knowledge led to the restoration of the basin in an ecohydrological approach. The local population was involved in the construction of very small dams along the micro-basin's river course. This system reduces runoff, revitalizes the plant cover and vegetation, increases infiltration, and replenishes the aquifer. The basin now provides more water, sufficient to increase the water supply to households in Catacocha from previously one to now six hours per day (UNESCO-IHP, n.d.).

Traditional system of Corongo's water judges, Peru

The Traditional System of Corongo's Water Judges is an organizational method developed by the people of the district of Corongo in northern Peru, embracing water management and historical memory. The system, which dates back to pre-Inca times, is primarily aimed at supplying water fairly and sustainably, which also translates into proper land stewardship, and thereby ensures the existence of these two resources for future generations (UNESCO Living Heritage, n.d.).

Water temples and *subak* of Bali, Indonesia

Water temples in Bali underpin the cooperative water management system of canals and weirs known as *subak*, which dates to the ninth century and allows for the cultivation of rice. Water temple networks composed of farmers and others make democratic decisions on water allocation and timing of water supply. Their decisions are supported by rituals, offerings and artistic performances that aim to sustain a harmonious relationship between the natural, human and spiritual worlds, or the ancient philosophical concept of Tri Hita Karana (UNESCO, 2018b; UNESCO World Heritage Centre, n.d.).

However, as noted by UNESCO (2017c, p. 7), *"not all kinds of education support sustainable development. Education that promotes economic growth alone may well lead to an increase in unsustainable consumption patterns"* that contribute to aggravating the challenges to water security, like water scarcity, water pollution or the transmission of discriminatory worldviews.

"The now well-established approach of Education for Sustainable Development (ESD) empowers learners to take informed decisions and responsible actions for environmental integrity, economic viability and a just society for present and future generations. ESD develops competencies that empower individuals to reflect on their own actions, taking into account their current and future social, cultural, economic and environmental impacts, from a local and a global perspective. Individuals should also be empowered to act in complex situations in a sustainable manner, which may require them to strike out in new directions; and to participate in socio-political processes, moving their societies towards sustainable development." (UNESCO, 2017c, p. 7). ESD provides an opportunity for learners, to receive a water-related education, including science, sanitation and hygiene, as well as to develop the relevant knowledge, skills, values and behaviours to encourage and promote water and sanitation sustainability.

Women, and particularly girls, are most affected by the lack of water supply and sanitation services, and efforts should also be made to provide them with opportunities to enhance their capacities and engagement. This means alleviating them of the water-fetching burden and providing dignity through adequate sanitation services. Lack of such services often prevents girls from attending school and developing the means to empower themselves at other levels of water management.

Youth in Ecuador

To make the learning processes about sustainable water management more effective, it should focus on cognitive as well as socio-emotional and behavioural learning. Cognitive learning includes, for example, the understanding of water as a fundamental condition of life itself, of the importance of its quality and quantity, and of the causes, effects and consequences of water pollution, water scarcity and unequal global distribution of access to safe drinking sources. This knowledge needs to be complemented with socio-emotional learning, which involves the ability to participate in activities to improve water and sanitation management in local communities, as well as the cultivation of a feeling of responsibility for water use and its related infrastructure and sanitation facilities. Behavioural learning includes being able to contribute to effective water resources management at a local level, for instance through technical and vocational education and training.

For ESD to be most powerful, educational institutions as a whole have to be transformed. Schools and other educational environments need to promote water sustainability and provide access to safe water and sanitation facilities. Educational structures, policy and management need to provide guidance, oversight, coordination, monitoring and evaluation to ensure an effective, sustainable and institutionalized educational response to ensure the respect of human rights and the implementation of SDGs for everyone.

CHAPTER 4

Political, legal and institutional dimensions

Plenary room of the European Parliament in Brussels

UNDP | Marianne Kjellén

UNDP-SIWI Water Governance Facility | Jenny Grönwall and Alejandro Jiménez

With contributions from: Carlos Carrion-Crespo (ILO); Florian Thevenon and Rakia Turner (WaterLex); Ignacio Deregibus and Heather Bond (IWRA); Antoine Delepière (UNDP); Alistair Rieu-Clarke, Sonja Koeppel and Nataliya Nikiforova (UNECE); Léo Heller (Special Rapporteur on the human rights to safe drinking water and sanitation); and Rio Hada (OHCHR)

This chapter outlines the legal, institutional and political mechanisms and tools aimed at promoting inclusive development in water resources management and ensuring that no one is left behind in relation to their basic rights to water and sanitation.

4.1
Introduction

There are many reasons and great complexity involved in processes of exclusion, through which people are alienated from their rights to influence and be part of society, and from the full enjoyment of the benefits of development (see Chapter 1). Ownership and control of resources across the world are highly unequal, and this directly contributes to exclusion and differentiation of income and livelihood opportunities (Alvaredo et al., 2018). There is no single solution to this broader inequity, which greatly transcends into the management and use of water resources, as well as the distribution of and access to water and sanitation services.

Addressing fundamental inequalities calls for greater incorporation of human rights into national legal systems in ways that benefit people who find themselves in the most disadvantaged or vulnerable situations. This requires a broader political consensus around the importance and relevance of human rights, which can then become a vehicle to guide action, including compliance and enforcement in practice.

The international human rights framework can serve as a basis for developing national policy and domestic law but needs to be supported by capable and accountable institutions to ensure inclusive and impartial policy implementation. Insufficient capacity (of the public sector) increases the risks of a widening 'policy implementation gap', causing well-intended initiatives to be ineffective or to be captured by vested interests.

For an equitable and sustainable management of water and sanitation, it is key to have inclusive institutional devices in place for dialogue, multi-stakeholder involvement and cooperation, and the fundamental connectivity between multiple layers of government as well as with broader society (private sector, civil society).

4.2
Policy, politics and processes

The adoption of the 2030 Agenda and its Sustainable Development Goals (SDGs) signals a firm global commitment to integrate environmental, economic and social development, and to ultimately leave no one behind. The 2030 Agenda's enveloped aspirations — the foremost being universality — imply that the processes to achieve the SDGs must be inclusive. Policies, laws and societal institutions comprise the enabling factors for driving processes and actions towards inclusiveness and ensuring that no one is left behind, but there are also limitations. Changing 'business as usual' might clash with existing political interests and power relationships. Indeed, inclusive development requires commitment and dedicated effort by new political alliances.

Water resources management, including the provision of water supply and sanitation services, requires sound and democratic institutions that build on the *rule of law*. At the national level, this involves a set of governance principles according to which all persons and institutions are subject and accountable, as well as laws that are publicly promulgated, equally enforced and independently adjudicated (United Nations Security Council, 2004). It entails a separation of powers between a *legislature* that makes laws, a *judiciary* that subsequently interprets the law (and, in common-law states, establishes precedents), and an *executive* that administrates and implements policy.

4.2.1 International policy principles

At the *international* level, laws protecting the environment and regulating the uses and benefits of shared water resources are based on certain recognized principles, as developed through the interactions and relationships between autonomous states alongside an ever-growing number of international organizations and companies. What is expected and accepted conduct towards others in a modern, globalized world is steadily evolving. Expectations reflect moral values as well as a gradually refined scientific understanding of, among other things, natural 'tipping points', 'planetary boundaries' and 'resilience'.

Changing 'business as usual' might clash with existing political interests and power relationships

Customary international law is often founded upon national practice. At the same time, there is an iterative process whereby international law can inspire national law, or must be incorporated in it through a legally binding agreement. Turning political agreements into legally binding rules through which rights-holders can hold duty-bearers answerable constitutes a challenge, not least when there is a transboundary dimension involved. At the global level, two legal instruments set forth key rules and principles for sharing transboundary waters: the 1992 *Convention on the Protection and Use of Transboundary Watercourses and International Lakes* (UNECE, 1992) serviced by the United Nations Economic Commission for Europe (UNECE) — the 'Water Convention', which was subsequently amended in 2003 (entering into force on 6 February 2013) to allow accession by all Member States of the United Nations (UN); and the 1997 *UN Convention on the Law of the Non-Navigational Uses of International Watercourses* — the so-called 'Watercourses Convention', adopted by the UN General Assembly (UN, 1997).

Key principles of these conventions include equitable and reasonable utilization of shared watercourses, obligations to take appropriate measures to prevent significant harm, and duty to cooperate in good faith. Additionally, an overarching principle that is imbedded in both instruments is the duty upon states to cooperate over their shared watercourses, this duty is also expressed through SDG Target 6.5. Such principles can serve as a key foundation upon which to foster cooperation between states and across actors at different levels on the basis of equity.

Most important for the equitable sharing of water at the level of individuals — by way of its distribution through water and sanitation services — is the acknowledgement of the human rights to water and sanitation. Complementary to this are the international labour standards, drawn up by the constituents (governments, employers and workers) of the International Labour Organization (ILO), which set out basic principles and rights at work, including the access to safe drinking water, sanitation and hygiene (ILO, 2017c).

Organizations such as UN agencies, the European Union and the Organisation for Economic Co-operation and Development (OECD) lay down what is termed *soft law instruments*: resolutions, general comments, principles, guidelines and codes of conduct. While 'soft law' instruments are neither legally binding nor enforceable in the way that treaties and customary international law are, they are deemed (more or less) authoritative and can hold weight in policy discourse and negotiations.[20] Additionally, they may reflect or influence the development of customary international law. Soft law instruments can also provide detailed baselines and frameworks that help clarify goals and ideals, in turn promoting streamlined implementation at regional and national levels. A practical example of the political importance of 'soft law' is how the various UN General Assembly resolutions on the right to water (see Chapter 1) have heightened political awareness and provided a basis for national policy-making and programme implementation.

In the current context of multi-level governance, the role of non-governmental organizations (NGOs) in expressing the opinions of civil society and promoting the public's active participation (including broad dissemination via social media) has become increasingly influential in policy formulation (Bache and Flinders, 2004; Piattoni, 2010).

Other important players include large corporations whose economic clout may bring about a great deal of influence over policy-making as well as policy outcomes. Actions and non-actions by corporations are subject to (non-binding) standards, foremost the Ruggie 'Protect, Respect and Remedy' Framework (HRC, 2008) and the UN Guiding Principles on Business and Human Rights (HRC, 2011a, 2011b), under which private actors have a responsibility to respect human rights, over and beyond national laws that are not in compliance with international human rights law. This entails avoiding activities with adverse impacts on human rights, as well as the responsibility to participate in remedial mechanisms. States have the obligation to enact national laws and regulations that actively monitor and address private actors' actions, to ensure that these do not impede human rights.

The human rights-based approach (HRBA), as presented in Chapter 1 and in Box 4.1, advocates for the fundamental standards, principles and criteria of the (binding) human rights frameworks. These include non-discrimination and participation that is active, free and meaningful, as well as representation by and for people in disadvantaged or vulnerable situations. HRBA serves to guide steps and processes across all types of development cooperation.

Box 4.1 The human rights-based approach (HRBA)

The 1986 UN Declaration on the Right to Development (UNGA, 1986) was an important step for developing the human rights-based approach (HRBA), which places human beings at the centre of development, and specifies responsibilities of different actors for integrating human rights into development.

In 2003, the United Nations Development Group adopted a Common Understanding to ensure that agencies, funds and programmes of the United Nations (UN) consistently apply the approach, including three fundamental elements (UNDG, 2003):

- Goal: All programmes of development cooperation, policies and technical assistance should further the realization of human rights;

- Process: Human rights standards contained in, and principles derived from, the 1948 Universal Declaration of Human Rights and other international human rights instruments should guide all development cooperation and programming in all sectors and in all phases of the programming process; and

- Outcome: Development cooperation should contribute to the development of the capacities of 'duty-bearers' to meet their obligations and of 'rights-holders' to claim their correlative rights.

---

[20] 'Hard law' refers to legally binding obligations that are precise and that delegate authority for interpreting and implementing the law. 'Soft law' is weaker in terms of obligation, precision or delegation, and may include political arrangements in which legalization is largely absent (Abbott and Snidal, 2000).

Taking an HRBA to water resources management recognizes that different water-related human rights and provisions of international law are duly interlinked, as the violation of one right may affect the enjoyment of a wide range of others, and vice versa. The principles of non-discrimination and meaningful participation are also important elements of the HRBA and good governance.

4.2.2 Good governance

If day-to-day politics can become caught up with power struggles, 'good governance' holds promises of rising above vested interests and exclusionary practices. The principles of HRBA overlap with those of good governance. Good governance relates to systems of governance that have qualities of accountability, transparency, legitimacy, public participation, justice and efficiency (Pahl-Wostl et al., 2008). This includes important elements of (political) legitimacy and democratic citizenship, with effective protection of human rights.

The term 'governance' (rather than 'government') denotes more inclusive and cooperative forms of governing, involving a wider set of actors that co-create development outcomes along with new forms of process-oriented societal co-steering through partnerships and dialogue (Mayntz, 1998; Tropp, 2007; Bäckstrand et al., 2010). The broader shift from 'government' to 'governance' has been seen from the 1980s in many Western countries, linked to the 'legitimation crisis', by which an organization does not possess the necessary administrative capacity to achieve its objectives (Habermas, 1975). Part of this transition has also been in conjunction with neoliberal policies and greater reliance on the contribution of the private sector (Pierre, 2000).

The broader change from (state-led) 'government' towards (whole-of-society) 'governance' also relates specifically to the challenges of water management. At one level, it has become clear that the government alone is not able to take on the full responsibility and development challenge of 'providing' water supply and sanitation services to all citizens, especially in low-income settings (Franks and Cleaver, 2007; Jiménez and Pérez-Foguet, 2010). This relates closely to the general change of governments' role towards policy setting and regulation, with the actual provision being carried out by non-state actors or increasingly decentralized or independent departments. Similarly, the reduced per capita availability of water also necessitates negotiation and water reallocation. This has reinforced the importance of governance in water management and reuse (Niasse, 2017).[21]

The actors that participate in decision-making processes also have a bearing on what issues are addressed and how they are formulated. As a duty-bearer, states have the obligation to facilitate public participation and protect peoples' rights to participate in decisions that affect them. Delegated power and representative democracy are more common types of participation, but these can raise equally important questions about legitimacy and approval of representation by its constituents. Effective participation needs to be free and meaningful, with genuine consultation processes: otherwise, participatory processes can turn into unjust and illegitimate exercises of power (Cooke and Kothari, 2001).

Because of the centrality of water to human survival, service providers, whether private or public, are often perceived as having disproportionate power, a perception regularly reinforced by information asymmetry among parties. Without institutions with sufficient capacity to monitor and enforce agreed norms, and/or in situations where users do not have adequate channels to signal their requests or express their dissatisfaction, incentives to implement necessary policies will likely be weakened, derailed, or even paralysed (OECD, 2015).

> **Good governance relates to systems of governance that have qualities of accountability, transparency, legitimacy, public participation, justice and efficiency**

---

[21] The role of water governance and the political nature of water management were emphasized in 2006 by the UNDP Human Development Report and the UN-Water World Water Development Report (UNDP, 2006; WWAP, 2006). As a guidance for governments, the OECD, through its Water Governance Initiative, has developed principles providing the 'must-dos' for governments to design and implement effective, efficient and inclusive water policies in shared responsibility with the broader range of stakeholders (OECD, 2015).

Another important aspect of good governance relates to accountability. Accountability is the set of controls that hold officials and institutions answerable for their actions and ensure that sanctions are applied against poor performance, illegal acts and abuses of power (UNDP-SIWI WGF/UNICEF, 2015). Well-functioning accountability mechanisms help institutions fulfil their mandates.

Human rights accountability exists when practices and procedures are in place that:

- Oblige persons in authority or their institutions to take responsibility for their actions, and to explain and justify their actions to those to whom they are answerable, against standards of behaviour and performance which reflect and affirm international human rights standards;

- Subject those in authority to forms of enforceable sanction or appropriate corrective action if their conduct is found to have breached human rights obligations. Procedures for appraising and sanctioning conduct, whether judicial, administrative or other, should also reflect and affirm international human rights standards; and

- Enable those living in poverty who have been deprived of their rights to access fair and transparent mechanisms to enforce their claim against those in authority, and to obtain appropriate redress if their rights have been violated (OHCHR/CESR, 2013, p. 12).

4.2.3 Water rights, value and conflicting interests

As suggested above, the role of governance and multi-stakeholder processes has become increasingly critical for resolving matters of water allocation and for protecting water resources from contamination or abuse. Integrated water resources management (IWRM) has been advocated for by international organisations for many years, and was included in Agenda 21 (UN, 1992). In 2015, all states committed to IWRM through the adoption of the 2030 Agenda (UNGA, 2015a). IWRM is closely associated with the Dublin Principles — adopted at the International Conference on Water and Environment ahead of the Rio Conference on Environment and Development in 1992 — which categorize water as a *"finite and vulnerable resource"* to be managed participatorily with *"decisions taken at the lowest appropriate level"* while acknowledging the *"pivotal role of women"* (ICWE, 1992).

Dublin Principle number 4, which emphasizes the economic value of water in all its competing use has been the subject of considerable debate. In spite of the recognition of the social and environmental value of water, it is the idea of water as an economic good which has been seen to lead the way to commodification (Castro, 2013) and has thereby restricted access to water resources, water supply and sanitation services by some of the people in the most disadvantaged or vulnerable situations.[22]

A set of more recent principles, contained in the *Outcome Document by the High-Level Panel on Water* (HLPW, 2018), contains a clearer recognition of water's multiple values, the first of which is: The first of the Panel's five principles for valuing water is:

> [To] Recognize and Embrace Water's Multiple Values. [We must] identify and take into account the multiple and diverse values of water to different groups and interests in all decisions affecting water. There are deep interconnections between human needs, social and economic well-being, spiritual beliefs, and the viability of ecosystems (HLPW, 2018, p. 17).

As explained in Chapter 1, IWRM promotes the coordinated development and management of water, land and related resources for maximum economic and social welfare in an equitable manner, without compromising the sustainability of vital ecosystems. Rather than a one-off exercise, it is an iterative process to take the

---

[22] Even though the explanation to the 4th principle suggests that water is also a basic right (*"Within this principle [no. 4 — 'Water has an economic value in all its competing uses and should be recognized as an economic good'], it is vital to recognize first the basic right of all human beings to have access to clean water and sanitation at an affordable price. [However] Past failure to recognize the economic value of water has led to wasteful and environmentally damaging uses of the resource"* — ICWE, 1992, p. 4), it is the push towards greater emphasis on the economic value that has generated a great deal of criticisms with respect to the Dublin Principles.

various uses of water and the range of people's water needs into account (GWP, n.d.). Contemporary applications of IWRM support the equitable, efficient and sustainable use of water, and are vital to balancing the social, economic and environmental dimensions of sustainable development. The IWRM approach calls for coordination among all involved sectors of management, development, regulation and decision-making processes related to water, land and related resources (GWP, 2000). As suggested in Box 4.2, however, it is far from easy to resolve resource conflicts between different uses and user groups.[23]

The practical means for allocating water resources is principally through water rights, which are regulated under national laws. Water rights are conferred to an individual or organization through property rights or land rights, or through a negotiated agreement with the state or landowner (see Box 1.4). In distinction from *human* rights to water, which relate to individual domestic use, a water right can be provided for a variety of uses, is temporary and can be withdrawn.

Both land and water allocation is commonly based on customary law. However, there may be several legal systems operating at various levels, which can also lead to conflicts between systems operating in parallel. In many cases, statutory law trumps community-derived rights (Cap-Net/WaterLex/UNDP-SIWI WGF/Redica, 2017). The resolution of such conflicts harbours great potential for furthering rights and access to water resources for communities who find themselves in a disadvantaged or vulnerable situation. Conflict resolution with this purpose seems to be on the rise. The 2016 Kenya Community Land Act (Parliament of Kenya, 2016) formally recognizes community ownership rights to registered and unregistered lands, including the tenure rights of women and people in disadvantaged or vulnerable situations. Further, in the same year, a ruling of the African Court on Human and Peoples' Rights recognized the customary land and forest rights (Rights and Resources Initiative, 2017). Societies that operate under a plural, or mixed, legal system, allow for statutory law to coexist with customary law. General Comment 15 (CESCR, 2002b, para. 21) is a reminder that states should refrain from *"arbitrarily interfering with customary or traditional arrangements for water allocation"* as part of their obligations to respect the human rights to water.

Given the importance of land ownership in many water rights allocation regimes, inequalities of land ownership are translated into unequal access to and benefits from water. This is manifested also in terms of gender differences in land ownership (see Prologue, Section 3.viii), compounded by unequal inheritance laws in some countries. Well-managed reform processes for agrarian land have the potential to enhance equity and to revolutionize the efficiency of the whole economy. The related matter of (secure) land tenure is critical. Insecure tenure tends to be a disincentive to investment, and further hampers productivity of the dispossessed, exacerbating the income inequality resulting from unequal access to resources, including water (Ostry et al., 2014; Niasse, 2017).

4.3
Walking the talk: Implementing plans and policies

Creating coherence between the various institutional levels is essential to ensure that policies deliver on their objectives. The public sector or other agencies involved in service delivery or policy implementation need to possess the relevant capacity and skills, while adhering to the core values of policy delivery (accountability, professionalism, integrity, impartiality, responsiveness, non-discrimination and participation).

Figure 4.1 illustrates how (potentially global) policy principles are institutionalized through laws and regulations; how they are institutionalized through the palette

---

[23] The problematic situation as regards water use conflicts between industry and indigenous peoples is further highlighted by Jiménez et al. (2015), finding mining and hydropower to be the most conflict-ridden types of projects, and that project closure or renegotiation affected a third of nearly 400 projects examined in the study.

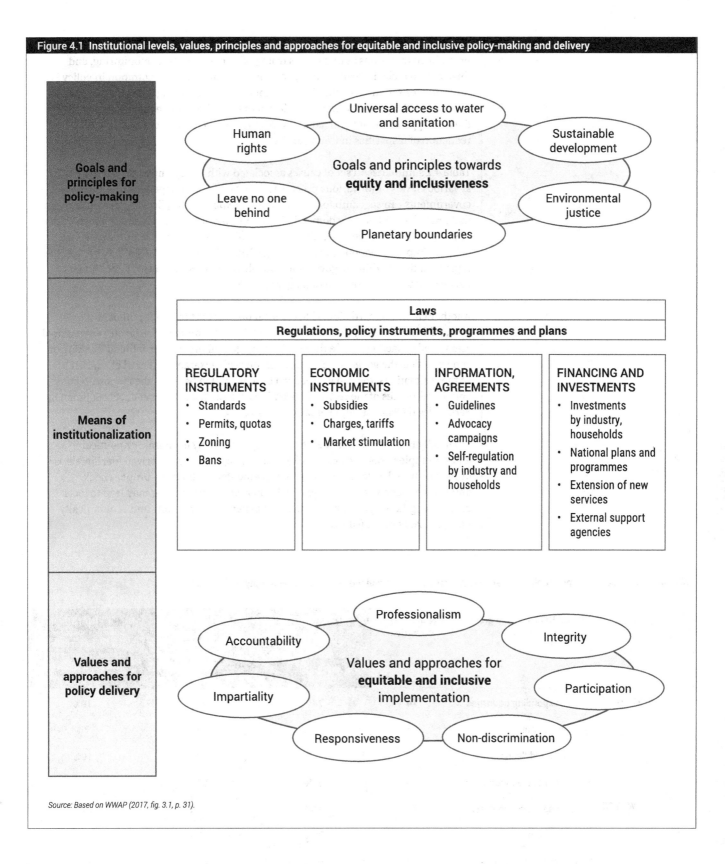

Figure 4.1 Institutional levels, values, principles and approaches for equitable and inclusive policy-making and delivery

Goals and principles for policy-making

Human rights

Universal access to water and sanitation

Sustainable development

Goals and principles towards **equity and inclusiveness**

Leave no one behind

Environmental justice

Planetary boundaries

Means of institutionalization

Laws

Regulations, policy instruments, programmes and plans

REGULATORY INSTRUMENTS	ECONOMIC INSTRUMENTS	INFORMATION, AGREEMENTS	FINANCING AND INVESTMENTS
• Standards • Permits, quotas • Zoning • Bans	• Subsidies • Charges, tariffs • Market stimulation	• Guidelines • Advocacy campaigns • Self-regulation by industry and households	• Investments by industry, households • National plans and programmes • Extension of new services • External support agencies

Values and approaches for policy delivery

Professionalism

Accountability

Integrity

Values and approaches for **equitable and inclusive** implementation

Impartiality

Participation

Responsiveness

Non-discrimination

Source: Based on WWAP (2017, fig. 3.1, p. 31).

of (mainly national) regulations, policy instruments, programmes and plans; and eventually implemented (locally) in an equitable and inclusive manner — most effectively so through transparent, responsive and professional civil servants or service providers.

4.3.1 The policy implementation gap

The misalignments or shortcomings that cause policies not to deliver the desired outputs and outcomes are commonly referred to as 'policy implementation gaps'. Such gaps (or insufficiencies) need to be overcome in order to operationalize policy intentions.

Table 4.1 illustrates the policy implementation gap as a progressive decline of proclaimed intentions as one moves from policy documents, to monitoring, and finally to financial measures. 'Pro-poor' measures are far more common in policy proclamations than in mechanisms for tracking or monitoring the rolling out of services for the poor. The actual fulfilment of the policy can be further hampered by the non-application of financial measures to implement pro-poor measures for the reduction of disparities in water services.

Table 4.2 summarizes a set of causes associated with policy implementation gaps at various levels or for various processes. Especially in aid-dependent countries, governments can succumb to pressure (either explicit or implicit) to develop reforms that might be neither truly demanded nor appropriately embedded in the social values of stakeholders. In such cases, the necessary high-level political commitment for effective implementation may be missing (IDB, 1999). The lack of stability of political representatives within the government involves changes in priorities and hinders perseverance and the pursuit of longer-term goals.

Another challenge partly linked to external pressure is the development of overambitious policies, setting objectives that are disconnected from current national reality and capacities. While these policies might adhere to international thinking on good practice, the goals assigned result in unrealistic targets (Ménard et al., 2018). In these situations, the gap is produced by a mismatch between the responsibilities and the resources of the responsible entities (Crook, 2003; Ribot et al., 2006; Jiménez Fernández de Palencia and Pérez-Foguet, 2011).

A partially related factor is the risk of policy capture by economic or political elites. Complex policy measures like decentralization, public–private partnerships or market-based water allocations, if implemented without the proper checks and balances and without adequate administrative capabilities, may lead to local elites strengthening their positions at the expense of politically and economically marginalized groups (OECD, 2015).

Table 4.1 Presence of pro-poor policies, tracking systems and financial measures in water supply and sanitation

	World Bank income group	Number of countries	GOVERNANCE Policies and plans have specific measures to reach poor population	MONITORING Progress in extending service provision to poor populations is tracked and reported	FINANCE Specific measures in the financing plan to target resources to poor populations are consistently applied
SANITATION	**All responding countries**	**74**	**74%**	**47%**	**19%**
	Low income	15	73%	33%	7%
	Lower middle income	29	66%	48%	10%
	Upper middle income	26	85%	58%	27%
WATER	**All responding countries**	**74**	**74%**	**55%**	**27%**
	Low income	15	73%	53%	20%
	Lower middle income	29	66%	48%	14%
	Upper middle income	26	85%	69%	38%

Legend: 80–100% / 60–79% / 40–59% / 0–39%

Note: The percentage shown are calculated with the total number of responding countries in the income group as denominator; results for high-income countries are not shown disaggregated due to the small number of responding countries in this income group. They are included in the overall results.

Source: WHO (2017b, table 12, p. 41). © WHO. Licensed under Creative Commons (CC BY-NC-SA 3.0 IGO).

Table 4.2 Types of gaps in policy implementation, and typical causes

Policy implementation gaps	Causes
Gaps in policy formulation process	• Lack of transparency, oversight and influence over policy formulation • External pressure to adopt blueprint policies not adapted to the context • Lack of high-level political commitment • Lack of participation in policy formulation • Policy capture by elites or influential groups
Gaps in operationalization of the policy	• Mismatch between the responsibilities and resources • Time needed to build capacity not adequately considered • Lack of legitimacy of institutions that implement policy • Misalignment between water policies and informal water institutions • Lack of capacity to monitor and enforce agreed norms • Ineffective channels for users to signal demands or express dissatisfaction
Gaps related to characteristics and behaviour of stakeholders	• Monopolistic position of providers • 'Third-party opportunism' • Quality of the representation of stakeholders • Policy processes 'captured' by specific interest groups • Corruption, inefficiency and inertia
Gaps related to the overarching country governance situation	• Political instability, protracted crisis and insecurity • Governments' lack of capacity to carry out basic functions • Lack of accountability in the public sector • Poor (self-)discipline and leadership in government • Lack of 'democracy': insufficient debate, lack of consultation and participation

Source: Adapted from Ménard et al. (2018, table 1, p. 9).

Apart from derailing policy implementation, corruption also reinforces existing inequalities

Corruption, excessive regulation and/or rigid conformity to formal rules tend to coincide with bureaucratic inertia, increase transaction costs, discourage investments, and potentially derail or hinder water management reforms. Certain practices that in contemporary societies are perceived as corrupt may in fact predate modern public administrations. For example, public servants have not always had salaries, without which rent-seeking (or other forms of financial compensation) will be a natural feature of the carrying out of the office. Nevertheless, corruption is a symptom of severe institutional weaknesses and poor governance (Menocal et al., 2015). Apart from derailing policy implementation, corruption also reinforces existing inequalities (Søreide, 2016), since payments trickle up to those with more (discretionary) power. This may also be manifested in the different powers and resources available to women and men (Purushothaman et al., 2012). Gendered roles and special responsibilities that are associated with women in many societies make them subject to diverse forms of corruption to obtain water for their household needs, some of which are very different from those men encounter and engage in. This includes the use of sexual favours or demands as a 'currency' of corruption (IAWJ, 2012; UNDP-SIWI WGF, 2017).

The next section explores the role that the legal system can play in closing the policy implementation gap and furthering human rights into policy implementation outcomes. The recognition of access to water and sanitation as human rights provides court systems with an additional means of justification.

4.3.2 Using legal instruments to further water-related human rights

Courts and judges play critical roles in making sure human rights are also applicable in domestic law. According to a principle adopted in some legal cultures, courts are to interpret domestic law in conformity with the applicable human rights treaties and thereby give an indirect effect to the provisions. Notwithstanding, the extent to which judges actually recognize international obligations varies (De Londras, 2010).

Box 4.3 The human rights to water in India's slums

India has many laws and rules regarding water but none of them contain any explicit 'rights to water'. Instead, the right to life under Article 21 of the country's Constitution has been interpreted by the Supreme and High Courts as including a right to clean and sufficient water.

In Mumbai, a study of an illegal slum area found that in 2012, the median price paid for water by residents was INR 135 (about US$2) per cubic meter of water; more than 40 times the standard municipal water charge paid by residents of notified slums and more than 30 times the charge paid by other city residents (Subbaraman and Murthy, 2015).

In 2014, the state High Court ordered that water supply to occupants of Mumbai's illegal slums should not be tied to land tenure (property rights) issues, thereby allowing cutting through what were previously considered intractable legal barriers to water access in non-notified slums. The court further clarified the right to water previously laid down in case law, and in international human rights law. Following the ruling, the city government developed a new policy for supplying water to non-notified slum residents.

However, the court directed the city government to prevent illegal construction and carry out demolition action against structures that came up after this date. It further stated that *"[a] citizen who stays in an illegal slum or structure cannot claim this right to get water supply at par with law abiding citizens who have constructed and occupied authorised structures"* (Pani Haq Samiti v. Brihan Mumbai Municipal Corporation, 2014, para. 18).

There are specific cases where international human rights have helped individuals or groups to enhance equity through, for instance, improved access to water and sanitation services, or helped to support moral claims and interests for protecting shared water resources. One compilation of such cases can be found in WaterLex/WASH United (2014). Another review from 2015 (Amnesty International/WASH United, 2015) commented on more than 80 individual UN Member States' positions with respect to resolutions and declarations on the Human Rights to Water and Sanitation (HRWS). As suggested in Boxes 4.3 and 4.4, below, the situation is generally complex, and the final results of court action may be elusive.

The case from India (Box 4.3) suggests that legal, institutional and political barriers can be greater obstacles to expanding water access than monetary or technical challenges, especially for poor urban communities. While the court ruled 'in favour' of the urban poor, it also created legal requirements on constructions, which forfeited the purpose to protect the poorest from exorbitant water prices.

Box 4.4 shows that wealthy countries can also struggle to make services available to all, especially to homeless or migrant populations. UN observers have a role as an authoritative observer to ensure that authorities live up to human rights obligations.

The examples presented in boxes 4.3 and 4.4 illustrate the importance of authoritative statements and rulings by judges and observers, in defence of less influential populations. Nevertheless, a policy implementation gap clearly exists, as the implementation of the eventually agreed or 'ruled' plans can linger. Continued monitoring and pressure on responsible actors is required.

4.3.3 Towards inclusive processes

Including all and leaving no one behind requires action of many different types and at many levels. Inclusive institutional devices that make room for 'voice' in the policy-making process are necessary conditions to craft realistic, implementable policies (Hirschman, 1970; OECD, 2011). Especially important in that respect is the capacity to tailor participatory processes in a way that mitigates power imbalances (COHRE/AAAS/SDC/UN-Habitat, 2007), particularly for ethnic minorities and indigenous peoples (Jackson et al., 2012; Jiménez et al., 2014).

Successful operationalization of policies also depends on their perception as being legitimate, which requires them to be clearly understood and effectively disseminated among all relevant stakeholders (SEI, 2013; OECD, 2015), particularly at the local level. Planning from the start for the full operationalization is unusual and may involve unexpected resistance. Yet, this is critical for overcoming the policy implementation gap, and essential for the realization of the 2030 Agenda.

Good water governance involves pro-active measures and mechanisms, ensuring guidance towards effective implementation along with sanctions against poor performance, illegal acts and abuses of power (Cap-Net/WaterLex/UNDP-SIWI WGF/Redica, 2017). Holding decision-makers accountable requires ability, willingness and preparedness among rights-holders, and others on behalf of them, to scrutinize actions and non-actions. In turn, this builds on transparency, integrity and access to information. An HRBA can be key in building capacities for taking responsibility, and acting in line with values like non-discrimination, professionalism, responsiveness, and so on (Figure 4.1).

Successful policy implementation requires cooperative relationships between parties, from transboundary negotiations to local deliberations. These

Box 4.4 The human rights to water and sanitation in French migrant camps

In 2017, a local court found that the authorities must provide access to water and sanitation facilities to refugees and migrants who have set up temporary camps in Calais, France. Upon appeal, this order was upheld by the Supreme administrative court, Conseil d'État, ruling that the treatment of refugees and migrants was inhuman. The court said in a statement that these living conditions reveal a *"failure by the public authorities, and exposes people to be subjected, in the most perceptible manner, to inhuman and degrading treatment."* (Conseil d'État, 2017a).

The court ordered the Prefect of Pas-de-Calais and the commune of Calais to set up drinking water points throughout the commune of Calais, to create free latrines on the territory of the commune of Calais, and to set up one or more facilities enabling all homeless persons of French or foreign nationality, who are on the territory of the commune of Calais, to take a daily shower (Conseil d'État, 2017a; 2017b).

Following this, the Government of France, through the voice of Minister of the Interior, announced that it is fully engaged in improving the reception conditions of migrants and refugees and that it is willing to organize distribution points to ensure better access to water (for meals, showers, toilets). The Special Rapporteurs of the United Nations (UN) on the human rights to safe drinking water and sanitation, on the human rights of migrants, and on the adequate housing, urged the Government of France to devise long-term measures to provide access to safe drinking water and sanitation for migrants in Calais and other areas (OHCHR, 2017a).

Nine months later, the situation is still worrying (OHCHR, 2018). After a visit by the UN Special Rapporteurs on the human rights to safe drinking water and sanitation in April 2018, they reported that "efforts have been made," but "they are not enough." According to estimates quoted by three UN human rights experts, some "nine hundred migrants and asylum seekers live in Calais, three hundred and fifty in Grande-Synthe, and an unknown number in other regions of the north coast of France live without access to emergency shelters and without regular access to drinking water".

Legal, institutional and political barriers can be greater obstacles to expanding water access than monetary or technical challenges

may be operating within different institutional layers and include stakeholders from government at various levels, the private sector and community-based organizations. The building of trust requires dialogue and takes time, but contributes to both the equity and the efficiency of initiatives.

Another path to inclusiveness is sharing knowledge and forming alliances on a global scale. Shared knowledge that is accessible to everyone helps to ensure that those in Developing and Least Developed Countries have the available resources to meet the SDGs, particularly on water management guidance. In a digital age where increasing parts of the global population have access to mobile phones and internet, providing open-access information on best practices for water policies through these mediums can have considerable impacts to ensure that no one is left behind (Bimbe et al., 2015).

Further attention needs to be afforded to the underlying reasons for exclusion and inequality: the unequal distribution of resources. In fact, redistribution has been found not only to be ethically or socially desirable; it is also economically efficient and conducive towards faster and more durable growth (Ostry et al., 2014). This emphasizes the point that redistribution and pro-poor measures are not only helping the poorest but contribute greatly to the overall growth of the economy and health of the society. Still, to ensure that no one is left behind, all realms of society need to subscribe to values of equity and inclusiveness, and these need to saturate higher-level policy-making as well as front-line service delivery and community work.

CHAPTER 5

Economic dimensions of WASH services

World Bank | Luis Andrés and Ye-rin Um

With contributions from: Alejandro Jiménez and Pilar Avello (UNDP-SIWI Water Governance Facility); Carlos Carrion-Crespo and Maria Teresa Gutierrez (ILO); and Lesley Pories (Water.org)

This chapter aims to advance the economic understanding of how national (and subnational) policies, plans and programmes can improve access to WASH services for all, and particularly for people in vulnerable situations.[24] The topics examined include: i) making an economic case for WASH; ii) assessing the affordability of WASH services; iii) reducing costs to improve affordability; iv) evaluating the role of subsidies; and iv) analysing the funding and financing of WASH services for vulnerable groups.

5.1
Introduction

A global vision of universal access to 'safely managed' water supply, sanitation and hygiene (WASH) services, as set under the Sustainable Development Goals (SDGs), calls for attention to vulnerable groups and equitable provision of WASH services. In many countries the water and sanitation coverage of lower-wealth quintiles has increased at a slower rate than that of the better-off quintiles (WHO/UNICEF, 2015b). Furthermore, vulnerable groups, including indigenous and tribal peoples, suffer disproportionately from inadequate access to safe drinking water and sanitation services (ILO, 2016) and are not being explicitly considered in countries' national WASH policies. Hence, in the discussions that led to the adoption of the SDGs' WASH targets, many sector stakeholders proposed that the service coverage of vulnerable groups be increased at a faster rate than that of other unserved populations (WHO/UNICEF, 2013). Effectively closing inequality gaps is a major challenge, as well as an indicator of progress on the 2030 SDG agenda.

WASH policies have implications for lessening inequality and enhancing the status of vulnerable groups. According to an ethics-based, human rights argument, society and the state have a duty to help people living in vulnerable situations access essential services such as WASH. To provide basic services is to respect human dignity. Going beyond this prescriptive statement, the value of WASH provision becomes even greater when the impact on redistribution is recognized. Indeed, addressing the basic needs (such as for WASH) of the

---

[24] The paper 'Counting the costs and benefits of equitable WASH service provision' (Hutton and Andrés, 2018) provided much of the basis for this chapter.

less well-off can address the underlying causes of inequalities. For instance, poor water supply and sanitation contribute to debilitating diseases such as diarrhoea and childhood stunting. Such health disturbances additionally result in decreased school attendance for children and time away from work for adults, further perpetuating cycles of poverty. Targeting WASH resources where access is low and populations are particularly vulnerable offers an efficient way to change the course of generational trends, by giving all children a better chance of reaching their full potential.

There are a number of factors at play in the current WASH investment gap affecting vulnerable groups. This is partly a question of information asymmetry — households and entire communities are not aware of some of the benefits they would enjoy as a result of better WASH services. Insufficient investment may also reflect the persistence of traditional practices and preferences, which are dictated by social customs as to what is considered normal or desirable. A third possibility is that although some households would like to improve their condition, they might not be able to act. They might not have the means to pay for the service, especially the up-front costs of investment, or they might choose to devote limited household resources to other priorities.

5.2
Providing WASH to vulnerable and disadvantaged groups: A cost–benefit analysis

Global cost–benefit studies have demonstrated that WASH services provide good social and economic returns when compared with their costs. Economic evaluation studies compare a programme's costs with its benefits to estimate cost–benefit ratios or annual rates of return. Evidence from global (Whittington et al., 2012; Hutton, 2012a) as well as country studies (Hutton et al., 2014) generally shows high returns on WASH spending, for example, with a global average benefit–cost ratio of 5.5 for improved sanitation and 2.0 for improved drinking water.

A central element of national planning, priority setting and budgeting is an understanding of the costs and benefits of reaching different population groups, especially vulnerable ones. However, evidence specific to subpopulation groups is rare; most studies present costs and benefits for the general population. In an evaluation of efforts to improve sanitation in the Philippines, the World Bank estimates lower cost–benefit ratios for poorer than for richer populations, due to the higher value of time assigned to the rich (World Bank, 2011). However, when the net present value[25] of sanitation interventions is compared with the average income of different income quintiles, the very poor have five times the relative return of the non-poor. A study of South Asia shows that costs per disease episode are relatively similar across wealth quintiles, but medical expenses represent a significantly greater share of income among poorer households (Rheingans et al., 2012). Jeuland et al. (2013) show that WASH-related mortality benefits, in the long term, are larger in poorer than in richer countries of South Asia and Sub-Saharan Africa. Hence, improvement in WASH services in these regions would have major implications for global equity.

WASH investments will do the most to reduce childhood deaths from diarrhoeal disease when they target geographic areas where vulnerable populations have little access to WASH services. A World Bank study (2017b) reveals that in developing countries across the six major regions of the world,[26] the greatest burden of disease associated with unimproved water and sanitation is borne by the poorest across national, urban and rural, and subnational populations. This is consistent with patterns of access to water, sanitation and health services (oral rehydration therapy and the provision of vitamin A), and the prevalence of undernutrition (measured by height and weight for age). Rural populations across all 18 countries and economies analysed in the study had a greater absolute and population-adjusted burden of WASH-related disease. However, the disparity in the degree of access to WASH infrastructure between the poor and non-poor was much greater among urban than rural households.

---

[25] Net present value is the difference between the present value of the future benefits flows from an investment and the amount of such investment.

[26] East Asia and the Pacific, Europe and Central Asia, Latin America and the Caribbean, Middle East and North Africa, South Asia, and Sub-Saharan Africa.

It is likely that the benefits of improved WASH services for vulnerable groups would change the balance of any cost–benefit analysis that accounts for changes in these groups' self-perceived social status and dignity, but further research is needed (Hutton and Andrés, 2018). A few existing studies indicate that health costs are more burdensome for poorer households than richer ones (World Bank, 2011; Rheingans et al., 2012; Jeuland et al., 2013). However, few studies explore the full range of economic and social benefits of access to improved WASH, or compare the barriers to WASH services faced by vulnerable groups with those of the general population.[27] Table 5.1 provides an indication of the relative impact of selected WASH initiatives for various vulnerable groups (see Box 1.3).[28] More data are needed for further analysis.

Table 5.1 **The relative possibility of gaining selected benefits from WASH interventions, by vulnerable population group**

Population group	Health	Living environment	Convenience and time savings	Dignity (social)	Educational outcomes*
People below national poverty line	↑↑↑	↑↑	↑	↑↑	↑
Slum dwellers	↑↑↑	↑↑↑	↑↑	↑↑	↑
Remote and isolated populations	↑	↑	↑	↑	↑
Ethnic [minority] groups	↑	↑	↑		↑
Women and female-heads of households	↑↑	↑	↑↑	↑↑↑	↑↑
Children	↑↑↑	↑	↑	↑↑	↑↑↑
Elderly, sick, and physically disabled people**	↑↑↑	↑	↑↑↑	↑↑↑	↑↑***
Emergency contexts	↑↑↑	↑↑↑	↑↑	↑	↑
Refugees	↑↑	↑↑	↑↑	↑	↑
Prison population	↑↑	↑↑	↑	↑↑	

*Due to reduced stunting, reduced illness-related absence, and higher enrolment and completion rates (especially among girls).

**Buildings and other facilities, including toilets, are often not accessible to persons with mobility limitations due to the lack of an accessible design, such as an entrance ramp, retrofitted bathrooms, or improved signage (ILO, 2017d).

***Educational gains for disabled children.

Note: The number of arrows is meant to illustrate the magnitude of the outcome expected for each population group.

Source: Hutton and Andrés (2018).

5.3
Affordability

It is clear that investing in WASH in general, and in WASH services for the vulnerable and disadvantaged in particular, makes economic sense. One of the reasons behind not providing adequate services to such groups is the assumption that they cannot afford to pay for them. Yet the vulnerable and disadvantaged, who are typically not connected to piped systems, often pay more for their water supply services than their connected counterparts (World Bank, 2017b) (see Chapter 6). As such it makes sense to explore the options for expanding access, and also to put into question what is meant by 'affordability' (see Section 1.2.3). This is especially critical given the core of SDG Targets 6.1 and 6.2: 'universal and equitable access to safe and affordable drinking water' and 'adequate and equitable sanitation and hygiene'.

---

[27] Jones et al. (2002) conducted a literature review to outline the various problems faced by disabled people in accessing WASH. A study assessing barriers to WASH among disabled people in Malawi found that being female, being from an urban area, and having limited wealth and education were likely to increase the number and intensity of the barriers faced by an individual (White et al., 2016).

[28] It should be noted that rural workers and their families are among the least protected in terms of access to basic health services, workers' compensation, long-term disability insurance, and survivors' benefits.

"Affordability is key for the realization of the human rights to water and sanitation. Economic sustainability and affordability for all people are not impossible to reconcile, but human rights require rethinking current lines of argumentation and redesigning current instruments. The main challenge is to ensure that targeted measures and instruments do, in fact, reach the people who rely on them most. For instance, tariffs must be designed in such a way that the most disadvantaged of those connected to formal utilities receive the assistance they need. It also requires ensuring that public finance and subsidies reach the most marginalized and disadvantaged individuals and communities, who are often not (yet) connected to a formal network, who may live in informal settlements without any formal title or in remote rural areas where self-supply is common, and who are often overlooked or deliberately ignored in current policymaking and planning." (HRC, 2015, para. 86).

The concept of affordability is not new, but no consensus has been reached on the methodology for measuring it, although various options were proposed in the Millennium Development Goal (MDG) era (Smets, 2009, 2012; Hutton, 2012b; WHO/UNICEF, 2017a). There has been limited analysis of WASH affordability that distinguishes different contexts, such as urban versus rural, households connected to a piped system versus those not connected, and consumers of various types of water sources, and the literature rarely encompasses sanitation and hygiene. In addition, there has been limited study of how greater expenditure on drinking water (or WASH in general) drives down the availability of disposable income for other non-water consumption and the inverse, that is, how non-water expenditure crowds out funds available for water (and WASH). Furthermore, to spend more on water does not necessarily imply that the water is of greater quantity, or for that matter quality, as this depends on its price, source, type of use, location and other factors. Affordability as a concept will need to be further defined before it can be effectively measured. For example, the prices of water or sanitation may decline and yet still be out of reach of certain vulnerable groups.

The affordability of water and sanitation services is an important cross-cutting concern that affects states' ability to deliver on the human rights to water and sanitation (WHO/UNICEF, 2013). The human rights to water and sanitation place obligations on states and utilities to regulate payments for services and to ensure that all members of the population can afford to access basic services. Expenditure on drinking water and sanitation typically includes infrequent, large capital investments, including the cost of connections, as well as recurrent spending on rehabilitation and maintenance, both of which need to be considered in any affordability threshold that may be established by governments or intergovernmental organizations. Rigorous assessments of affordability also need to consider populations' wealth or income, as well as WASH sector subsidies or other social transfers provided by the state.

Evidence from willingness-to-pay studies points to the limitations of setting rigid benchmarks that define what is and what is not affordable to (poor) households. Households are often willing to pay significantly more than current tariffs if they are guaranteed a level of water supply that meets their expectations. *"Some households are willing to pay more than 3–5% of their monthly income for a utility service, while others would refuse to pay that much. In this sense, an affordability threshold analysis does not help determine how many households in a particular utility's service area would see cost-recovery prices as a barrier to continuing to use improved water services, nor whether affordable prices would be enough to induce unconnected households to use the services"* (Komives et al., 2005, p. 45).

An alternative way of defining water affordability is to establish an affordability threshold that is based on a monetary value of the subsistence water 'basket'. This basket could accommodate, for instance, the service level mandated by SDG Targets 6.1 and 6.2, or it may be adapted to the level of access and quality set in national policies or standards. The goal is that populations should, at a minimum, be getting water at the 'defined' level of services. In other words, the defined price of a particular water basket is affordable for a population group, based on that particular group's income level. The assessment should consider that different population groups have different degrees

> To spend more on water does not necessarily imply that the water is of greater quantity, or for that matter quality, as this depends on its price, source, type of use, location and other factors

of access to services, at different prices. Ensuring that water is affordable to all population groups in a given country will require tailored policy recommendations for specific targeted population groups.

Understanding affordability could be facilitated through the use of a broad framework that classifies population groups into one of four main categories, depending on service level and ability to pay. It is important to note that this categorization should be based on: i) a targeted minimum service level, since the current level of service might fall below this threshold; and ii) a population group's ability to pay for the targeted service level, excluding any subsidy (Hutton and Andrés, 2018).

5.4
Increasing efficiency and reducing unit costs

Service costs can often be reduced without any impact on the service level

An obvious but often neglected way of increasing affordability is to lower the costs of providing the service. This also has the benefit of improving the overall financial performance of the service provider and making it more creditworthy, a route to mobilizing additional financing (discussed more in later sections). Service costs can often be reduced without any impact on the service level. There are many ways to achieve this, and five examples are discussed below. The financial resources freed up by efficiency gains can in turn enhance the provision of WASH services to groups in vulnerable situations.

First, technological innovation and dissemination can lead to major cost reductions over time. For example, as water and wastewater treatment technologies advance, greater efficiency can be achieved, in which the costs per unit treated fall. In addition, the falling prices and increasing performance of plastic products — not only for latrine slabs but also for their superstructure — enable the production of latrines at a lower cost. Hence, producers save costs in different parts of the production process by investing in new technologies. Digital payment for service platforms, already on the uptake in many countries in the developed and developing world, also stand poised to facilitate reduced transaction costs on the part of payment and/or tariff collection, particularly in remote areas that are harder to access.

Second, much can still be done to reduce unit costs through input and scale optimization. Identifying better-priced factors of production is the most conventional way of cutting costs. Purchasing materials in bulk and exploiting economies of scale, which involves spreading relatively fixed costs (e.g. overheads) over a larger production base, are good examples. While the evidence is mixed on the optimal size of a utility's service area (as unit costs are very context-specific), authorities need to make evidence-based decisions when dividing up cities or districts into service zones, considering among other things the factors that are driving costs.

Third, more competition can be introduced into the provision of WASH services, which is a natural monopoly due to its intensive capital investment requirements. Many markets are highly regulated and monopolistic, with very limited competition. In some cases, such as piped water or wastewater networks, it does not make economic sense to have alternative networks competing for the same customers. However, regulations on broader market entry can be reduced. Enabling more producers and suppliers in the marketplace will increase competition, with benefits that include lower costs, product or process innovation, and the availability of a diverse range of products in the marketplace.

Fourth, enhancing management practices can improve production efficiency. Production inefficiencies are caused by poor planning (e.g. overstocking, underutilized resources), lack of accountability, and product wastage and leakage (e.g. non-revenue water). By institutionalizing modern management practices and identifying cost-effective interventions, costs can eventually be cut back and services can be delivered to consumers at a lower cost. This is helped by opening markets up to competition, in order to increase incentives for good performance.

Fifth, production efficiency can be improved by good governance and increased transparency. Governance aspects of utility management are also essential for reducing the costs of service delivery and improving organizational management (Box 5.1). The positive impact of good governance (and the negative impact of corruption) has been proved to affect the efficiency of water utilities (Estache and Kouassi, 2002) (see Chapter 4). When addressing these issues, water utilities should allow for worker participation through social dialogue and collective bargaining.[29] Corruption, in particular, is not only a blockage that needs correcting but a disincentive for much-needed external investment. Increased transparency may lead to increased investment from other sectors over time, as well as deepened buy-in from potential clients — if people are more confident or have avenues for resolution of their service quality complaints, they are more likely to be willing to pay tariffs on time or to connect to a provider in the first place. Fonseca and Pories (2017) observe that budget transparency is critical at all stages along the chain, from national to local government, in order to ensure equity and efficiency. The finance-themed 2017 UN-Water Global Analysis and Assessment of Sanitation and Drinking Water (GLAAS) report (WHO, 2017b) has documented WASH government budgets, sub-sector allocations, and disparities between budget and expenditure in an effort to better monitor and hold governments accountable for how WASH priorities are determined and ultimately implemented. The emerging UN-Water GLAAS TrackFin Initiative (Tracking Financing to WASH) is another example that encourages budget transparency, by identifying and tracking financing to the WASH sector at the national or subnational level in a consistent and comparable manner. As of June 2018, TrackFin has been initiated in 15 countries with the support of a number of development partners, and countries around the world continue to show interest (WHO, n.d.).

5.5
Designing subsidies and tariffs

Subsidies will continue playing a key role, so they should be well designed, transparent and targeted. Subsidies are a subset of funding flows between governments, utilities and customers. National governments provide fiscal transfers (in the form of budgetary allocations) to subnational government entities (e.g. states, counties, parastatal organizations) that play either a direct or an indirect role in water and sanitation service delivery. Under a broader definition, subsidies can also take the form of implicit transfers through underpriced products or services. The process by which developed countries achieved universal access to water and sanitation clearly demonstrates that domestic public finance, including targeted subsidies, has been and remains critically important, even in strongly market-led economies (Fonseca and Pories, 2017). Thus, even with improved efficiency, it is likely that subsidies will continue to be important to achieve universal coverage (including vulnerable groups) in the WASH sector. When designing and allocating subsidies, there are a number of points to be considered so that scarce public resources reach those groups most in need.

First, the cost or programme components to be subsidized must be carefully chosen. A common choice that policy-makers face is between: i) subsidizing activities to promote household WASH investments and changes in social norms and behaviours; or ii) subsidizing the costs of service, with a broad distinction between subsidizing capital investment versus operation and maintenance (O&M) costs. Historically, subsidies have played a major role in financing water investments (i.e. capital infrastructure), with a large share of O&M expenditure expected from each household (Danilenko et al., 2014). Because subsidies are most often linked to capital expenditures and those are most often focused on relatively well-off communities, the non-poor have often been the beneficiaries of subsidy interventions intended to reach the poor (Fuente et al., 2016). Subsidizing capital

---

[29] For example, the multi-employer collective agreement between the Water Employees Trade Union of Malawi (WETUM) and the existing Water Boards, signed in 2014, provides for discussions regarding productivity, capacity building, gender mainstreaming and discrimination, HIV and AIDS in the workplace, corruption, water sector policies, and youth participation (Water Boards/WETUM, 2014).

Box 5.1 El Salvador: Integrity Pact promotes transparency around pipe replacement contracts

With the aim of building trust and increasing transparency around public procurement, the National Water and Sewerage Administration of El Salvador (ANDA) has signed three Integrity Pacts around the tenders for pipe replacement in the greater San Salvador area. Integrity Pacts are a tool developed by Transparency International and constitute an agreement between the government agency offering a contract and the companies bidding for it. In this agreement, they declare that they will abstain from bribery, collusion and other corrupt practices for the duration of the contract. To ensure that the Pact is being followed by the parties, the Integrity Pact includes a delegated 'monitor' overseeing the bidding and execution process, providing recommendations, and delivering a public statement. The role of the monitor is typically taken up by civil society groups.

The Integrity Pacts were signed by ANDA as the commissioning agency, the contractors as the bidders, and the Foundation for Studies on the Application of Law in El Salvador (FESPAD) in the role of monitor. The UNDP-SIWI Water Governance Facility (WGF) signed the Pact as the international witness and can give advice about the implementation of the Integrity Pact. The financing of the Pact formed part of the activities included in the "Agreement on Technical Cooperation on Improving Integrity in the Management of ANDA" between the UNDP-SIWI WGF and ANDA to improve the management of the organization through the lens of integrity. The work was supported by the Spanish Agency for International Cooperation and Development (AECID).

FESPAD´s bidding process evaluation report[1] was presented to the public in a press conference in 2016, in the presence of AECID and ANDA. FESPAD´s final report was due to be presented in a press conference by the end of 2018.

The signing of the Integrity Pacts forms part of a series of initiatives undertaken by ANDA to progress towards a more open, transparent and accountable management of the organization, with the aim of increasing resource use efficiency, reducing the losses due to corrupt practices and building trust to attract better offers from the private sector. This includes a series of workshops and activities to help the organization and its staff understand what integrity entails, how it can be pursued, what bad practices are hindering its full realization, and what can be done collectively to increase ANDA´s integrity management. Examples of measures include the adoption of results-based management or performance indicators for staff evaluation. The workshops were conducted in collaboration with cewas, a Swiss non-for-profit organization, drawing on the methodology of the Integrity Management Toolbox.

Contributed by UNDP-SIWI Water Governance Facility.

[1] The evaluation report in Spanish can be accessed in the following link: fespad.org.sv/wp-content/uploads/2016/06/Primer-informe-de-observaci%C3%B3n-social-a-ANDA_etapa-1-1.pdf.

---

infrastructure may still make sense if vulnerable groups are clustered in a specific location that can be targeted. Sanitation services may be more natural candidates for subsidies than water services, since willingness to pay for such services is often lower and the wider social benefits are higher (World Bank, 2002). Under the community-led total sanitation (CLTS) approach, subsidies are calibrated to stimulate demand for sanitation, allowing the market to respond to households' increased willingness to pay.

Second, subsidies that promote greater community participation are being proven effective, as they empower vulnerable groups to allocate resources toward their own priorities. Incorporating transparent mechanisms for underserved people to easily provide inputs into the design and decision-making processes behind infrastructure projects could potentially allow them to compete with the more informal mechanisms that richer populations use to influence decision-making. Involvement of community-based organizations and user groups can lead to greater accountability and improved performance, with benefits for poor and vulnerable households, through their contribution to planning, implementation (e.g. raising awareness) and monitoring and evaluation (Andrés and Naithani, 2013). These mechanisms are becoming part of the policy toolkit as they are tested and mainstreamed.

Third, setting tariffs — ideally the major funding source of service provision — requires striking a balance between several key objectives. In general, the design of water tariff structures aims to accomplish the following four objectives (World Bank, 2002):

- **Cost recovery.** From the service provider's point of view, cost recovery is the main purpose of a tariff. Cost recovery requires that, on aggregate, the tariff faced by consumers should generate revenues equal to the financial cost of supplying the service over time.

> Subsidies that promote greater community participation are being proven effective, as they empower vulnerable groups to allocate resources toward their own priorities

- **Economic efficiency**. Economic efficiency requires that prices signal to consumers the financial, environmental, social and other costs that their water use decisions impose on the rest of the system and on the economy. In practice, this means that the volumetric charge should be set equal to the marginal cost of bringing one additional cubic meter of water into a city and delivering it to a particular customer. An efficient tariff creates incentives that ensure that, for a given water supply and sanitation cost, users obtain the largest possible aggregate benefits.

- **Equity**. Equity means that the tariff treats similar customers equally, and that customers in different situations are not treated the same. This usually means that users pay monthly water bills that are proportionate to the costs they impose on the utility by their use of the service.

- **Affordability**. WASH services differ from many other services in that they are considered a basic right and should be provided to people regardless of cost or ability to pay.

Designing tariff structures is challenging precisely because these four objectives conflict, and trade-offs are inevitable. For example, providing underpriced water through private connections in order to achieve the objective of affordability conflicts with the objectives of cost recovery and efficient water use. It may not appear equitable to charge population groups that are relatively expensive to serve (due to, say, their outlying location) the same as, or less than, other customers. At the same time, it might not be equitable to charge the poor the same water price as other customers given the difference in their ability to pay.

If, to meet affordability and equity objectives, subsidies are to be delivered through water tariffs, then vouchers or cash distribution might be better than an increasing block tariff (IBT). Despite the widespread implementation of IBTs in low- and middle-income countries, there is now broad consensus that IBTs do not effectively target subsidies to the intended low-income customers due to several factors (Brocklehurst and Fuente, 2016; Burger and Jansen, 2014; Fuente et al., 2016). First, prices in most low- and middle-income countries are not sufficient to cover the full cost of water and sanitation services, resulting in most customers being subsidized. Second, contrary to conventional wisdom, metered water consumption might not be correlated to income since poor households might have bigger family sizes. Third, low-income customers are typically more likely to have a shared connection than wealthier customers and thus face the highest price in IBTs. Finally, like all usage subsidies, IBTs apply only to those households connected to a piped network and therefore exclude the poorest households, who often lack access to piped water and sanitation services (Andrés and Fuente, 2017). Instead of IBTs, a uniform volumetric tariff — where customers are charged the same amount per unit of water they use — combined with a negative fixed charge or rebate for the target group is recommended. The rebate could be delivered through vouchers or cash distributions. While the mechanisms for identifying the targeted population tend to be challenging and expensive, making use of robust mechanisms that identify deserving households or individuals could be a viable option. In Mexico, for instance, energy subsidies are being channelled this way, through a programme called Oportunidades ("Opportunities") that provides conditional cash transfers to the poorest segments of the population (Andrés and Naithani, 2013).

Large WASH service providers can use commercial financing and indirectly support vulnerable groups through cross-subsidization

---

5.6
Funding and financing: Mobilizing commercial sources of investment

A lack of funding and financing mechanisms is a critical bottleneck to achieving the SDG WASH targets for vulnerable groups. Funding refers to the financial resources of the WASH sector, which are made up of: i) tariffs and fees paid by the WASH users; ii) domestic tax revenues passed from the central or local governments to the WASH sector; and iii) grants from international donors, charitable foundations and non-governmental organizations (NGOs) interested in supporting the sector. By contrast, financing is what the WASH sector borrows from the donors or financial market and then repays in the future, using funding. There is much scope for change in both the funding and financing mechanisms so as to close the investment gap for vulnerable groups.

Commercial financing involves a wide range of sources and terms, many of which are utilized in the WASH sector in developing countries to some degree. This type of financing comes from various domestic and international sources, such as water equipment suppliers, microfinanciers, commercial banks or private and institutional investors. Such providers of commercial finance are generally willing to take on varying levels and types of risk, which can be complementary. Accessing commercial finance is not equivalent to privatizing the sector, since both public and private operators can and should utilize commercial finance for their infrastructure needs. Unfortunately, commercial financing in emerging markets currently makes up only a small portion of WASH investment worldwide — no aggregate numbers are available, but the WASH sector on average attracted only 3% of all private sector participation in infrastructure (energy, transport and water) projects in the years 2009–2014 (Goksu et al., 2017).

For households in vulnerable situations, a common bottleneck is the availability of funds to pay up-front capital costs, and microfinance is growing but still rare. In order to pay capital costs, many households are willing to take out a repayable loan, which can be paid off over subsequent years. Ikeda and Arney (2015) have highlighted the potential role microfinance can play in addressing the water and sanitation financing gap. However, there are still many barriers to expanding microfinance to vulnerable groups, including the unavailability of service in rural areas, especially those distant from commercial centres. Furthermore, capital costs for water (and especially sanitation) infrastructure may not be considered an eligible or viable purpose for getting a loan, and even if they are, interest rates may be high, and vulnerable households in particular are likely to lack collateral to offer against a loan.

Some success stories in microfinance exist. A number of initiatives have successfully made microfinance loans accessible to vulnerable groups, addressing the barriers above. Moreover, repayment data from WASH microfinance programmes around the world prove that the poor are not only willing to take loans to finance their WASH assets but also consistently repay these loans (Water.org, 2018). A well-known example is that of Bangladesh's Grameen Bank, which has successfully reached rural populations with affordable loans for WASH, specifically targeting women (Khandker et al., 1995). Another example is in Viet Nam, where many women's unions have helped households to invest in their own toilets through a revolving fund (Kolsky et al., 2010). Suppliers have also provided microfinancing for pumps, meters and solar pumps. These examples (including Box 5.2) show that if financial actors learn to perceive many substrata within 'the poor' as an untapped market to harness, tailored goods and services that cater to specific needs and price points can emerge and change the nature of how low-income groups address WASH.

Where small-scale local WASH service providers are significant, certain features of the business environment need to be in place. These may include: i) financial products that allow small- and medium-sized enterprises (SMEs) to manage pre-financing; ii) a business support sector that can help SMEs achieve the formalities required to borrow and to meet water sector licensing requirements; iii) an enabling environment for the capital market; and iv) an efficient water services sector that provides investors with access to competitive services, such as site surveying, well drilling and component purchasing (World Bank, 2016b).

Large WASH service providers can use commercial financing and indirectly support vulnerable groups through cross-subsidization. These service providers usually cover a large service area where both the better-off and vulnerable groups reside. Where this is the case, pricing mechanisms might allow for cross-subsidization between population groups, using a uniform volumetric tariff with a rebate. If the service provider is creditworthy — characterized by strong technical and financial performance, a sound governance structure and solid business strategy and plans — and located in a country where a robust financial market exists, additional resources can be brought in through commercial financing. Loan or bond proceeds can be used to expand service coverage and enhance service levels for all population groups. Ideally, the tariff level paid by the customers who do not receive the rebate should be high enough to repay the principal and interest at commercial terms. In some cases, other funding sources such as domestic tax revenues and grants may supplement the tariff receipts.

Well-designed public–private partnerships (PPPs) can improve access to WASH services for vulnerable groups. A PPP is one of the legal structures in infrastructure delivery, and it often utilizes commercial finance. WASH PPP projects specific to certain vulnerable groups may not be feasible due to a lack of bankability, but efforts can be made to protect and promote their representation in projects that serve a wider population. For example, during the feasibility stage, data can be collected in a disaggregated way to further understand the different needs, capacities and concerns of various population groups. Legal frameworks governing PPPs can be reviewed to ensure no biases exist against particular groups in vulnerable situations. Furthermore, a consideration of certain vulnerable groups could be embedded in output specifications for the private sector. For example, in a PPP project in Ghana, minimum design and construction terms required separate toilet blocks for males and females, and disposal units catering to women's needs (World Bank, 2016c).

'Crowding in' private investment for WASH requires a significant change in the mindset that works for traditional funders. Experts within the WASH sector repeatedly highlight the need to attract private finance and have called for the strategic use of development assistance funding to serve as a guarantor for larger private investment. Blended finance shows strong promise, but for it to truly address the funding gap all actors must be willing to accept roles and approaches outside their traditional operating procedures. Specifically, monitoring the outputs of blended finance programmes requires flexibility and awareness of the degree of efficiency required by the private sector, as well as recognition and acceptance of the fact that private investment alone will not be able to serve the majority of the target populations. As illustrated in Box 5.3, blended finance approaches will require potentially complex combinations of development finance, private finance and government subsidies to ensure that all target groups are being reached and no one is being left behind.

> Blended finance shows strong promise, but for it to truly address the funding gap all actors must be willing to accept roles and approaches outside their traditional operating procedures

Box 5.3 Kenya: Using blended finance to improve water services

Kenya's national development plan seeks to make basic water and sanitation available to all by 2030. Building on utilities reforms that started in 2002, the Kenyan government decided to mobilize commercial financing to help bridge the financing gap for investments in water infrastructure.

The World Bank Group and international development partners supported the country through a series of measures from 2007 to 2017. These included helping scale up the financial and operational performance of water service providers, supporting creditworthiness assessments, and piloting financing initiatives focused on delivering improved water supply and sanitation services to low-income homes. Technical assistance supported by multi-donor World Bank Group trust funds — including the Public–Private Infrastructure Advisory Facility (PPIAF), the Global Partnership on Output-Based Aid (GPOBA), and the Water and Sanitation Program (WSP) — to borrowers and lenders has facilitated the process. The support from the European Union and the credit guarantees by the United States Agency for International Development (USAID), which provided partial risk cover to domestic lenders, helped scale up the efforts.

As of 2018, approximately 50 transactions have been completed, which raised more than US$25 million in private capital. Investments in low-income areas were encouraged through results-based grants of US$21 million provided by GPOBA, which enabled water service providers to obtain commercial funds for delivering water services to low-income areas. These results-based projects have already provided water access to over 300,000 people, with another 200,000 expected to benefit by the time the last project closes in December 2019.

Source: World Bank (2018).

5.7
Conclusions

In sum, the social and economic returns of investing in WASH services are significant. When resources are limited, it makes most sense to target those areas where vulnerable populations have little existing access. Here, tremendous benefits can be realized with long-term implications — for example, if childhood diarrhoeal disease and subsequent deaths can be mitigated, this would transform the economic prospects of the next generation. If subsidies are to be applied, they might have a larger impact in the sanitation sector, compared to the water supply sector. Improvements in sanitation have far-reaching impacts, and populations are more likely to pay for drinking water than for improved sanitation. WASH services in general would also benefit from the same principles seen to benefit the private sector: competition, rigorous analysis of consumers' willingness and ability to pay for a service (including questioning the common assumption that the poor cannot pay), and the implementation of new technology, where applicable.

To address the investment gap in the WASH sector, institutions must coordinate at the planning stage and carefully consider priorities. Policy-makers are confronted with myriad factors to consider during the investment decision-making process. The problem of conflicting priorities is particularly acute in infrastructure decisions, which often involve large investments, lock-in technologies and long-term maintenance commitments. Planning authorities will need to base their programming on what service level can be achieved using both public funds and tariffs recovered from users. If the financial resource constraints are considerable, it will not be feasible to achieve all elements of 'safely managed' services in the short or medium term. Planning authorities will also face difficult decisions about whether to allocate funds to upgrade an existing basic service to a safely managed one, or to provide a basic service to a community with no access to it at all (World Bank, 2017b). Coordination among related agencies and adequate budget allocation is critical to ensure that project delivery aligns with set priorities.

Incentives to improve the provision of services to vulnerable groups may originate from the transparency and accountability of decision-making processes. Government officials are guided by incentives when making decisions about the allocation of financial resources to investments and management. Examples from many countries show that, if civil society receives information and is consulted, a higher level of transparency is achieved and government decision-makers at different levels take the needs of stakeholders, including groups in vulnerable situations, more directly into account. Improving the provision of WASH services to vulnerable groups can often be achieved by cross-subsidization, by which better-off users help cover the costs of the provision of the service to those who can least afford it. Stakeholders are much more likely to agree to changes, even those that may affect them in the short run, when their interests have been considered and options have been discussed. Therefore, transparency, access to information and the involvement of stakeholders are essential to ensure that WASH services reach vulnerable groups (World Bank, 2013).

Given that poor and vulnerable groups are not homogeneous, WASH policies need to distinguish between different populations and prepare specific actions to address each of them. First, it is important to realistically identify the minimum service levels needed for vulnerable groups to exercise the human rights to safe water and sanitation. This policy needs to be backed up with a service-pricing mechanism, a financing strategy and an implementation plan to ensure that the service level is affordable and sustainable for vulnerable groups. Given scarce resources, governments should encourage service providers to increase their efficiency — both to keep costs down (and hence make services more affordable) and to improve their financial performance (and hence the opportunity to access new, commercial, sources of financing). The policy's success will depend on the effectiveness of the targeting mechanisms, the availability of subsidies and the strength of domestic financial markets, among other things. While there are many examples of public actions to make water services more affordable, more evaluations are needed of their successes and weaknesses, and conditions under which they do or do not work.

CHAPTER 6

Cities, urbanization and informal settlements

Reflection of slums on a high-rise building in Rio de Janeiro, Brazil

UN-Habitat | Graham Alabaster

With contributions from: Jenny Grönwall (UNDP-SIWI Water Governance Facility)

This chapter focuses on urbanization and the fact that many of the inequities in access to water and sanitation services will be most keenly felt in urban and peri-urban areas. This chapter therefore concerns those who reside in an urban agglomeration of any size, and who have a significantly lower level of service than the average for the whole administratively defined area in which they reside.

6.1
Defining who are left behind in urban settings

There is cause for concern that a significant proportion of unserved and under-served urban residents in vulnerable situations are not counted ('below the radar') in current methods used for estimating service coverage. There are many generic urban settings where this is apparent, including the peri-urban areas of large cities (which include intra-urban slums and low-income areas), and the secondary urban centres, small towns and large villages where a significant proportion of the urban population resides.

Peri-urban areas, although they often comprise the residential area for the labour force of the city, are often not included in service schemes due to the fact that their residents in many cases don't pay taxes and their housing rental arrangements are part of the informal economy (UN-Habitat, 2003). This is not acceptable under the International Covenant on Economic, Social and Cultural Rights, as *"no household should be denied the right to water on the grounds of their housing or land status"* (CESCR, 2002b, para. 16(c)). In these settings, the wealthier enjoy in many cases high levels of service at (often very) low cost, whereas the poor pay a much higher price for a service of similar or lesser quality. Examples include cities in Sub-Saharan Africa, such as Nairobi, where the low tariffs paid in the middle-class neighbourhoods are far lower than the cost of water supplied to slum dwellers (Crow and Odaba, 2009). The administrative inefficiency of formal service providers is such that water tariffs are unrealistically low and do not even cover the cost of production. In such settings, weak utilities fail to collect water user fees and consequently enter a vicious cycle of inadequate cost recovery, poor investment in operations and maintenance, and poor levels of service (UNDESA, 2007). People living in informal settlements have to pay a much higher cost for water, often 10 or 20 times the cost of their more affluent neighbours (UNDP, 2006). The poor end up paying dearly for what the rich get (almost) for free.

Many smaller urban centres in secondary urban settings do not have a centralized reticulation of piped systems, or it may only cover a small part of the city/town. This limited system may be run at a loss by the local council and is therefore a poor investment choice for private utilities (Bhattacharya and Banerjee, 2015). The wealthier often rely on groundwater resources, often on an individual or household basis (Healy et al., 2018), with numerous private boreholes, without regulation. Aside from the impact on the environment, inequities usually arise, and again the most disadvantaged and vulnerable groups miss out. The lack of well-maintained water reticulation or off-site services for water supply is further exacerbated by the lack of effective sanitation facilities. Many poorly designed or poorly located on-site systems rapidly contaminate both surface water and groundwater, and poor solid waste management leads to blocked drainage systems and flooding (Vilane and Dlamini, 2016). The levels of basic service that low-income residents have access to are often far from satisfactory, and available at a much higher cost than for residents from other areas of the same city. Most slum dwellers pay between 10–25 times more for water in the city of Nairobi than what the utility would charge (Migiro and Mis, 2014; Ng'ethe, 2018). Sanitation services are often shared or poorly maintained and there are few connections to sewers. Solid waste collection and garbage disposal is often non-existent and waste is removed primarily through waste picking and informal recycling. Connections to the power grid are often illegal and extremely dangerous.

Understanding both the patterns of urbanization and some of the factors that contribute to the inequities are critical in order to develop differentiated services at appropriate levels (see Chapter 5).

> **The levels of basic service that low-income residents have access to are often far from satisfactory, and available at a much higher cost than for residents from other areas of the same city**

6.2
Challenges of monitoring inequalities in service

The definitions of 'urban' versus 'rural' can be rather difficult to distinguish.[30] These terms are often used for technical purposes and do not necessarily bear any relation to size, population density, or indeed to governance structures. Most national statistics, when disaggregated by rural and urban, use such imprecise definitions. As a result, when aggregated at national level, there is seldom any pattern and it is impossible to compare one country figure with another (see Figures 7, 10 and 13 of the Prologue). For example, many small towns, while classified as rural, display urban characteristics in terms of population density and service provision models. The speed with which many of these 'rural towns' are growing is unprecedented — for example, annual growth rates in excess of 5% are typical in urban agglomerations in Sub-Saharan Africa (UN-Habitat, 2005). The existence of different government structures (even in the same geographical region) adds to this complexity, such that caution is needed when making policy decisions based on national statistics. Within urban areas, the inter-urban differences in service levels are perhaps a better indicator of overall delivery.

Failing to understand the complexity of urban settings is especially problematic as aggregated national information or (even city-level data) can mask the minimal levels of service and intra-urban differentials. Some of the problems lie in the 'informal status' of certain urban settings, and their consequent exclusion from 'official' statistics, whereas other problems result from the sampling frames used in household surveys for the more well-established monitoring exercises such as the WHO-UNICEF Joint Monitoring Programme (WHO/UNICEF, 2017a). The UN-Habitat Urban Inequities Survey (UIS) (UN-Habitat, 2006) is one such survey method that is designed to highlight these inequities in service provision. Figure 6.1 clearly indicates the impact of a water-focused UIS in the urban centre of a small town in Uganda. The graph shows the situation with respect to service coverage both before and after a water, sanitation and hygiene (WASH) intervention. The largest coverage percentage represents the published Joint Monitoring Programme (JMP) figure for the respective years, based on data from the Demographic and Health Surveys (WHO/UNICEF, 2010). The data were further analysed by applying

---

[30] An overview of urban typologies in the context of wastewater and sustainable urban drainage issues is provided in Table 5.1 of the World Water Development Report 2017 (WWAP, 2017, p. 51).

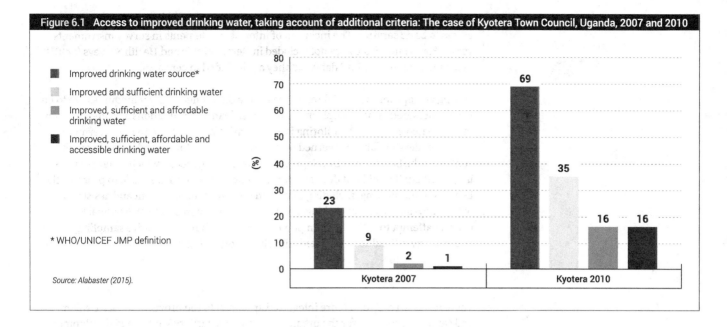

Figure 6.1 Access to improved drinking water, taking account of additional criteria: The case of Kyotera Town Council, Uganda, 2007 and 2010

Legend:
- ■ Improved drinking water source*
- ▨ Improved and sufficient drinking water
- ▣ Improved, sufficient and affordable drinking water
- ■ Improved, sufficient, affordable and accessible drinking water

*WHO/UNICEF JMP definition

Source: Alabaster (2015).

some additional criteria, going beyond the JMP definition[31] of 'improved'. The additional criteria in the UIS (which incidentally were not considered in the JMP definitions in place at the time) included the following, more stringent (but nonetheless reasonable) criteria:

- the cost should not exceed 10% of the household income;
- the volume available should be no less than 20 litres per capita per day; and
- the time taken to collect the minimum volume should not be greater than 1 hour.

If these conditions (which are often not met in smaller urban centres) are applied, the impact is dramatic, with coverage decreasing from 23% to 1% in 2007 as compared to a decrease from 69% to 16% in 2010.

The grave reality is that small urban centres such as Kyotera in Uganda are typical of the more than 250 smaller urban areas in the Lake Victoria basin, where service levels are significantly less than reported by global monitoring programmes (Alabaster, 2015). The cost of such a comprehensive monitoring exercise is of course prohibitive, but it is likely that the same inequities exist in many other smaller urban settlements in Africa and other regions. The example clearly illustrates the importance of disaggregated data and how those who are left behind are 'lost' in aggregated national statistics.

The use of self-supplied groundwater among poor urban dwellers represents another case where certain groups remain 'invisible' and are thus at greater risk of being 'left behind' (Box 6.1).

6.3
Mapping and data collection in informal settlements

Community-led documentation and mapping have helped residents of informal settlements to negotiate with governments and to generate new knowledge that makes their vital interests and challenges more visible (Satterthwaite, 2012).

Many of the world's poorest and most disadvantaged individuals are not recognized or counted as they have no physical address (Patel and Baptist, 2012). In Sub-Saharan Africa, for example, it is accepted that close to 60% of urban populations live in low-income settings (UN-Habitat/IHS-Erasmus University Rotterdam, 2018). These individuals are not

---

[31] According to the 2010 WHO/UNICEF JMP report (WHO/UNICEF, 2010), 'improved' sources of drinking water include piped water on premises (piped household water connection located inside the user's dwelling, plot or yard; public taps or standpipes; tube wells or boreholes; protected dug wells; protected springs; and collected rainwater). For monitoring purposes, the use of improved drinking water sources had been equated to access to safe drinking water, but not all 'improved' sources in actual fact provide drinking water that is 'safe'.

recognized as part of the formal system, and most importantly find difficulty in gaining access to basic services. The inclusion of informal settlements in survey instruments varies. For example, they are not included in Demographic and Health Surveys (or 'DHS' — the main source for JMP data), but they are included in censuses.

Having an appropriate spatial reference for the data is necessary if inequities are to be fully understood, as the people in the most disadvantaged situations are often 'hidden' in aggregated statistics. Monitoring is an expensive business and many governments may be understandably concerned over the cost of monitoring and reporting in the context of the Sustainable Development Goals (SDGs) process, which so far remains unquantified. It is without doubt important that more efforts are made to promote the benefits of monitoring, including improved resources management and assistance with policy- and decision-making. Most survey instruments used by National Statistical Officers attempt to estimate slum populations through representative sampling, but in reality many difficulties associated with slum monitoring persist.

6.4
Integrated urban planning and community engagement

There is often a call for a more integrated approach to the provision of basic water and sanitation services for the urban poor. In this regard, risk-informed development towards more resilient and sustainable communities is also important, because the poor or those who live in informal settlements are more likely vulnerable to disasters. This is feasible in formally arranged cities and towns, but integrated planning in low-income areas of large cities or smaller urban centres is often neglected, despite the opportunities that come from increased community engagement. Box 6.2 below gives an important example of the benefits of integrated infrastructure projects. The particular case of Kibera highlights the added value of fully engaging the community in the planning process, and also in the management of facilities. This planning is not undertaken in the conventional sense, in the same way a new city would be designed, but relies on modifying existing services (in this case not just with water and sanitation) to accommodate community preferences (UN-Habitat, 2014).

Box 6.1 Self-supply and groundwater dependence among urban poor dwellers

While the water community is moving beyond the simple classification of water sources as 'improved' or 'unimproved' and striving instead to ensure access for all under the 2030 Agenda, it remains clear that some states are unable to provide regulated, piped supplies to everyone. This is partly associated with trends in urbanization, where rapid, unplanned or inadequately managed expansion leads to sprawl and unequal sharing of the benefits of development (Grönwall, 2016).

Hundreds of millions of people in low-income urban settlements rely on wells and boreholes as their primary or back-up source of domestic water (Grönwall et al., 2010). Those groundwater sources are vital in that they provide opportunities for low-cost self-supply systems developed and maintained by households, but awareness about point-of-use treatment lags behind considerably.

The paradigms underpinning good water governance, the human right to water and the 2030 Agenda, classify a self-supplying household as 'underserved', while they do not provide an all-applicable answer to who is accountable during this supposedly transient stage before the household becomes connected to the public system (Grönwall, 2016).

Such a classification has led some city planners and decision-makers to avoid allocating (surface) water sources to these groups, as their contextual entitlements are not clearly on the agenda. The implicit justification is that, in particular, shallow, dug wells do not provide safe water, and that little can or should be done to protect or improve them as they essentially characterize a transient phase that needs to be eliminated by the continued expansion of piped water systems.

An additional problem is the reliance on aggregate statistics and insensitive indicators, such as those normally used to classify a households' primary source of drinking water. These contribute to masking the realities faced by millions of low-income urban dwellers, and ultimately lead to their omission from improved service delivery planning. For example, a household survey in the low-income township of Dodowa on the fringe of Accra concluded that residents there relied on dug wells almost twice as much (on average) as was reported by the census data in other parts of the District (Grönwall, 2016). The direct dependence on groundwater from their own wells or those of neighbours therefore had been 'invisible', as was the potential impact of sewage on the aquifers themselves.

6.5
Costs of service provision in high-density low-income urban settlements

One of the key factors in the selection of water and sanitation services is the per capita cost. Although capital cost seems to be among the main selection criteria, operational costs are not always considered. Many low capital-cost technologies have high operational costs. For example, the capital cost of a pit latrine may be low, but the associated desludging and disposal costs are high.

The population density of those served can dramatically affect costs, and although the unit cost for on-site technologies remains the same, the per capita cost of networked systems diminishes considerably (see Table 6.1) as population density increases. For example, the per capita cost of a private tap in a deeply rural area is over 30 times the cost of the same service in a dense urban settlement. This is also very apparent in the provision of low-cost sewerage systems: at densities greater than 30,000 people per km^2, networked sewers are a cheaper option than on-site systems (Foster and Briceño-Garmendia, 2010). The trunk facilities of a sewer may be available to all, but for the poor, the cost of connection is often beyond their means.

Box 6.2   The Kenya slum upgrading project: Providing integrated infrastructure in Soweto East, Kibera, Nairobi

The Kenya Slum Upgrading Project was launched in 2003, reflecting the Government of Kenya's commitment to look more closely at improving the lives of slum dwellers. In the context of this project, a survey was undertaken to document all of the 13 distinct villages that make up Kibera. Extensive consultations with communities were held through the "Settlements Executive Committee" (SEC), which helped to plan the project's progressive upgrade. Then, a pilot project was developed that would use the provision of water and sanitation facilities as an entry point for slum upgrading in the village of Soweto East. Additionally, the new idea of improving the road through the village was explored and then facilitated. Importantly, it was deemed very critical that the new developments be compatible with the lifestyles of residents and not imposed on them.

Many hours were spent in consultation with community stakeholders to decide on the best options and, most importantly, to plan how the work would be carried out. This was a special challenge, as space in Kibera is at a premium and the new facilities would need some residents to be relocated.

The construction was carried out over a period of 18 months. By 2008, when one of the first sanitation blocks was complete, the village of Soweto East took on a new life and showed transformations that were not expected. For example, it was appreciated that the odour from excreta had been reduced.

Within a short period of time, the road had become the public open space of choice; both day and night would see much activity. During the day, traders were lining the new street and at night time residents enjoyed socializing in their new town square.

We can see how unblocking the main artery to Soweto East has brought new life to the community. It has rejuvenated areas and, most importantly, has improved the lives of Soweto East residents. In 2018, all except one of the original toilet blocks were fully functioning. The Government of Kenya has replicated the concept of using roads. They have additionally adopted the expansion by linking it to a youth employment scheme.

Although it was a single pilot project, it has given some good ideas for future slum upgrading. It has demonstrated how creating good living space, both inside and outside the household, can greatly improve living standards. On top of that, it has shown the importance of community engagement. Through this process, many invaluable lessons were learned by a dedicated, multi-disciplinary and multi-agency project team. Given the challenges that have come with accelerated urbanization in developing countries, as described above, these lessons are important.

Source: UN-Habitat (2014).

Table 6.1 Capital cost (US$ per capita) of infrastructure provision, by density

Infrastructure type	Large cities						Secondary cities	Rural hinterland	Deep rural
Density (people/km²)	30 000	20 000	10 000	5 008	3 026	1 455	1 247	38	13
Water									
Private tap	104.2	124.0	168.7	231.8	293.6	416.4	448.5	1 825.2	3 156.2
Standpost	31.0	36.3	48.5	65.6	82.4	115.7	124.5	267.6	267.6
Borehole	21.1	21.1	21.1	21.1	21.1	21.1	21.1	53.0	159.7
Hand pump	8.3	8.3	8.3	8.3	8.3	8.3	8.3	16.7	50.4
Sanitation									
Septic tank	125.0	125.0	125.0	125.0	125.0	125.0	125.0	125.0	125.0
Improved latrine	57.0	57.0	57.0	57.0	57.0	57.0	57.0	57.0	57.0
Unimproved latrine	39.0	39.0	39.0	39.0	39.0	39.0	39.0	39.0	39.0

Source: Adapted from Foster and Briceño-Garmendia (2010, table 5.6, p. 131). © World Bank. openknowledge.worldbank.org/handle/10986/2692. Licensed under Creative Commons (CC BY 3.0 IGO).

6.6
Attracting sustainable investment at the local level

Accountability and transparency are basic governance attributes, which promote good financial management

Weak institutional structures at the local level are often cited as the root cause of the inability to attract investments (see Chapters 4 and 5). This applies both to donor financing and to domestic sources of finance, both private and public. In the past, urban development projects were usually financed by loans, underwritten by national governments. A larger proportion of this kind of financing was directed towards capital cities and provincial centres, while small urban centres were neglected. The justification for this has been the small centres' inability to effectively coordinate and administer finance, as well as their lack of institutional capacity.

Corruption plagues many institutions in urban areas. Accountability and transparency are basic governance attributes, which promote good financial management. If cost recovery is managed, urban development projects stand a better chance of success.

Pre-investment activities can offer greater opportunities to leverage resources from both multilateral development banks and bilateral donors. The preparation period of many projects that receive funding from Development Banks, both as grants and as loans, can be enhanced by interventions to make the investments more sustainable in the long term (UN-Habitat, 2011). Such activities include, for example:

- Preparation of business development plans for service providers;
- Development of baseline assessments for project design;
- Development of impact monitoring frameworks;
- Capacity building to improve the utility capacity for servicing loans and sustaining capital investments; and
- Participatory methods to ensure the involvement of groups in disadvantaged or vulnerable situations.

Many of these approaches offer great potential to prepare organizations for inward investment. This is particularly of interest for sub-sovereign lending (UN-Habitat, 2011).

In the area of capacity building, participatory approaches can sharpen the focus of project development and ensure more effective targeting of beneficiaries. One such example is the fast-track capacity building of small water utilities to increase revenue generation and cover operations and maintenance expenditure (IWA/UN-Habitat, 2011).

6.7
Financing WASH in urban settings

Development banks often provide significant resources and expertise to augment the capacity of governments to design and implement rural, urban and peri-urban water and sanitation programmes. The ability to take on and service loan financing depends on the capacity of the institutions and their stability. Trends in financing have focused predominantly on sovereign lending, but with sector reform and decentralization, service providers are also considering sub-sovereign lending. In many of the larger urban areas, utilities have the capacity to service loans, but in the smaller urban settlements, where the main growth during the coming decades will take place, there is little capacity for repayment of loans, as such settings do not enjoy the economies of scale. Flexible types of financing and grant/loan packages will be necessary in smaller rapidly growing urban centres (see Chapter 5). Mixed technologies and service levels can coexist in the same urban agglomerations but need to be carefully planned and progressively upgraded as cities densify and the economic conditions improve in lower-income areas.

6.8
Centralized vs. decentralized urban water supply and sanitation systems

The density of population frequently dictates the choice of infrastructure and the decision to use networked systems or provide off-site facilities

Traditional approaches to sanitation and wastewater management in urban areas tend to favour large-scale, centralized collection and treatment. This has historically required significant investments. In order to get cost recovery, a sufficient number of users must be connected. For the poor, the costs of connection are often prohibitive. As mentioned in Section 6.5, the density of population frequently dictates the choice of infrastructure and the decision to use networked systems or provide off-site facilities. In reality, urban areas that fall somewhere between large urban centres and rural settlements need hybrid approaches. The density may be too low to justify the cost of household connections, and not high enough to permit conventionally designed systems. Mara and Alabaster (2008) propose a new paradigm to connect groups of households (and not individual households) in peri-urban low-income areas and large villages, to reduce the investment cost while still allowing a good service level for the poorest.

Although water supply systems are sometimes better served with smaller, easily managed networks, the challenges of wastewater and sludge management are often more complex. The main reason is the unwillingness to pay for sanitation services. There have been numerous attempts to use resources recovery to offset some of the costs of service provision (WWAP, 2017), but, as with all 'waste', if it needs to be transported, the costs thereof often negate the benefits gained. From this perspective, the idea of decentralized wastewater treatment systems (DEWATS) is becoming popular. Not only are investment costs substantially lower, but the operational costs also. Using DEWATS also means that carriage of wastewater can be simplified. For example, pumping can often be avoided and low-cost sewerage technologies can be used.

Aside from efficient collection and treatment of wastewater, local reuse for crop irrigation or fish production can lead to a market, based on the value of the treated wastewater (WWAP, 2017). If the systems are simple to operate and maintain, they can often be managed by relatively unskilled labour, sometimes by community groups.

A typical DEWATS system is shown in Figure 6.2. A combination of simple unit processes is usually favoured, most often without the need for external power. DEWATS also have the advantage that they can be connected to networks, or can be decommissioned easily, should conditions dictate that larger-scale centralized systems are more cost-effective, or that urban expansion puts heavy pressure to use the land. They are particularly appropriate where low-income populations are at risk from wastewater and faecal sludges directly contaminating water supplies.

One of the main challenges is land provision. In dense low-income settlements, land is a premium and giving up space to treatment facilities is difficult. In these situations, the use of low-cost sewerage to transport the wastewater to the periphery of the settlement is favoured.

Figure 6.2 Typical DEWATS system

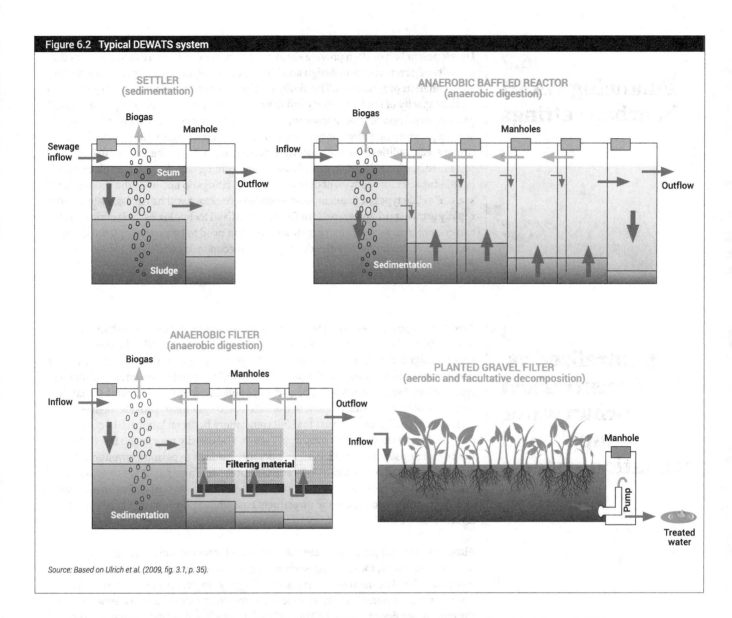

Source: Based on Ulrich et al. (2009, fig. 3.1, p. 35).

6.9

Conclusions and policy recommendations

Substantial inequality exists between slum and non-slum households in access to water and sanitation facilities. Rapid urbanization coupled with inadequate control over physical development and investments on the part of local authorities means that pockets of slum areas will continue to emerge in small urban centres. This trend of slum development has to be gauged and factored into the planning of water and sanitation infrastructure. In particular, urban development and structure plans need to be instituted, with clear strategies on slum upgrading that account for water and sanitation services. New approaches to monitoring need to be developed to better account for intra-urban differentials.

The provision of urban sanitation infrastructure lags far behind infrastructure for water provision in most urban settings, but the poorest residents of slum areas are the most affected. This sanitation deficit can erode the benefits of improved water provision in many ways, with dire consequences on the environment and public health. Where there is a significant improvement in water, this needs to be matched with a commensurate investment in sanitation. Significant financial and political commitment has to be channelled towards bridging the widening gap between water and sanitation provision through novel business models and strategies that make urban sanitation an attractive and cost-effective investment option for local government and businesses. This will need appropriate blended financing approaches and a strengthening of local authority systems.

The widespread use of on-site sanitation technologies, designed mainly for the collection and storage of human excreta, still predominates in urban areas, particularly in slum areas. These on-site facilities place a significant economic and social burden on poor households.

There is a need for a paradigm shift in urban sanitation monitoring strategies from unitary monitoring to system monitoring. This means that improvements in urban sanitation will be measured not only by 'the number of on-site installations' in the urban space, but by 'on-site installations with functional systems for the collection, transportation, treatment and safe disposal/reuse of human excreta'. This way, the main functions of a sanitation system (i.e. protection of human health and improvement of environmental quality) can be met. In framing a monitoring framework, particularly the use of sanitation products will gain significant prominence in urban areas during the coming decades, as worldwide, the so-called ecological sanitation technologies and the use of wastewater/human excreta are being promoted.

Access to water through pipes into dwellings remains low, even though such facilities have the potential to reduce children diarrhoea and lessen the burden of water collection on women and children. In small urban centres, significant investments in piped water systems that are connected to household dwelling units or are located on plots are needed to alleviate diarrhoeal diseases and the burden of water collection on women and children. Better household water management that safeguards the quality of drinking water has to be promoted for the minimization of recontamination, particularly in areas where households' dependence on other improved water sources is widespread. This has to be combined with point-of-use water quality monitoring.

One of the root causes for non-inclusion of informal settlements in the provision of services relates to the legal tenure/ occupation of the land on which they are located

The proportion of urban households with access to improved water supply and sanitation services decreases substantially when adjusting for additional indicators related to water (quantity, time and cost) and sanitation (distance, cleanliness, hand-washing and safety) (UN-Habitat, 2006). Some of these criteria, although not considered in early JMP reporting, are highly relevant and now reflected in new JMP methodologies as developed for the SDGs (WHO/UNICEF, 2017a). Additionally, in 2010, through Resolution 64/292 (UNGA, 2010), the United Nations General Assembly explicitly recognized the human right to water and sanitation and acknowledged that clean drinking water and sanitation are essential to the realization of all human rights. This creates new opportunities to enhance and improve monitoring, which will have to be progressively recognized in national laws and ordinances. Where data are available, the monitoring of water provision should be based on indicators that systematically integrate aspects of physical and economic accessibility of water (time/distance to collect water, and amount spent to collect water), quantity of water (adequate amount of water for household use), quality of water (uncontaminated water), and reliability of water (uninterrupted water supply). Where data are available, the monitoring of sanitation provision should be based on indicators that systematically integrate shared toilets, and account for factors directly related to the use (distance, cleanliness and safety), hygiene (hand-washing facilities), emptying, treatment and disposal/reuse. It is fully recognized that gathering quality data on the aforementioned key indicators for the construction of an integrated monitoring framework can be an extremely expensive and technically daunting process for the National Statistical Offices in developing countries. Innovative data collection systems that build on existing local structures (including water and sanitation committees and civil society) and make use of telecommunication applications in synch with geographic information systems or similar platforms for the establishment of user-friendly data portals offer new and potentially affordable opportunities. The implementation of such data collection systems has to proceed with an incremental inclusion of indicators, subject to the availability of resources.

The new paradigm proposed to supply groups of households (and not individual households) in peri-urban low-income areas and large villages, reducing the investment cost while still allowing a good service level for the poorest, offers promise as a way forward to ensure that the very poorest are not 'left behind' (Mara and Alabaster, 2008).

The critical issue of population density will greatly influence both capital and operational costs of both water supply and sanitation systems in low-income urban areas. The use of DEWATS will most likely enable the use of networked systems, where previously only on-site systems would be considered.

One of the root causes for non-inclusion of informal settlements in the provision of services relates to the legal tenure/occupation of the land on which they are located. To address this issue, aside from institutional recognition, there is a need to enact laws and policies to dissociate the tenure status from service provision.

CHAPTER 7

Rural poverty

Women walking among their fields in the Nyalungana swamp reclamation project in the Democratic Republic of the Congo

FAO | Patricia Mejías-Moreno and Helle Munk Ravnborg

With contributions from: Olcay Ünver, Benjamin Davis, Maya Takagi, Daniela Kalikoski, Giorgia Prati and Jacqueline Ann Demeranville (FAO)

This chapter examines the linkages between rural poverty and water, with a focus on the role of supplemental irrigation in rainfed agricultural systems in contributing to poverty reduction among smallholder farmers and ensuring food security at local and national levels.

7.1
Introduction: Three paradoxes to better understand rural poverty and water

Paradoxes proliferate in the rural areas of the world. A look into three of these paradoxes provides important guidance for efforts to achieve water security for the millions of people living in poverty in the rural areas of the world.

Paradox 1: Supplying the bulk of food, and yet poor and hungry

More than 80% of all farms in the world are family farms smaller than 2 hectares (HLPE, 2013; FAO, 2014). At the global level, smallholder family farmers operate around 12% of the world's farmland area, whereas in low and lower–middle income economies, they are estimated to operate around a third of the total farmland (FAO, 2014). In Africa, farms up to 2 hectares are estimated to constitute 75% of the farms and operate 24% of the farmland (HLPE, 2013). Smallholder family farmers constitute the backbone of national food supplies, contributing to more than half of the national agricultural production in many countries (FAO, 2014).[32]

Yet, it is in the rural areas that poverty, hunger and food insecurity are most prevalent (FAO/IFAD/WFP, 2015a). Extremely poor households are more likely to depend on agriculture and natural resources for their livelihoods and food security: 76% of the extreme poor and 60% of the moderate poor in rural areas over the age of 15 report primary employment in agriculture (Castaneda Aguilar et al., 2016). Jobs in the agricultural sector are highly water-dependent (WWAP, 2016), and access to water for irrigation is a major determinant of land productivity, as irrigated land is twice as productive as rainfed land (Rapsomanikis, 2015).

---

[32] In a cross-section of countries consisting of Bangladesh, Bolivia, Kenya, Nepal, Nicaragua, Tanzania and Viet Nam, small family farms provide more than half, and in the case of Kenya up to 70%, of the total agricultural production.

Approximately three-quarters (74%) of people living in extreme poverty[33] live in rural areas (FAO, 2017b) and the vast majority of the rural poor are in fact smallholders who themselves suffer from food insecurity and malnutrition.

In 2017, there were 821 million chronically food-insecure and malnourished people in the world, up from 804 million in 2016. Africa remains the continent with the highest prevalence of undernourishment, affecting almost 21% of the population (more than 256 million people). Women tend to be more undernourished than men. Conflict and climate variability and extremes are making poverty reduction and food security more challenging. The risk of hunger is significantly greater in countries with agricultural systems that are highly sensitive to rainfall and temperature variability and severe drought, and where the livelihood of a high proportion of the population depends on agriculture. Severe droughts linked to the strong El Niño of 2015–2016 affected many countries, contributing to the recent increase in undernourishment at the global level. For example, the drought caused by El Niño resulted in losses of 50–90 % of the crop harvest in the dry corridor, especially in El Salvador, Honduras and Guatemala (FAO/IFAD/UNICEF/WFP/WHO, 2018).

The extremely poor in rural areas also face social exclusion and discrimination, because of race, ethnicity and gender (De la O Campos et al., 2018). Indigenous peoples make up a disproportional number of the world's poor (see Section 3.2.4) and account for around one-third of the extremely rural poor (UNDESA, 2009). Globally, women are 4% more likely than men to live in extreme poverty (UN Women, 2018). Women in agricultural rural areas have less access to productive resources, including water, than men (FAO, 2011).

Paradox 2: Substantive investments in water infrastructure in rural areas, and yet the rural poor lack access to water

Roughly 70% and, in the world's Least Developed Countries, over 90% of freshwater withdrawals take place in rural areas, primarily for the irrigation of agricultural crops (AQUASTAT, n.d.). A significant part of the water withdrawn is embedded in food and fibres, most of which are processed and consumed elsewhere, either in urban areas or in other parts of the world.

Globally, investments worth billions of dollars have been made in establishing water infrastructure in rural areas, in large part for irrigation development and for energy production (e.g. Zarfl et al., 2015; Crow-Miller et al., 2017). Irrigation can contribute to poverty reduction by enhancing the productivity of labour and land and leading to higher incomes and lower food prices (Faurès and Santini, 2009). However, with investments in water-related infrastructure highly centred on the most productive areas, most of the rural poor in other areas have not benefited from similar levels of investment and infrastructure, hindering their access to water for agriculture, drinking and domestic purposes.

Most of the people using unimproved sources of drinking water and lacking basic sanitation services live in rural areas. In 2015, of the 159 million using surface water (streams, lakes, rivers or irrigation channels), 147 million lived in rural areas, and over half lived in Sub-Saharan Africa, where 10% of the population still drank untreated surface water. Using surface water also implies that poor people in rural areas, particularly women and girls, spend a considerable amount of time collecting water (see Section 2.1.2). While three out of five people with safely managed sanitation lived in urban areas (1.7 billion), the ratio drops to two out of five in rural areas (1.2 billion) (WHO/UNICEF, 2017a).

Paradox 3: Smallholder farmers being water-productive, and yet overlooked

Access to water for agricultural production, even if only for supplemental watering of crops, can make the difference between farming as a mere means of survival and farming as a reliable source of livelihoods. This importance is accentuated even further in the current context of climate change, with its increasingly unpredictable and

> **Indigenous peoples make up a disproportional number of the world's poor and account for around one-third of the extremely rural poor**

---

[33] The international poverty line for extreme poverty is $1.90 a day 2011 purchasing power parity (PPP).

erratic rainfall patterns. Across the world, millions of smallholder family farmers find ways of accessing, storing and conducting water to their crops to make up for water deficits during periods of dry spells or to secure food supplies during the dry season. Yet, despite their often high level of water (and land) productivity (Comprehensive Assessment of Water Management in Agriculture, 2007) and their crucial role in contributing to national food security, smallholders tend not to be the ones receiving attention as part of ongoing efforts to formalize the allocation of water use rights nor through the allocation of public subsidies for the establishment and operation of irrigation infrastructure.

7.2
Emerging challenges

7.2.1 Access to safe and affordable drinking water in rural areas

Millions of people in rural areas, particularly women and children in low- and middle-income countries, spend long hours fetching water from unsafely managed sources. When water sources run dry, they also often face the competition for the limited amounts of available water for domestic and productive uses, such as watering crops or animals.

Access to safe drinking water and improved sanitation is used as an indicator in several multidimensional poverty indices.[34] Despite progress made to improve access to drinking water over recent decades, the drudgery and unreliability that millions of rural women and men still face across the world owes to the fact that water infrastructure has been spread too thinly and is thus insufficient to ensure comprehensive coverage. Moreover, the institutional capacity, including domestic resource mobilization and budget allocations — both at national and subnational levels — has been insufficient to cater for maintenance needs of the installed water infrastructure. However, the burden is far from evenly distributed. Significant — and structural — inequalities exist in drinking water access, not only between rural and urban areas, but also within rural territories (WHO/UNICEF, 2017b).[35]

Very often, differences in economic wealth and skills as well as ethnicity and gender spill over into power imbalances and abilities to influence political, technical and legal decisions. Thus, empirical evidence starting to emerge (e.g. from Latin America and the Caribbean) shows significant disparities in access to improved drinking water among rural territories in a wide range of countries. Additional inequalities exist within rural territories (e.g. along the lines of ethnicity), with indigenous households being less likely to enjoy access to safely managed drinking water than non-indigenous households (WHO/UNICEF, 2016). Empirical data from rural districts in Viet Nam, Nicaragua, Bolivia and Zambia show that non-poor households are not only more likely to enjoy access to publicly funded domestic water supply infrastructure than poor households, but they also are more likely to enjoy access to such infrastructure within the immediate vicinity of their homes (Cossio Rojas and Soto Montaño, 2011; Huong et al., 2011; Mweemba et al., 2011; Paz Mena et al., 2011; Funder et al., 2012). Furthermore, they are more likely to benefit from such infrastructure to water their crops and animals during the dry season, often to the detriment of neighbouring, particularly poor, households' access to water (e.g. Funder et al., 2012; Ravnborg and Jensen, 2012).[36]

Despite common scheme-level regulations that water provided should only be used for domestic purposes, the potential economic gains associated with breaking the rules often outweigh the risk of sanctions. A large body of research shows that, particularly in rural areas, the distinction between domestic and productive water is difficult to

---

[34] For example, the Global Multidimensional Poverty Index developed by the Oxford Poverty & Human Development Initiative. For more information, please see: ophi.org.uk/multidimensional-poverty-index/.

[35] Data on inequality in access to drinking water services are also becoming increasingly available from national large-scale surveys such as the Multiple Indicator Cluster Surveys (MICS) (WHO/UNICEF, n.d.). The MICS 2013 survey from Bangladesh is an example of this (BBS/UNICEF Bangladesh, 2014).

[36] Testimonies of this are also given in video reports from Zambia and Nicaragua available at www.thewaterchannel.tv/media-gallery/810-media-8-competing-for-water-when-more-water-leads-to-conflict and www.thewaterchannel.tv/media-gallery/839-media-2-competing-for-water-the-challenge-of-local-water-governance.

uphold (HLPE, 2015) and that instead water should be considered — and governed — as a multiple-use resource. Thus, water infrastructure development that fails to provide sufficient water to cater for the full spectrum of domestic needs, also during the dry season, and that does not cater for even a minimum of productive uses of water, can easily contribute to exacerbating rather than reducing socio-economic inequalities (Araujo et al., 2008; Gómez and Ravnborg, 2011; Funder et al., 2012; Hellum et al., 2015).

7.2.2 Water for crops in the context of climate change

The major effects of climate change in rural areas will be felt through impacts on water supply, food security and agricultural incomes. In some regions, shifts in agricultural production are likely to take place, not only as a result of changes in temperature and rainfall, but also through changes in the availability of water for irrigation. Climate change will have a disproportionate impact on the welfare of the poor in rural areas, including female-headed households and those with limited access to modern agricultural inputs, infrastructure, and education (IPCC, 2014).

Increased rainfall variability and unpredictability, as well as more frequent and prolonged droughts and floods, will accentuate the need for increased attention to water management in agriculture. This is even to be more accentuated in the drylands, where the extreme variability, rather than the total amount of rainfall, is the key limiting factor for improving agricultural yields (Rockström et al., 2007).

Water management for smallholder family farmers needs to consider both rainfed and irrigated agriculture. Approximately 80% of the global cropland is rainfed, and 60% of the world's food is produced on rainfed land. Soil management is an essential element in rainfed and irrigated agriculture. Well-managed soils are capable of absorbing and retaining water and are more resilient towards erosion following heavy downpours. Soil management also limits soil evaporation and has been shown to be complementary to other strategies such as supplemental irrigation in rainfed agricultural systems during periods of dry spells (Comprehensive Assessment of Water Management in Agriculture, 2007; Rockström et al., 2007).

Research from different parts of the world shows that supplemental irrigation in rainfed agricultural systems may not only ensure crop survival, but also double or even triple rainfed yields per hectare for crops such as wheat, sorghum and maize (Oweis and Hachum, 2003; Rockström et al., 2007; HLPE, 2015). Research also shows that water productivity is highest at the lower end of the yield spectrum (Comprehensive Assessment of Water Management in Agriculture, 2007), and can be higher in systems of supplemental irrigation than in full-irrigation systems (Oweis and Hachum, 2003). Thus, the case for strengthening small-scale farmers' — men and women's — access to supplemental irrigation is strong, in terms of ending poverty and hunger, reducing inequalities, and improving resource productivity.

Strengthening small-scale farmers' ability to provide their crops with water during periods of deficits also requires the infrastructure necessary to withdraw, harvest, or store crops, and to conduct water to them. It is also important to formally recognize their right to do so.

In many parts of the world, farmers have over the course of generations developed systems of informal irrigation. Technologies are available and are constantly being improved (Box 7.1). These range from simple drip irrigation systems constructed from water-filled plastic bottles placed to irrigate seedlings, to elevated water drums from where water is led to the plants through pipes and drip tape, to organizationally more demanding systems of furrows and elevated seed beds in valley bottoms, possibly combined with solar, treadle or diesel pumps (e.g. Comprehensive Assessment of Water Management in Agriculture, 2007).

Opening up new opportunities for the rural poor in relation to managing water in the context of climate change will require increased investment in water infrastructure, such as water harvesting (Box 7.2) or irrigation, improving the advisory services for crop

> Climate change will have a disproportionate impact on the welfare of the poor in rural areas

Box 7.1 Adapting small-scale irrigation to climate change in West and Central Africa

The Food and Agriculture Organization (FAO) of the United Nations, in collaboration with the International Fund for Agricultural Development (IFAD) and national partners, is implementing the project "Adapting small-scale irrigation to climate change in West and Central Africa" to improve sustainability and adaptation of small-scale irrigation across the region. The objective of this project is to provide tools to enable stakeholders involved in water management, from policy-makers to small-scale farmers, to make the right decisions about climate change adaptation strategies in small-scale irrigation systems.

The project is being implemented in Côte d'Ivoire, the Gambia, Mali and Niger, and has conducted the climate resilience assessment of smallholder farmers across 21 irrigation sites.

Information was collected from 691 households who are mostly reliant on agriculture as their main source of livelihood and for whom rainfall still constitutes the main source of water for crops. Farmers have noticed that precipitation patterns have changed in the past 10 years. Water shortage due to decreased rainfall, the late start of the rainy season, and the presence of extreme events such as floods and droughts has impacted farmers' capacity to produce food. Indeed:

- 45% have experienced an increase in crop failure;
- 38% have seen a decrease of their farm income;
- 17% have observed a reduction in the availability of water for irrigation; and
- 13% of families have seen at least one of their relatives forced to migrate.

Climate variability and extreme events pose challenges to development, and farmers in West and Central Africa have identified key aspects to be strengthened to enhance their capacity to adapt to climate change through:

- increased investment and access to financing mechanisms to make equipment, sustainable energy sources and technology for small-scale irrigation available to them;
- improved irrigation and water conservation practices and increased water availability;
- diversified sources of revenue outside agriculture;
- improved soil fertility of irrigated land to avoid soil degradation;
- enhanced access to information and knowledge; and
- better access and connectivity to local markets.

Source: FAO (forthcoming).

Box 7.2 One million cisterns for the Sahel

In the Sahel, climate change exacerbates rainfall irregularity and climatic shocks, including droughts and floods. The consequences can be devastating for the poorest rural households, who struggle to cope with these shocks and see their vulnerability worsen. Efficient and sustainable management of water resources is more than ever a priority to improve the resilience of vulnerable communities.

The programme 'One million cisterns for the Sahel' aims to promote and facilitate the introduction of rainwater harvesting and storage systems for vulnerable communities, especially women. The objective is to enable millions of people in the Sahel to access safe drinking water, have a surplus to enhance their family agricultural production, improve their food and nutrition security, and strengthen their resilience. Besides ensuring access to clean water during the dry season, the programme promotes the participation of the communities in the construction of cisterns through cash-for-work activities. Local communities are trained in the construction, use and maintenance of cisterns, thus becoming qualified for civil construction works and infrastructure maintenance to enable income diversification and improved housing conditions.

It is inspired by the 'Programme One Million Cisterns', implemented in Brazil through the 'Zero Hunger' programme.

Source FAO (2018b).

and water management, and planning and implementation of drought preparedness plans. These actions, when coupled with better access to social protection, including social security schemes (pensions and insurance) and more targeted social assistance programmes, result in a better enhancement of the economic and productive capacity of poor smallholder farmers and their families. New ways of providing the often modest capital needs for undertaking necessary investments at farm level are also required. The rapid expansion of internet connectivity, even in rural areas, combined with conventional broadcasting and written and face-to-face communication, open up such new opportunities, not only for developing technology information platforms, but also for connecting (groups of) farmers to distant but organized groups of consumers and investors (e.g. through crowdfunding platforms). Leaving no one behind will require continuous support to such platforms, and assistance to ensure that young and disadvantaged men and women can access and benefit from them.

7.2.3 Rural migration

Mobility is a widespread phenomenon in rural societies. Rural households have traditionally adopted migration as a strategy to manage risk, diversify livelihoods and adapt to a changing environment. It is estimated that around 40% of international remittances are sent to rural areas, suggesting that a significant share of international migrants comes from rural communities (IFAD, 2017). About 85% of international refugees are hosted by developing countries, with at least a third — and in Sub-Saharan Africa more than 80% — in rural areas (FAO, 2018a), which further emphasizes the rural and agricultural dimension of migration and forced displacement.

Rural migration is closely related to structural factors that often characterize rural settings, including poverty, food insecurity and limited income-generating activities, as well as lack of employment and decent working conditions. Rural–urban inequality can further push people to migrate to urban areas in search of better jobs and living conditions, including access to education, health services and social protection. There is growing evidence that the depletion of natural resources, such as water, due to a combination of excessive use, environmental degradation and climate change, can be a major driver of migration (FAO/GWP/Oregon State University, 2018). The advancing threat of climate change with the risk of substantial negative effects on agriculture and rural areas, in particular for people living in poverty, is increasingly perceived as a driver of displacement and potentially vast migratory flows (Stapleton et al., 2017; FAO, 2018a; Rigaud et al., 2018). Water stress can result in declining agricultural production and directly and indirectly influence migration patterns.

Migration has different impacts on the rural areas of origin, transit and destination, which may be positive or negative and differ according to the context. In rural areas of origin, emigration of working-age people will affect the supply of labour and the demographic composition of the remaining population. At the same time, rural out-migration can reduce pressure on natural resources, foster a more efficient allocation of labour and lead to higher wages in agriculture. For rural areas in low- and middle-income transit countries, migration and protracted forced displacement can constitute a challenge for local authorities to provide public services, while increasing pressure on natural resources, such as water.

Migration can be one of many adaptation strategies to water stress. It can contribute to agricultural and rural development in the areas of origin through financial remittances that can help overcome lack of access to credit and insurance, and foster investments in climate-resilient livelihoods. For example, in Sri Lanka, rural remittance-recipient households tend to have improved recourse to farm inputs and better equipment (such as tube wells and water pumps) than non-migrant households (FAO, 2018a). Migration can also contribute to the transfer of knowledge and skills, which could enhance a more sustainable use of natural resources in both receiving and sending communities.

Leaving no one behind requires efforts to give people in rural areas the choice to remain where they live rather than to be forced to move due to the impossibility of sustaining their livelihoods. Providing alternatives to migration includes creating stronger rural

Water stress can result in declining agricultural production and directly and indirectly influence migration patterns

communities that are more resilient to water stresses and other environmental and non-environmental risks, as well as investing in local diversification and promoting policy coherence and coordination. To tackle the challenges and harness the opportunities of migration, comprehensive policies on migration and rural development that integrate the water–migration nexus will be needed, as well as increasing support to origin, transit and hosting communities to enhance resilience to water-related vulnerability.

7.2.4 The invisibility of small-scale irrigation: Dealing with water rights and investment

Only a minority of the world's small-scale users of water for irrigation hold a legally sanctioned water right (Ravnborg, 2016).[37] Historically, small-scale irrigation has escaped official statistics (e.g. Comprehensive Assessment of Water Management in Agriculture, 2007; Kodamaya, 2009) and only recently, lessons learned from experience with water use for irrigation have found their way into agricultural census designs,[38] thus beginning to provide a more comprehensive overview of small-scale irrigation. Also, many small-scale water users have been reluctant to register their water use in fear of the imposition of water use fees. Yet, this 'invisibility' of small-scale irrigation may now put the water security of small-scale water users at risk as legally sanctioned water rights regimes are rolled out in many countries (Hodgson, 2004; 2016; Van Koppen et al., 2004; 2007; 2014; Pedersen and Ravnborg, 2006; HLPE, 2013; 2015; Ravnborg, 2015; 2016; Van Eeden et al., 2016) as part of ongoing water governance reforms, and as the use of available water is gradually conceded to agricultural corporations, industries, and other major users.

There appears to be a (re)surge of large-scale water development projects, such as the construction of storage and inter-basin water transfer infrastructure (e.g. Molle et al., 2009; Crow-Miller et al., 2017), often with multiple objectives, including power generation and agricultural development. Much of this infrastructure development takes place in low- and middle-income countries (Zarfl et al., 2015; Crow-Miller et al., 2017), where the water security of small-scale users is often at risk. These risks can escalate if public transparency throughout the planning and implementation process is limited. While water infrastructure development projects often provide broad-based societal gains, most notably in the form of improved power supply, other gains such as irrigation development tend to primarily benefit larger agricultural corporations. The mismatch between those to whom benefits accrue (e.g. in terms of construction contracts, land developed for irrigation, cheaper electricity, etc.) and those who pay for the costs (e.g. farmers, herders and others losing their access to land and water, as well as tax payers) has frequently made many of such investments politically contentious, not to mention the environmental costs.

Leaving no one behind in the effort to ensure secure and equal access to water in rural areas, while providing opportunities for future water investments, will require continued efforts to increase the visibility of small-scale users with regards to water for irrigation, as well as greater recognition of their contribution to national food security. Water allocations to large-scale users, whether for irrigation or other purposes, must not take place at the expense of small-scale farmers' legitimate needs, irrespective of their ability to demonstrate formally sanctioned water use rights. The current dominant resource-focused approach, based on the allocation of water use rights to the most productive and largest users, has to be complemented with a user- and use-oriented focus that assigns equal priority to all users on a territorial basis, irrespective of amounts of water used, and that takes the intended use (e.g. food security, etc.) and the associated water productivity into consideration. This invokes internationally agreed conventions and principles, including the 2004 *Voluntary Guidelines to support the progressive realization of the Right to adequate food in the context of national food security* (FAO, 2005) and the 2010 UN recognition of the human right to water and sanitation (UNGA, 2010).

While water infrastructure development projects often provide broad-based societal gains, most notably in the form of improved power supply, other gains such as irrigation development tend to primarily benefit larger agricultural corporations

---

[37] Depending on the country, such formal water rights could be what Hodgson refer to as 'traditional', e.g. land-based, formal water rights, or 'modern', e.g. administrative or permit-based, formal water rights (Hodgson, 2016).

[38] As part of the World Programme for the Census of Agriculture. For further information, please see www.fao.org/world-census-agriculture/en/.

A high level of transparency and democratic control, with investments that involve public resources (be they financial or other), is required to maximize the public gains from such investments. Future investment plans for water infrastructure should combine large- and small-scale interventions and be people-centred (Faurès and Santini, 2009). Finally, support to small-scale agriculture should be specifically recognized in national and regional development programmes.

7.2.5 Water quality: An ever-growing concern

Water quality is a growing concern in rural areas in both low- and high-income countries.

In many countries, the biggest source of water pollution today is agriculture, while worldwide, the most common chemical contaminant found in groundwater aquifers is nitrate from farming. Pesticide accumulation in water and in the food chain, with demonstrated ill effects on humans, led to the widespread banning of certain broad-spectrum and persistent pesticides (such as DDT and many organophosphates), but some such pesticides are still used in poorer countries, causing acute and likely chronic health effects (FAO/IWMI, 2018). This puts farmers and agricultural workers, often belonging to the poorer segments of the population, at risk.[39] The fact that part of these chemicals or their derivates may filtrate into the groundwater or may reach surface water bodies through runoff from fields, as well as through common practices of preparing and cleaning spraying equipment in or near streams and rivers, gives rise to growing concern among experts, authorities and rural citizens (UNDP, 2011b; HLPE, 2015).

---

[39] Emblematic cases include the sugarcane workers in Nicaragua and other areas in Central America (Ravnborg, 2013).

Streams and rivers play important roles for ecosystem health. Many people living in poverty and in areas with inadequate water infrastructure (mainly women and girls) rely on rivers and streams for doing their laundry. Children swim in rivers and streams, and cattle drink from them. Hence, chemical pollution from agriculture, mining and industry generates risks to ecosystems, but also to human health, both through the direct use of this water for domestic purposes or via the watering of crops and animals (Turral et al., 2011; UNDP, 2011b; HLPE, 2015). The poorest rural populations, who depend on surface water or unimproved water sources such as shallow wells and unprotected springs for domestic purposes, are therefore at risk of being left behind with respect to access to safe water. Agricultural labourers living in the vicinity or downstream of areas cultivated with the intensive use of agricultural chemicals are exposed to similar risks.

The lower prevalence of improved water sources and safely managed sanitation in rural areas (WHO/UNICEF, 2017b) also causes rural populations to be more exposed to faecal contamination than their urban neighbours. As a case in point, recent data (2016) from Ecuador show that while 15% of the urban population is exposed to E. coli from their drinking water source, this is the case for 32% of the rural population (INEC, n.d.). Unfortunately, however, using water from improved sources provides no guarantee that water is free from faecal contamination (WHO/UNICEF, 2017b). Data on the presence of toxic chemicals in water used for domestic purposes, whether supplied from improved or from surface water sources, are lacking at the global and (in many cases) national levels.

7.3 Promoting pro-poor multisectoral policies

Agriculture will continue to play a crucial role in the transformation and development of rural societies, and particularly in ending extreme poverty. As explained above, any intervention in the water and agriculture sectors will need to strengthen the livelihoods of the poorest and the people in the most vulnerable situations in rural areas, ensuring food security and access to drinking water and sanitation services. Nevertheless, agricultural development by itself will not be sufficient to end rural poverty, and those in the agricultural sector need to work hand in hand with other development actors.

Water-related ecosystems, including wetlands, rivers, aquifers and lakes, are crucial for ensuring goods and services like drinking water, food, energy and climate resilience. Natural resources like water, as well as ecosystem services, are the basis of all agricultural systems. Interventions that preserve ecosystems can also benefit the rural poor by securing their livelihoods and building resilience to climate change. A better integration between agricultural and environmental policies is a prerequisite to achieving sustainable development. Such integration, in order to be successful, needs to put the rural poor at the forefront.

Agricultural, water and broader sustainable development programmes also need to be coupled with other measures to ensure equality and social safety nets. For instance, social protection programmes can be linked to actions aimed at improving agricultural production and rural infrastructure development to ensure the reduction of poverty and hunger while stimulating economic growth, particularly among the poorest communities. It has been estimated that, to end hunger by 2030, additional investments in agriculture amounting to US$265 billion per year between 2016 and 2030 will be required at the global level, US$41 billion of which should be committed to social protection to reach the poorest in rural areas; and US$198 billion to pro-poor investment in productive and inclusive livelihood schemes, including regarding water (FAO/IFAD/WFP, 2015b).

CHAPTER 8

Refugees and forced displacement crises

Zaatari camp in Jordan

UNHCR | Murray Burt and Ryan Schweitzer

With contributions from: Eva Mach, Daria Mokhnacheva and Antonio Torres (IOM); Léo Heller (Special Rapporteur on the human rights to safe drinking water and sanitation); Alejandro Jiménez (UNDP-SIWI Water Governance Facility); Maria Teresa Gutierrez (ILO); Amanda Loeffen and Rakia Turner (WaterLex); Dominic de Waal (World Bank); and the Turkish Water Institute (SUEN)

This chapter focuses on the main drivers of displacement, including armed conflict and persecution as well as disasters and climate change, and describes the challenges and potential response options for providing safe drinking water and sanitation services to refugees and internally displaced people.

8.1
Refugees and forced displacement: A global challenge

The world is witnessing the highest levels of human displacement on record. By the end of the year 2017, an unprecedented 68.5 million people around the world have been forcibly displaced from their homes as a result of conflict, persecution, or human rights violations (UNHCR, 2018a). In addition, an average of 25.3 million people are displaced each year by sudden-onset disasters (IDMC, 2018), a trend likely to continue with the adverse effects of climate change. Infrastructure development related to megaprojects and mega-events has also led to the involuntary resettlement of affected populations (Picciotto, 2013).

Away from home, refugees and internally displaced people (IDPs) are among the most vulnerable and disadvantaged groups, often faced with barriers to access basic water supply and sanitation services, due to various factors related to their ethnicity, religion, gender, age, caste, class, physical or mental state, or other conditions. Displacement has impacts on the security and safety, financial means, health and well-being, education and employment opportunities, gender relations, nutrition and food security, social networks, family relationships, and legal rights of the displaced. Definitions of several key terms used in this chapter are provided in Box 8.1.

8.1.1 Displacement due to conflict and persecution
Of those displaced due to armed conflict or persecution, **40 million are recognized as IDPs**, forcibly displaced within their own country, while **25.4 million are refugees**, who have fled across an international border, and **3.1 million are asylum seekers** awaiting their refugee status determination (UNHCR, 2018a). In addition, it is also estimated that there are **more than 10 million stateless people** who have been denied a nationality and fulfilment of basic rights such as water, sanitation, education, healthcare, employment and freedom of movement. During 2017, 16.2 million people were newly displaced due to conflict (UNHCR, 2018a). This included 11.8 million individuals displaced within the borders of their own countries (IDMC, 2018) and 2.9 million new refugees and asylum seekers (UNHCR, 2018a).

Box 8.1 Definitions of key terms

Forced displacement is the movement of people who have been forced or obliged to flee or to leave their homes or places of habitual residence, in particular as a result of, or in order to avoid the effects of, armed conflict, situations of generalized violence, violations of human rights, or natural or human-made disasters (CHR, 1998).

A **refugee** is someone who has been forced to flee his or her country because of persecution, war or violence. A refugee has a well-founded fear of persecution for reasons of race, religion, nationality, political opinion or membership in a particular social group. Refugees are recognized under various international agreements. Some are recognized as a group or on a '*prima facie*' basis while others undergo an individual investigation before being given refugee status. The 1951 Convention (UN, 1951) and the 1967 Protocol (UN, 1967) provide the full legal definition of a refugee. The five countries hosting the most refugees at the end of 2017 (in descending order) were Turkey, Pakistan, Uganda, Lebanon and the Islamic Republic of Iran (UNHCR, 2018a).

An **asylum seeker** is a person who is seeking sanctuary in a country other than their own, and are waiting for a decision about their status. The legal processes related to asylum are complex and variable, which is a challenge when it comes to counting, measuring and understanding the asylum-seeking population. When an asylum application is successful, the person is awarded refugee status.

Internally displaced people (IDPs) are people who are forced to flee their homes as a result of, or in order to avoid the effects of, armed conflict, situations of generalized violence, violations of human rights, or natural or human-made disasters, and who have not crossed an internationally recognized state border (CHR, 1998). Unlike refugees, IDPs are not protected by international law or eligible to receive many types of aid because they are legally under the protection of their own government. In 2017, the three countries with the largest internally displaced populations (in descending order) were Colombia, the Syrian Arab Republic, and the Democratic Republic of the Congo (UNHCR, 2018a).

A **stateless person** is someone who does not have a nationality of any country. Some people are born stateless, but others become stateless due to a variety of reasons, including sovereign, legal, technical or administrative decisions or oversights. The Universal Declaration of Human Rights underlines that "*Everyone has the right to a nationality.*" (UNGA, 1948, article 15). Countries with the largest stateless populations in 2017 (in descending order) were Bangladesh, Côte d'Ivoire, Myanmar, Thailand, and Latvia (UNHCR, 2018a).

Protracted conflicts within fragile states such as the Democratic Republic of the Congo, South Sudan and Yemen are causing forced displacement at an unprecedented level and with a global impact. The United Nations High Commissioner for Refugees (UNHCR) defines a protracted refugee situation as one in which 25,000 or more refugees from the same nationality have been in exile for five or more years. Two-thirds of refugees are in protracted refugee situations, with an average duration of more than 20 years (UNHCR, 2018a), with some specific protracted situations now exceeding 30 years, such as Palestinian refugees in Egypt and Afghans in Pakistan.

The global number of forcibly displaced people has increased by 50%, from 42.7 million in 2007 to 68.5 by the end of the year 2017 (Figure 8.1). Almost a quarter of these displaced people live in refugee/IDP camps, but the overwhelming majority are hosted in cities, towns and villages (UNHCR, 2018a). These refugees, asylum seekers, IDPs and stateless persons are often not officially recognized by local or national government and are therefore excluded from development agendas.

8.1.2 Displacement due to disasters and climate change

In 2017, 18.8 million people across 118 countries were forced to leave their homes due to disasters brought on by sudden-onset natural hazards (IDMC, 2018). While figures can vary greatly from year to year depending on the occurrence and magnitude of disasters, the overall risk of being displaced by disasters has doubled since the 1970s mainly due to population growth and increased exposure and vulnerability to natural hazards. Climate change, in tandem with poverty, inequality, urban population growth, poor land use management and weak governance, is increasing the risk of displacement and its impacts.

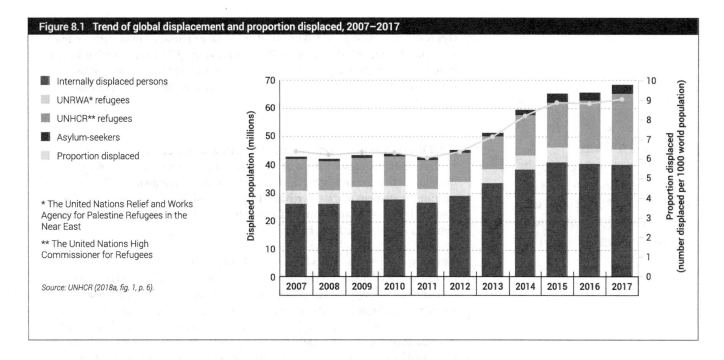

Figure 8.1 Trend of global displacement and proportion displaced, 2007–2017

■ Internally displaced persons

□ UNRWA* refugees

■ UNHCR** refugees

■ Asylum-seekers

□ Proportion displaced

* The United Nations Relief and Works Agency for Palestine Refugees in the Near East

** The United Nations High Commissioner for Refugees

Source: UNHCR (2018a, fig. 1, p. 6).

Regional patterns suggest that most disaster displacement happens in Asia and the Pacific, with 84% of the total displacement between 2008 and 2016 (IDMC, 2017). Disasters triggered by weather-related hazards led to 95% of all new displacements in 2017 (IDMC, 2018), even more than during the period from 2008 and 2016, when 86% of total displacements were weather-related (IDMC, 2017). Excluded from these figures are those people that move due to slow-onset events and stressors (e.g. chronic drought, sea level rise, desertification, or ecosystem loss, among others), as factors behind such movements are often complex.

8.2
Marginalization of the displaced: Main drivers

There are many factors which influence the marginalization of displaced persons. For example, refugees may be marginalized due to their ineligibility to vote, or stateless people may be marginalized because they do not have identification documents. The following sections highlight main drivers of marginalization as related to water, sanitation and hygiene (WASH) services.

8.2.1 Water as a direct and indirect driver of displacement

Vulnerability in relation to water supply can be a direct and indirect driver of displacement, and it can also be linked to the scale, duration and location of the displacement, and the buffering capacity of the environment in the host community to support the increased demand.

Climate change is expected to increase the frequency and intensity of drought and resultant population displacement. The Intergovernmental Panel on Climate Change (IPCC) has highlighted the considerable risks posed by heat waves, droughts, floods, cyclones and wildfires, as well as the vulnerability of water supplies and food production capacity (IPCC, 2014). Regardless of the geographical location, poor and marginalized populations are more exposed to the adverse consequences of extreme events such as extreme water scarcity or drought. For example, in Viet Nam in 2017 there were 633,000 new displacements, many of which were caused by storms, which are examples of the extreme weather predicted under the government's climate change models. These storms can disproportionately affect the poor, migrants or IDPs, who often lack the income to cover the costs to rebuild or do not have access to the social service systems (IDMC, 2018).

In arid and semi-arid climates, military targeting of water supply points has been used to increase water resource scarcity with the purpose of forced displacement.

For example, in Sri Lanka, an armed group closed the sluice gates of the Mavil Oya reservoir which provided irrigation water for thousands of farmers in the government-controlled area of the Eastern Province (UN, 2011). Bombardment in southern Lebanon in July and August of 2006 damaged or destroyed water supply infrastructure, displacing 25% of the 4 million inhabitants (Amnesty International, 2006).

8.2.2 Drivers of marginalization after mass displacement

Mass displacement places strain upon water resources and related services, including sanitation and hygiene, at transition and destination points for both existing populations and new arrivals. This can result in marginalization of the displaced population and restricted access to adequate services manifested in a number of ways, as outlined below.

Water supply and sanitation service level inequality

Unplanned rapid population growth in the areas receiving displaced persons can overwhelm existing WASH infrastructure. The immediate result is that the new arrivals (e.g. refugees, IDPs) cannot access services and resort to practices such as open defecation or drinking from unsafe surface water sources. This is most recently documented in Colombia where over 440,000 Venezuelans have been registered between May and June of 2018 and where WASH infrastructure in the border towns is unable to cope with the massive influx (UNHCR, 2018b).

The average length of protracted refugee situations (i.e. those with 25,000 or more persons of concern, displaced for 5 years or more) now exceeds 20 years (UNHCR, 2004; 2018a). However, host governments often refuse to accept that the displacement situation may become protracted, and insist that refugees and IDPs remain in camps with 'temporary' or 'communal' facilities at a lower level of service than the surrounding host community. As a result, WASH service level inequality may develop, where refugees and IDPs receiving lower levels of WASH service when compared to the hosting community. For instance, refugees in camps in Jordan receive approximately 35 litres of water per day (UNHCR, 2018c), while the target that the Jordanian government uses for citizen in towns outside of Amman is 100 litres of water per day (Ministry of Water and Irrigation of Jordan, 2015).

The reverse situation may also occur, where refugees receive higher-quality WASH services than what is available for nearby communities. For example in Maban (South Sudan), refugees receive 20 litres of chlorinated piped water per day, close to their homes, while the host community relies on handpumps that may only provide 15 litres per day and that may be located very far from their homes (UNHCR, 2018c).

Social discrimination

Adequate WASH services may exist in areas where displaced people are hosted. However, specific groups or individuals may be denied access to those services due to their nationality, ethnicity, religion, sexuality, political opinion or other conditions. As a result of this social discrimination, these groups or individuals resort to accessing water from unsafe sources and may be forced to practice open defecation or other unsafe sanitation behaviours (see Box 8.2).

Economic marginalization

Even if adequate WASH services exist, specific groups may not be able to afford access to those services. This form of marginalization is directly linked to legal status and the 'right to work' or 'freedom of movement'. As a result of restrictive legal policies, refugees and stateless persons are often the most marginalized in this regard (see Box 8.3).

In some countries, particularly those that follow an 'encampment' policy for refugees and IDPs, water supply and sanitation services may be provided free of charge by the international humanitarian community. At the same time, the local population is expected to pay for the same services provided through the national

---

In arid and semi-arid climates, military targeting of water supply points has been used to increase water resource scarcity with the purpose of forced displacement

---

Box 8.2 Examples of social discrimination

Burkina Faso and Mauritania: Domestic workers within the Malian refugee populations were prevented from using the same toilets as the general refugee population, forcing them to revert to open defecation, which exposed them to violence. They were not allowed by other community members to attend hygiene promotion sessions, and were required to pass on any relief items they obtained to their 'masters'.

Kenya and Djibouti: New arrivals were stigmatized and faced discrimination by the refugees who had been living in these camps and settlements for several years. This discrimination included limiting the access time to WASH facilities, such as water points and communal latrines.

Source: House et al. (2014).

or municipal system. This is the case in a number of areas such as the refugee camps in Gambella (Ethiopia) and Kakuma (Kenya) (UNHCR, 2018d). This can result in tensions between displaced populations and their hosting communities.

Environmental degradation

Hosting refugees or IDPs in areas that are environmentally sensitive can lead to tensions with the host community regarding the perceived or actual depletion/degradation of resources (e.g. aquifer depletion, surface water pollution and deforestation). In such cases, competition for scarce resources, including water, food, fuel and building materials, can cause conflict with the host community and further marginalization of the refugee or IDP population. For example, aquifer drawdown as a result of pumping water for IDP camps in Darfur (Sudan) resulted in drying of host community pastoralist wells, causing further conflict, marginalization and increased displacement (Bromwich, 2015).

In other cases, the resource depletion due to the displaced population may be perceived, and not real. For example, in Dadaab (Kenya) and in various camps in Yemen, rumours circulated that water pumping for the camp's water supply was adversely impacting the groundwater aquifers. However, detailed studies showed that water extracted for these camps' water supply did, in fact, not have a significant impact on groundwater resources (Zahir, 2009; Blandenier, 2015). Nevertheless, the perception of resource depletion can still result in tensions between the hosting and the displaced communities, and in the marginalization of the displaced.

8.3
Providing displaced people with access to water and sanitation

8.3.1 Crisis preparedness and response actions
Contingency planning and preparedness actions

Preparing countries for emergency situations and the arrival of refugees and IDPs requires consolidated efforts aimed at strengthening standards, policies and institutions relating to displacement, and empowering local actors to respond to emergency situations. The creation of specific water supply and sanitation risk management plans can help ensure adequate service provision during situations of rapid population increase while taking account of social, economic and environmental challenges. Successful contingency planning and preparedness actions also include preparation for the coordination of humanitarian actors that may be involved in such response actions, either through the coordination mechanisms of the United Nations (UN) — e.g. the UNHCR Refugee Coordination model, the Cluster Coordination system — or an equivalent national crisis coordination system. Increasing resilience and adaptive capacity of water supply and sanitation systems are also essential components to be considered in these plans (see Box 8.4).

Box 8.3   Refugees' right to work

A 2016 study on 20 countries that host 70% of the world's refugee population found widespread inconsistencies in the laws, policies and practices with regard to the legal right to work for refugees. The right to work was often exclusively linked to the recognition of refugee status, which is governed by a complex system that is difficult to navigate. This is compounded by bureaucratic and administrative hurdles which can include work and/or residence permits required from refugees; the financial costs of permits; and registration and banking regulations that negatively affect self-employed refugees and impede payment of wages (Zetter and Ruaudel, 2016).

The vast majority of refugees work in the informal sector under much less satisfactory and more exploitative conditions than nationals. In fragile economies, which host a large number of refugees, the informal sector can be constrained and provide limited opportunities for refugees. For example, there are approximately 666,000 registered Syrian refugees in Jordan, and the vast majority (80%) are hosted in cities and towns. These refugees do not have the right to work and without an income, they are at risk of having reduced levels of access to WASH services (UNHCR, 2018a).

Immediate crisis response actions
States and other relevant stakeholders can benefit from close collaboration with national and international humanitarian partners to provide appropriate services to the displaced. Immediate crisis response actions principally involve:

- Timely provision of life-saving WASH services including: access to potable water, access to safe sanitation (e.g. toilets, bathing facilities, kitchens, laundries and menstrual hygiene management), access to solid waste management and vector control.

- WASH service-strengthening measures in hosting areas for the short term and system-strengthening measures for the medium term, based on ongoing assessments. These include: providing additional staff, equipment and supplies in order to increase production and maintain uninterrupted service delivery for displaced people and their host communities.

- Ongoing assessment of the WASH services and systems to monitor the impact of displacement on national services and on the host community.

An example of effective crisis response is highlighted in Box 8.5.

8.3.2 Potential responses in ongoing situations
Inclusion of refugees, asylum seekers, stateless and internally displaced people within national systems, and plans for SDG 6 to create water supply and sanitation service level equality
Moving towards achievement of Sustainable Development Goal (SDG) 6 target of safe drinking water and sanitation for all' implies the inclusion of refugees, asylum seekers, stateless people and IDPs in national development plans, and ensuring that financing is adequate to reach these populations. Specifically, states have a responsibility to:

- Assess and monitor the impact of population growth as a result of displacement on national WASH systems, including access to water, the quantity and quality of water, and access to sanitation services, in order to identify appropriate measures to increase access to services where required.

- Review and strengthen national policies relating to the inclusion of refugees and IDPs in national WASH systems, ensuring that they have the same level of access to WASH services as nationals.

- Include the needs of refugees and IDPs in national WASH-related strategies, initiatives and action plans, national and local development plans, as well as in strategies and plans designed to meet targets for SDG 6 'safe drinking water and sanitation for all' and other WASH-related SDGs.

- Include refugees and IDPs in donor proposals and financing mechanisms to ensure adequate quantity and quality of WASH services for refugees and hosting communities, as well as refugee inclusion in the monitoring of outcome data. At the same time, donors and financiers (both humanitarian and development) need to commit multi-year, predictable funding for relevant stakeholders (including Ministries of Water) to ensure that the immediate and ongoing needs of both refugees/IDPs and affected host communities can be met, as well as to promote resilience.

- Incorporate WASH needs of refugees and IDPs into national contingency plans for further displacement and disaster preparedness plans.

- Improve monitoring and impact evaluation relating to WASH services for refugees and IDPs by including them in national surveys, and disaggregate national WASH data and SDG 6 reporting by refugee/displacement status on WASH services utilization and access.

- Ensure that WASH monitoring for refugees and IDPs includes relevant indicators that account for the normative criteria of the human rights to safe drinking water and sanitation (accessibility, availability, affordability, acceptability and quality).

Refugee status should not be grounds for unjustified restrictions on freedom of movement, nor for stigmatization, removal and other forms of discriminatory practices

- Eliminate service level inequality between the refugees/IDPs and the hosting community by harmonization of service levels in refugee and IDP camps, as well as in urban hosting areas, with national standards.

Removing social discrimination and creating access equality: Harmonizing service levels with surrounding community/national standards

In order to remove social discrimination and create water supply and sanitation service access equality, states in partnership with relevant stakeholders need to review and strengthen national laws and policies in order to promote the principle that refugees and IDPs should have access to WASH services just like any other person, and refugee status should not be grounds for unjustified restrictions on freedom of movement, nor for stigmatization, removal and other forms of discriminatory practices.

Box 8.5 Meeting water, sanitation and hygiene (WASH) needs of Syrians under temporary protection in Turkey

Turkey hosts the largest number of refugees in the world, with over 3.9 million registered refugees, of which 90% are from Syria (UNHCR, 2018e). Only 178,255 out of the 3.6 million Syrians in Turkey live in the 20 state-run centres operated in southeastern Turkey, with the rest hosted in cities, towns and villages throughout the country, causing the populations in many areas to dramatically increase (Ministry of the Interior of Turkey, 2018).

Figure | Distribution of Syrian refugees in the scope of temporary protection in Turkey by top ten provinces on 21 September 2018

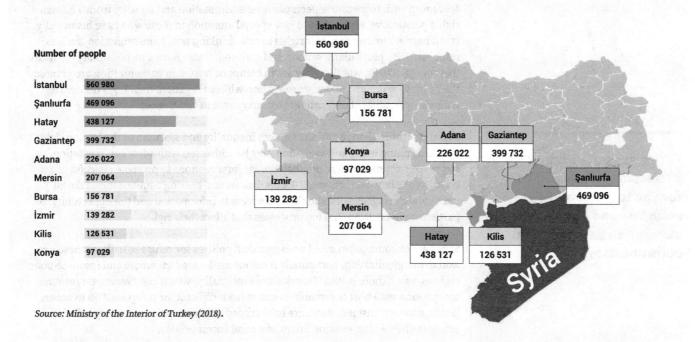

Number of people

İstanbul	560 980
Şanlıurfa	469 096
Hatay	438 127
Gaziantep	399 732
Adana	226 022
Mersin	207 064
Bursa	156 781
İzmir	139 282
Kilis	126 531
Konya	97 029

Source: Ministry of the Interior of Turkey (2018).

The dramatic population growth has resulted in stress on already scarce water resources, requiring additional administrative, technical, financial and human capacity to maintain existing water infrastructure and to construct additional infrastructure. Turkey has adopted the principle that humanitarian assistance must be paired with development investments that can respond to the scale, scope and protracted nature of the refugee influx. Of the US$31 billion that has been spent, 5% has focused on water, sanitation and hygiene (WASH) infrastructure and services, at the shelter centres and for those living outside the centres. New dams, reservoirs and pipelines were constructed, enhancing the water and wastewater treatment capacities, mainly in the border provinces of Gaziantep, Şanlıurfa, Kilis and Hatay. In addition, capacity-building projects have sought to integrate Syrians into the social and economic life in Turkey to ensure an inclusive and sustainable WASH management and promote regional development.

Contributed by the Turkish Water Institute (SUEN), based partly on metrics synthesized from internal documents.

Refugees in Zaatari camp in Jordan

Moreover, with respect to aspects of non-discrimination and equality from a human rights perspective, states need to give special attention to those who have historically faced barriers to exercise their rights to safe drinking water and sanitation, such as refugees/IDPs, particularly women and children. States have a responsibility to ensure that refugees/IDPs, whether they are in camps or hosted in communities, are granted the rights to water and adequate sanitation without regard to their legal residence, nationality or other classifications that may serve as hindrances.

Social discrimination resulting in access inequality and violation of the human rights to safe drinking water and sanitation may be addressed with advocacy, mediation, improved communication, or other similar interventions to promote peaceful co-existence between refugee/IDP populations and hosting communities. Like all individuals, refugees/IDPs should have access to information and the opportunity to participate in decision-making processes that affect their rights.

States are encouraged to pursue policies for the inclusion of refugees and IDPs within existing urban and rural communities

States are encouraged to avoid 'encampment' policies for refugees/IDPs, as these can lead to marginalization, particularly if camps are located in remote and resource-poor regions, and if there is WASH service level inequality, which can exacerbate resource competition with host communities and make it difficult for refugees/IDPs to access labour markets. Instead, states are encouraged to pursue policies for the inclusion of refugees/IDPs within existing urban and rural communities.

In the case of refugees/IDPs living in informal settlements in urban and peri-urban areas, it is difficult to differentiate between different types of vulnerable populations (refugees and other urban poor), and making such distinctions may not be beneficial at all. In many contexts, it will also be difficult or even impossible to identify the 'most vulnerable' groups. Interventions should therefore aim at improving access to water supply and sanitation services for the broader populations in vulnerable situations, including both refugees and urban poor.

While the monitoring of access to services in refugee camps is well established, little information is available on the situation of people living outside the camps, among host communities. It is often helpful to increase the knowledge about their situation through, for example, surveys and other methods, instead of relying entirely on data provided by the state (which often do not differentiate between refugees and other populations).

Ensuring the right to work and supporting economic growth to pay for water supply and sanitation services

Both issues of water supply and sanitation service affordability and water tariff inequity for refugees/IDPs may be solved in the short term through international humanitarian 'cash' assistance, and in the long term, if hosting governments give refugees the 'right to access the labour market' and to generate income so they can pay for the services.

The 1951 Convention relating to the Status of Refugees (UN, 1951) requires hosting governments to allow refugees the 'right to work' and 'freedom of movement'. This has the effect of allowing refugees to access livelihoods opportunities and to reduce the burden of subsidizing their access. This means that refugees would be able to pay for water supply and sanitation services in the same way as national citizens, which may reduce social tensions or discrimination, while empowering refugees to integrate into their host communities.

> **Globally, most nations have a restrictive approach to refugees' rights to work and freedom of movement**

Although displaced persons are often perceived as a problem or threat, they could be seen as an opportunity that host countries can benefit from, be it economically, culturally, socially, or other. Host countries often economically benefit as displaced persons are 'consumers, producers, buyers, sellers, borrowers, lenders and entrepreneurs' (Betts and Collier, 2017). For example, Somali refugees have been financially investing in Kenya in both formal and informal business of varying sizes from petty traders to larger companies in a wide variety of sectors including real estate, transportation, finance, import-export and others (Abdulsamed, 2011). In addition to the economic benefits, there are also many social and cultural benefits that refugees and migrants can offer the host community.

Globally, most nations have a restrictive approach to refugees' rights to work and freedom of movement. Many countries retain a strict policy of encampment or apply movement restrictions, thereby increasing refugees' difficulties in accessing employment and livelihood opportunities. However, there are good examples of progress (see Box 8.6).

Development actors can insist that governments recognize human rights of refugees and give them parity with other residents. However, this must go hand in hand with proactive steps to harmonize relations between refugees and their host communities. Tensions are often due to legitimate concerns from the host community about the impact of increased numbers of job-seekers on local labour markets, impacts on environmental resources, etc. Easing pressure on host communities and enhancing the self-reliance of refugees are two of the key objectives of the Global Compact on Refugees (UNHCR, 2018f).

Box 8.6 Positive examples of supporting economic growth

Uganda – Refugees are allowed freedom of movement and the right to work. Some are given land for subsistence farming. Refugees and host communities share access to education, health and water, sanitation and hygiene (WASH) services and the service levels in refugee-hosting communities has been improved. In addition, refugees starting businesses and working has boosted the economy in these areas (UNHCR, 2017).

Jordan aims to provide up to 200,000 work permits for refugees, thereby creating new work opportunities for refugees and Jordanians in selected labour market sectors and locations (mainly Special Economic Zones), and regularizing the situation of refugees working in the informal economy (Zetter and Ruaudel, 2016).

Turkey – The government granted work permits to Syrians and other foreign nationals who are under temporary protection (Council of Ministers of Turkey, 2016). The Turkish Employment Agency organizes training programmes to enhance the work qualifications in areas of specific need in the labour market.

Ethiopia's new "out of-camp" policy demonstrates a conditional relaxation of legislative restrictions on the movement and place of residence for refugees. The International Labour Organization (ILO) and the United Nations High Commissioner for Refugees (UNHCR) have partnered with Ethiopia's Administration for Refugees and Returnee Affairs to promote self-employment in camps and surrounding host communities (ILO, 2018b).

Ensuring environmental sustainability of services

Environmental sustainability is integral to achieving the SDG targets. This will require implementing a wide range of interventions, many of which are linked to integrated water resource management activities, developing water safety plans, conducting environmental impact assessments to understand the effects of displacements, as well as ensuring robust systems for environmental monitoring, in particular water resource monitoring. In protracted situations, sustainable access to WASH services for refugees, IDPs, as well as host communities can be enhanced by technology solutions which are both environmentally sustainable and cost-effective.

During the immediate phase after displacement, media attention and political interest are high and funding sources plentiful. However, both decrease with time, which makes it important to select WASH technologies that minimize long-term operation and maintenance costs, as well as environmental impacts. Examples of such technologies, which have been adopted in recent refugee situations, include photovoltaic solar energy for water pumping (instead of diesel generators), waste reuse, and recycling solutions such as biogas, conversion of waste to cooking fuels or fertilizer, and solid waste recycling. Such technologies help to reduce carbon emissions, environmental impacts and operation costs (see Box 8.7). There are additional technologies which can be explored (e.g. decentralized wastewater treatment systems (DEWATS), as described in Chapter 6), but all technological solutions need to be implemented in coordination with national and local governments to ensure the appropriate capacity within the local communities to take over management of these systems. While there are opportunities to use innovative technologies and approaches in humanitarian contexts, a need to continue with 'traditional' emergency response approaches (e.g. water trucking) will also remain.

8.4
Fragile states and states in fragile situations

A fragile state is a low-income country characterized by weak state capacity and/or weak state legitimacy, leaving citizens vulnerable to a range of shocks. The World Bank deems a country to be 'fragile' if it: i) has had a UN peacekeeping mission in the last three years; and ii) has received a 'governance' score of less than 3.2 (as per the Country Performance and Institutional Assessment (CPIA) index of The World Bank) (World Bank, n.d.).

Two billion people now live in countries where development outcomes are affected by fragility, conflict and violence. By 2030, 46% of the global poor could live in fragile and conflict-affected situations, as defined by The World Bank Group's (WBG) Fragile, Conflict and Violence Group, which annually releases the World Bank Harmonized List of Fragile Situations (World Bank, n.d.). Fragility and conflict can cross national borders, and the consequences of conflict, such as forced displacement, further hinder the capacity of countries and regions to find their path out of poverty.

Box 8.7   Future is bright with solar

The cost of solar photovoltaic panels reduced by a factor of 100 since 1977, with the current cost at less than US$1 per Watt of solar electricity (ECHO Global Solar Water Initiative, 2017). Despite this, adoption of solar within the humanitarian context remains low, due to a shortage of technical expertise, inability to communicate benefits to donors and decision makers, focus on numerical targets for immediate beneficiaries reached, and a lack of standards, best practices and policy guidelines. The Global Solar Water Initiative, funded by the European Civil Protection and Humanitarian Aid Operations (ECHO), has sought to address these gaps by collating and sharing information on good practices, commissioning research, providing technical resources for implementation, and improving technical expertise through trainings.

Displacement crises can escalate very rapidly, as illustrated by the South Sudanese case. As of the end of 2016, one in four people in South Sudan have been forced from their homes. This translates to a total of 3.3 million, with 1.9 million IDPs and 1.4 million refugees in neighbouring countries. South Sudan and the neighbouring countries are among the poorest and Least Developed Countries in the world, with limited resources to deal with the needs and challenges associated with hosting displaced people. In the Democratic Republic of the Congo, which has been subject to a long-standing and complex humanitarian crisis, the year 2016 saw 1.3 million IDPs in the eastern part of the country. During the same year, 630,000 were displaced in Libya, 623,000 in Afghanistan, 598,000 in Iraq and 467,000 in Yemen. All these countries are listed as fragile states (UNHCR, 2018a).

It has been argued by the Overseas Development Institute that fragile states require approaches that are fundamentally different from the development models exercised in more resilient countries, because of the different context of risk (Manuel et al., 2012).

One such successful mechanism is community-driven development (CDD), which gives control over planning decisions and investment resources for local development projects to community groups. Often used by the World Bank in conflict situations, CDD is fast, flexible and effective at re-establishing basic services, which can range from health to clean water to education, and has helped rebuild social capital and trust within communities and between communities and governments (Wong and Guggenheim, 2018).

It is important to acknowledge that for many parts of the world, without huge investment in sustainable development, peace and security, refugees are the 'new normal.'

> **It is important to acknowledge that for many parts of the world, without huge investment in sustainable development, peace and security, refugees are the 'new normal.'**

CHAPTER 9

Regional perspectives

Aerial view of water tanks on the rooftops of Rocinha slum in Rio de Janeiro, Brazil

UNECE | Chantal Demilecamps

UNECLAC | Andrei Jouravlev

UNESCAP | Aida Karazhanova, Ingrid Dispert, Solène Le Doze, Katinka Weinberger and Stefanos Fotiou

UNESCWA | Carol Chouchani Cherfane and Dima Kharbotli

WWAP | Angela Renata Cordeiro Ortigara and Richard Connor

With contributions from: Shinee Enkhtsetseg (WHO Regional Office for Europe); Simone Grego (UNESCO Multisectoral Regional Office in Abuja); Abou Amani (UNESCO-IHP); and Noeline Raondry Rakotoarisoa (UNESCO-MAB)

Different regions of the world face particular challenges in the attempt to provide safe, affordable and sustainable water supply and sanitation services for all. This chapter highlights some of these major challenges and potential responses from the often unique perspectives of the five major global regions.

9.1
The Arab region

9.1.1 Regional context

The Arab region is the most water-stressed region in the world. Total renewable water resources for the world average 7,453 m³ per person per year, while it stands at only 736 m³ per person per year in the Arab region based on latest available data from AQUASTAT (n.d.). Water scarcity on a per capita basis has been increasing and will continue to increase due to population growth and climate change. These trends have contributed to increased groundwater depletion, loss of arable land for agricultural production, and the movement of people when water resources are insufficient to support health, welfare and livelihoods.

In the entirety of the Arab region, some 51 million people (or 9% of the total population) lacked a basic drinking water service in 2015, 73% of whom lived in rural areas (Figure 9.1) (WHO/UNICEF, 2018b).

Least Developed Countries (LDCs) in the Arab region suffer the greatest equity gap with respect to ensuring access to basic water supply and sanitation services, and particularly in rural areas. In Mauritania, 86% of the urban population has access to basic drinking water services, compared to only 45% in rural areas. Disparities in rural and urban access to basic drinking water services were also noted in Yemen (85% in urban versus 63% in rural areas) and Sudan (73% in urban versus 51% in rural areas) in 2015 (see Figure 9.2) (WHO/UNICEF, 2018b), and have likely worsened since then given the ongoing conflicts.

The situation is not only limited to LDCs, however. In Morocco, access to basic water services in urban areas reaches 96% versus only 65% in the rural parts of the country (WHO/UNICEF, 2018b).

At the end of 2016, around 41% of the internally displaced people (IDPs) worldwide were living in the Arab region, with numbers reaching over 16 million. Humanitarian access has been a significant challenge, with roughly 4.9 million people of this total living in hard-to-reach areas, including almost one million in besieged areas (UNESCWA/IOM, 2017).

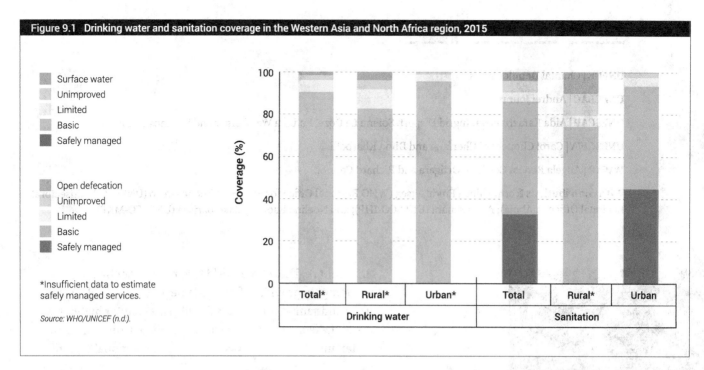

Figure 9.1 Drinking water and sanitation coverage in the Western Asia and North Africa region, 2015

Surface water
Unimproved
Limited
Basic
Safely managed

Open defecation
Unimproved
Limited
Basic
Safely managed

*Insufficient data to estimate safely managed services.

Source: WHO/UNICEF (n.d.).

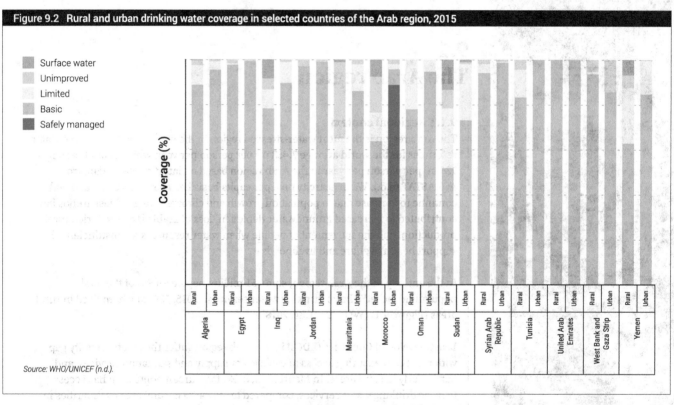

Figure 9.2 Rural and urban drinking water coverage in selected countries of the Arab region, 2015

Surface water
Unimproved
Limited
Basic
Safely managed

Source: WHO/UNICEF (n.d.).

By December 2016, the Syrian Arab Republic had more IDPs (6.3 million) than any other country in the world, many of them having endured multiple displacements (UNESCWA/IOM, 2017). High levels of internal displacement owing to conflict and violence also persist in the Arab region's LDCs, namely Somalia, Sudan and Yemen. Sudan hosts the largest number of IDPs among the Arab LDCs, with over 3.3 million at the end of 2016 (UNESCWA/IOM, 2017), as shown in Table 9.1.

In addition, natural disasters linked to climate change impacts have resulted in the displacement of over 240,000 people across the Arab region in 2016, the vast majority of them in the Arab LDCs (98%): 123,000 in the Sudan, 70,000 in Somalia, and 36,000 in Yemen (UNESCWA/IOM, 2017). This means that special attention must be focused on enhancing the resilience of this group of displaced people, to ensure that no one is left behind.

Table 9.1 Internally displaced persons due to conflict and generalized violence in the Arab region (stock at year end), 2012–2016

Country	2012	2013	2014	2015	2016
Syrian Arab Republic	3 000 000	6 500 000	7 600 000	6 600 000	6 325 978
Sudan	3 000 000	2 424 700	3 120 000	3 264 286	3 320 000
Iraq	2 100 000	2 100 000	3 276 000	3 290 310	3 034 614
Yemen	385 000	307 000	334 090	2 509 068	1 973 994
Somalia	1 350 000	1 100 000	1 106 751	1 223 000	1 106 751
Libya	50 000	59 400	400 000	500 000	303 608
Palestine	144 500	146 000	275 000	221 425	193 277

Source: UNESCWA/IOM (2017, Box 1, p. 22).

> The challenge of ensuring access to water services for all under water-scarce conditions is exacerbated in conflict settings where water infrastructure has been damaged, destroyed and targeted for destruction

9.1.2 Providing access to safe water and sanitation services under conditions of war and conflict

The challenge of ensuring access to water services for all under water-scarce conditions is exacerbated in conflict settings where water infrastructure has been damaged, destroyed and targeted for destruction, as in parts of Iraq, Libya, Palestine, Somalia, Sudan, the Syrian Arab Republic and Yemen. Not only have water reservoirs, pumps, treatment facilities and distribution networks been affected by military conflicts and occupation by foreign forces, but also have wastewater treatment facilities and irrigation networks been destroyed during military incursions. Operation and maintenance of water facilities is also limited during periods of insecurity and occupation, which have affected the availability of fuel for pumping water (e.g. in Yemen), the import of replacement parts (e.g. in Palestine), or access of employees to operate water facilities (e.g. in Iraq).

Even prior to the current conflict in Yemen, its capital city Sana'a was expected to run dry due to population pressures and unsustainable production and consumption patterns (UNESCWA, 2011), with experts projecting *"if current trends continue, by 2025 the city's projected 4.2 million inhabitants will become water refugees, forced to flee their barren home for wetter lands. In preparation, some officials have already considered relocating the capital to the coast. Others have proposed focusing on desalination and conservation to buy time."* (Heffez, 2013). Instead, Yemen suffers the destruction of conflict and the plague of war with recurrent cholera outbreaks due to insufficient water for safe sanitation and hygiene, and extreme water scarcity caused by groundwater depletion and quality concerns. Lack of water for hygiene and sanitation has become dire with the reporting of the International Committee of the Red Cross (ICRC) that 1 in every 200 Yemenis is suspected of having been infected with cholera as of June 2017 (ICRC, 2017; OHCHR, 2017b).

A large proportion of refugees tend to remain in protracted situations for decades (see Section 8.1.1). Humanitarian assistance has become increasingly intertwined with development work aimed at providing more permanent water supply and sanitation facilities in refugee camps and informal settlements. This has at times caused conflict and tensions with host communities, who often do not have equal access to water services as those served by humanitarian organizations. Additional attention has been paid to this problem in recent years with governments, donors and humanitarian agencies recognizing that leaving no one behind means serving refugees and IDPs as well as host communities, as shown in Box 9.1.

Box 9.1 The Zaatari Syrian refugee camp in Jordan

The Zaatari refugee camp is located in the heavily water-stressed area of northern Jordan. It was initially set up in a haste in a response to the sudden influx of refugees coming from Syria, and hence it lacked proper planning and basic infrastructure. This resulted in outbreaks of measles, scabies, diarrhoea, hepatitis A and other diseases in the months following its establishment, mainly attributed to deficient amounts of clean water and poor sanitation (UNESCWA/IOM, 2015). Tensions were also manifested with neighbouring communities, who had long faced water scarcity constraints and were now seeing their limited resources being diverted and unsustainably consumed.

In response, international humanitarian organizations and non-governmental organizations (NGOs) started working with the Jordanian Ministry of Water and Irrigation and with host communities to improve access to clean water supply and sanitation services in the Zaatari refugee camp as well as in neighbouring areas. This included the rehabilitation of existing water wells and drilling of additional wells to respond to the increasing water demands (UNESCWA/IOM, 2015). Details on water infrastructure works are included in the table below.

Project	Description	Population served
Zaatari refugee camp	Digging 2 new wells and building their associated pump stations	120 000
Tabaqet Fahel well	Renovation and expansion of the well	63 000 (80 liters per day per capita)
Zabdah reservoir	Water saving through renovation to fix leaks and install insulation	27 000 (80 liters per day per capita)
Abu Al Basal pipeline	Installation of a 2.5 km pipeline for better water conveyance and distribution	

Source: Mercy Corps (2014, p. 14).

Rehabilitation works were also performed on ageing water networks and transmission lines servicing the area. The wastewater collection infrastructure was rehabilitated, and wastewater treatment plant capacities were expanded to accommodate the growing volumes of wastewater generated. In addition to helping the refugees, these collective and cooperative efforts also contributed to improving water infrastructure and services to host communities in this water-stressed region (UNESCWA/IOM, 2015).

9.2
Asia and the Pacific

Achieving access to clean water and sanitation for all, as framed by Sustainable Development Goal (SDG) 6 of the 2030 Agenda for Sustainable Development, remains a challenge in Asia and the Pacific as a whole.

In 2016, 29 out of 48 countries in the region qualified as water-insecure due to low availability of water and unsustainable groundwater withdrawal, and 7 of the 15 countries with the largest estimated annual groundwater extractions are in Asia and the Pacific (ADB, 2016). The increase in demand for irrigation for agriculture has led to severe groundwater stress in some areas, especially in two of Asia's major food baskets — the North China Plain and Northwest India (Shah, 2005). Many large and medium-sized cities in the region face the risk of water shortages, due to outdated water supply systems and inadequate infrastructure to harvest and store rainwater (UNESCAP/UNESCO/ILO/UN Environment/FAO/UN-Water, 2018). High levels of water pollution worsen the situation in terms of drinking water availability, caused by the alarming rates of untreated wastewater released into surface water bodies — 80 to 90% in the Asia and the Pacific region — and high levels of chemical contamination in runoff water in some areas (UNESCAP, 2010). Water scarcity is compounded by the effects of climate change and worsened by the impacts of disasters.

Despite observable progress in terms of access to safe drinking water, one in ten rural residents and 30% of the population living in landlocked developing countries did not have access to it in 2015 (OECD, n.d.). That same year, 1.5 billion people did not have access to improved sanitation facilities (UNESCAP, 2017).

However, vast sub-regional disparities can be observed. For example, while 89% of the population in urban areas in Eastern and South-Eastern Asia has access to safely managed drinking water services, in Central and Southern Asia this ratio drops to 61% (WHO/UNICEF, n.d.) (Figure 9.3). Progress is stalling in North Asia, Central Asia and the Pacific, and in LDCs (UNESCAP, 2016). Landlocked countries are facing the most significant difficulties ensuring access to clean water and sanitation for all, with 30% of the population living in landlocked developing countries not having access to safe drinking water in 2015 (OECD, n.d.).

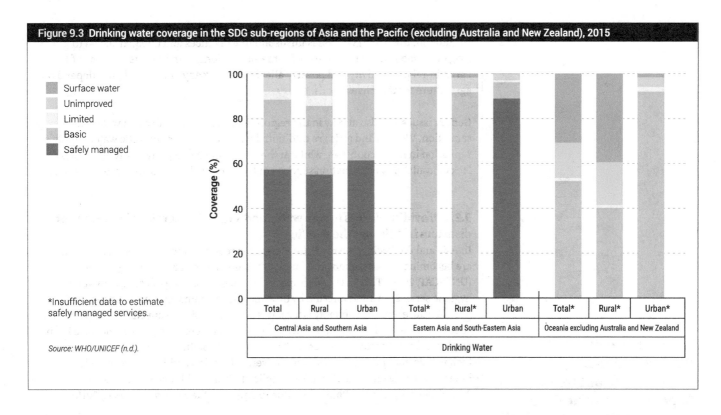

Figure 9.3 Drinking water coverage in the SDG sub-regions of Asia and the Pacific (excluding Australia and New Zealand), 2015

Legend:
- Surface water
- Unimproved
- Limited
- Basic
- Safely managed

*Insufficient data to estimate safely managed services.

Source: WHO/UNICEF (n.d.).

Similar disparities can be observed across the region in terms of sanitation (Figure 9.4). There is also unequal access to improved sanitation between urban and rural areas in the region: the gap was approximately 30% in 2015. Levels of improvement in terms of access to sanitation differ considerably (WHO/UNICEF, n.d.). Since 2000, the proportion of people in rural areas with access to basic sanitation has increased by 0.8% per year, compared with 0.5% per year in urban areas (UNESCAP, 2017). This is mainly due to the fast growth of the region's urban population, which has more than doubled since 1950, and the issues faced by cities in developing the adequate infrastructure to keep up with the escalating water and sanitation needs. This inequality of access between rural and urban areas varies among sub-regions, as shown in Figures 9.3 and 9.4. Within cities, it is the poor urban populations that tend to be left behind.

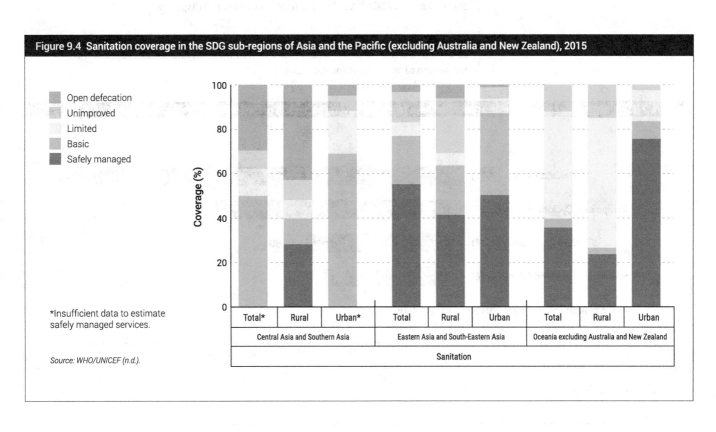

Figure 9.4 Sanitation coverage in the SDG sub-regions of Asia and the Pacific (excluding Australia and New Zealand), 2015

Legend:
- Open defecation
- Unimproved
- Limited
- Basic
- Safely managed

*Insufficient data to estimate safely managed services.

Source: WHO/UNICEF (n.d.).

In addition, the region witnesses unsustainable practices and unequal access to irrigation water in the rural areas of some sub-regions, with impacts in terms of agricultural productivity and poverty alleviation, as many of the rural poor depend on agriculture for their livelihoods.

Gender issues are also at play in the region in terms of access to clean water and sanitation. Women and girls are traditionally responsible for domestic water supply and sanitation in many countries, whilst at the same time being particularly affected by the lack of availability of sanitation services in terms of health and safety (see Section 2.2).

9.2.1 Providing access to safe water and sanitation services in the face of disasters in Asia and the Pacific

In Asia and the Pacific, the most disaster-prone region in the world, natural disasters are becoming more frequent and intense, and disaster risk is outpacing resilience (UNESCAP, 2018). This has major impacts for the provisioning of water, sanitation and hygiene services in areas affected by disasters, due to damaged water and sanitation infrastructure and water quality issues. It is also a very significant challenge to provide adequate water and sanitation services to the areas that receive people who have been displaced from disaster-struck areas. The magnitude of these displacements is extremely high in Asia and the Pacific, with respectively 4.4 million and 1.2 million people internally displaced in the People's Republic of China and India in 2017 due to floods, and 2.5 million people in the Philippines due to typhoons the same year (IDMC, 2018).

Disasters cause disproportionately more significant losses to poorer countries and people, as these often lack resilience and the capacity to mitigate the impact of disasters. In addition to hitting the poorest, disasters can also cause the near poor — those living on between US$1.90 and US$3.10 per day — to fall into poverty, as shown in Figure 9.5 (UNESCAP, 2018). With over 50% of urban residents living in low-lying coastal zones, these cities and towns in Asia and the Pacific are particularly vulnerable to climate change and natural disasters. Disasters are also found to have impacts on gross domestic product (GDP), school enrolment rates, and per capita expenditure on health (UNESCAP, 2018). Analysis by the United Nations Economic and Social Commission for Asia and the Pacific (UNESCAP) among 19 countries in Asia and the Pacific indeed suggests that each disaster in the region leads to a 0.13 point increase in the Gini coefficient (UNESCAP, 2018), thus increasing income disparity.

The impacts and costs of these events are exacerbated by such factors as non-resilient or unplanned urbanization and degradation of the ecosystems that support the regulation of water flows and quality.

Disasters cause disproportionately more significant losses to poorer countries and people, as these often lack resilience and the capacity to mitigate the impact of disasters

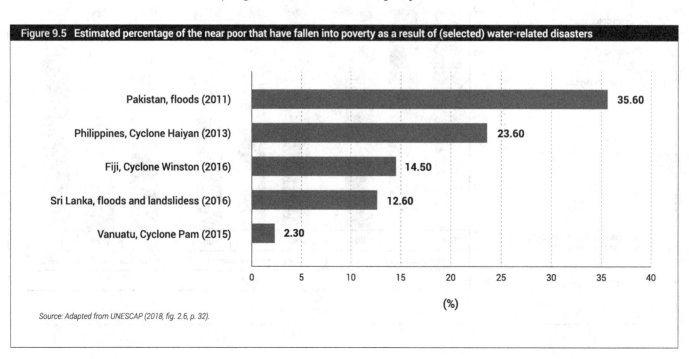

Figure 9.5 Estimated percentage of the near poor that have fallen into poverty as a result of (selected) water-related disasters

Pakistan, floods (2011) — 35.60
Philippines, Cyclone Haiyan (2013) — 23.60
Fiji, Cyclone Winston (2016) — 14.50
Sri Lanka, floods and landslidess (2016) — 12.60
Vanuatu, Cyclone Pam (2015) — 2.30

(%)

Source: Adapted from UNESCAP (2018, fig. 2.6, p. 32).

Improving the resilience of water and sanitation services is therefore key to maintaining access in a climatically uncertain future. Scaling up disaster risk reduction and associated investments is critical to meet current and future needs.

In addition to its support to member states in Asia and the Pacific for their overall disaster risk reduction, UNESCAP promotes the adoption of nature-based solutions for disaster risk reduction (Eco-DRR) for water, in particular in coastal cities, islands and coastal settlements. In coastal areas, mangroves and coral reefs provide a natural line of defence against tsunamis and storms. They also improve water quality and prevent salt water inundation and floods, while providing multiple other environmental, economic and social benefits. Eco-DRR proves a worthwhile approach in the region: a cost–benefit analysis in Viet Nam estimated that investing in 12,000 hectares of mangroves to protect the coast was much cheaper than infrastructural developments (US$1.1 million compared to US$7.3 million for the maintenance of dykes) (Tallis et al., 2008).

UNESCAP's Disaster Related Statistical Framework (ECOSOC, 2018) provides a comprehensive framework for producing the basic statistics used in assessments and other applications, including for the relatively smaller-scale but more frequently occurring forms of disasters. When coupled with the development of community-based participatory mapping, it may be adapted to operationalize clean water and sanitation in urban areas and provide a sufficient level of granularity to allow a focus on those usually 'left behind' by natural disasters.

9.3
Europe and North America

Millions of people in this region drink contaminated water, often without knowing it. As of 2015, those 'left behind' in the region include 57 million people who do not have piped water at home, and 21 million people who still lack access to basic drinking water services. In addition, 36 million people lack access to basic sanitation, using unsafe, shared or unsustainable sanitation (WHO/UNICEF, n.d.). The World Health Organization (WHO) estimates that, every day, 14 people die of diarrhoeal disease due to inadequate water, sanitation and hygiene (Prüss-Ustün, 2016). Access to safely managed sanitation services remains a challenge in many countries, especially in rural areas (Figure 9.6). For example, in the regions of Central Asia and the Caucasus, 72% of the people without access to basic water services and 95% of the people using surface water live in rural areas (UNECE, n.d.a).

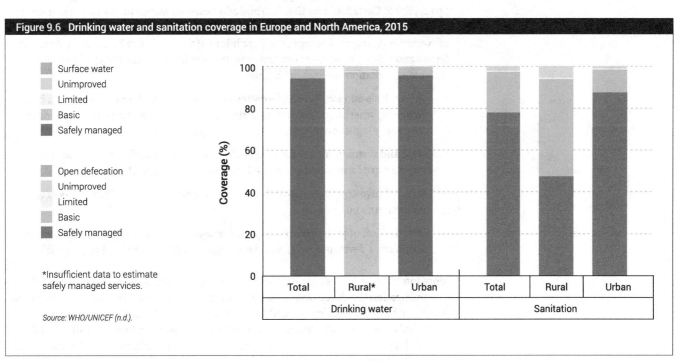

Figure 9.6 Drinking water and sanitation coverage in Europe and North America, 2015

Surface water
Unimproved
Limited
Basic
Safely managed

Open defecation
Unimproved
Limited
Basic
Safely managed

*Insufficient data to estimate safely managed services.

Source: WHO/UNICEF (n.d.).

While the situation is particularly severe for a major part of the population in Eastern Europe, the Caucasus and Central Asia, many citizens in Western and Central Europe, as well as in North America, also suffer from the lack of or inequitable access to water and sanitation services. Inequities are frequently related to sociocultural differences, socio-economic factors and the geographical context (see Box 2.4).

Inequities in access therefore must be fought on three fronts: by reducing geographical disparities, by addressing specific barriers faced by marginalized groups and people living in vulnerable situations, and by reducing affordability concerns.

9.3.1 The Protocol on Water and Health: Driving progress in reducing inequities in access to water and sanitation

The Parties to the Protocol on Water and Health of the United Nations Economic Commission for Europe and the WHO Regional Office for Europe (UNECE/WHO Europe, 1999) have committed to ensure equitable access to safe drinking water and adequate sanitation through accession to or ratification of the Protocol. The Protocol indeed requires its Parties to ensure access to water and sanitation for everyone, and specifically to promote equitable access to water and sanitation *"for all members of the population, especially those who suffer a disadvantage or social exclusion"* (UNECE/WHO Europe, 1999, article 5l).

Since 2011, the Protocol on Water and Health has developed tools and carried out country-level activities to support countries in their efforts to improve equitable access to water and sanitation.

The publication *No one left behind: Good practices to ensure equitable access to water and sanitation in the pan-European region* (UNECE/WHO Europe, 2012) presents good practices and lessons learned from throughout the pan-European region on the policies and measures to be enacted to provide equitable access.

An analytic tool, the *Equitable Access Score-card* (UNECE/WHO Europe, 2013) supports governments (at the national, regional and municipal level) and other stakeholders to establish a baseline measure of the equity of access, to identify priorities and to discuss further actions to be taken to address equity gaps. It has already been applied in 11 countries of the pan-European region (Armenia, Azerbaijan, Bulgaria, France (Paris Greater Area), Hungary, the Republic of Moldova, North Macedonia, Portugal, Serbia, Spain (city of Castellón) and Ukraine) and additional countries have expressed interest in applying it. Based on the outcomes of such assessments (UNECE, n.d.b), a number of countries (Hungary, Portugal, the Republic of Moldova, North Macedonia, Armenia, Serbia and others) have taken concrete measures to improve the equity of access to water and sanitation services, including:

- the analysis and evaluation of existing plans, policies and programmes (e.g. in Armenia, where a review of the legislative framework around water was conducted to identify legislative barriers in ensuring equitable access);

- legal and institutional reforms (e.g. in Serbia, where specific equitable access targets were formulated under the Protocol on Water and Health);

- targeted investments (e.g. North Macedonia, where toilets in village schools were renovated); and

- introduction of policy reforms (e.g. in Portugal, where new regulations on water tariffs were developed, with mandatory rules for the general and social tariffs).

More information on these and other initiatives is available in Boxes 9.2, 9.3 and 9.4. The publication *Guidance Note on the Development of Action Plans to Ensure Equitable Access to Water and Sanitation* (UNECE/WHO Europe, 2016), so far used in North Macedonia (Box 9.3) and Armenia (Box 9.4), helps governments to take a structured approach to the development and implementation of actions to ensure equitable access to water and sanitation.

Box 9.2   Continuous progress to improve equitable access to water and sanitation in France

In 2013, the greater Paris area engaged in a detailed assessment of the level of equity of access to water and sanitation in the area, applying the Equitable Access Score-card. The exercise unveiled problems of access for a minority, namely for homeless people and nomadic communities, and also highlighted that the main challenge was to avoid disconnection from the water grid for people who cannot afford to pay for the service (Eau de Paris/SEDIF/SIAAP/OBUSASS/Ministry of Social Affairs and Health, 2013).

In France, several measures have been adopted at the national level to fight inequities in access. The second *National Plan on Household Sanitation 2014–2019* aims to improve household sanitation (which concerns nearly 20% of the French population) through a better understanding of the challenges faced, improvements in the operation of sanitation facilities and a reduction of the financial barriers to the population. The *3rd National Plan on Health and Environment 2015–2019* (Ministry of Solidarities and Health and Ministry of Ecological Transition and Solidarities, n.d.) aims, among others, to strengthen the health–environment dynamics in the territories, in particular by supporting equitable access to safe drinking water and sanitation and by promoting water safety planning and legal protection of 33,000 water catchments. Social pricing of water is subject to an experimental scheme provided by law (Brottes Law) and reported to the National Water Committee (French Parliament, 2013).

Box 9.3   Working with local authorities to improve equitable access to water and sanitation in North Macedonia

A Score-card self-assessment of equitable access to water and sanitation, carried out in 2015–2016 by the National Institute of Public Health and the non-governmental organization (NGO) Journalists for Human Rights in 3 regions, helped understanding the challenges faced in ensuring equitable access, beyond official statistics. Lack of menstrual hygiene management in schools, lack of access to drinking water and sanitation for homeless people, and absence of toilets in religious facilities were identified as major problems, together with the limited financing of the water and sanitation sector. Working closely with local authorities and regional Centers of Public Health, as well as through local media, a campaign was launched to improve the situation: the results of the assessment were not considered as criticisms to the local government, but as an incentive to improve detected weaknesses and to promote access to water and sanitation for all, especially in public institutions and schools. Some school toilets were already renovated in certain municipalities.

Source: National Institute of Public Health/Journalists for Human Rights (2016).

Box 9.4   A National Action Plan to ensure equitable access to water and sanitation adopted in Armenia

To address the main challenges identified in ensuring equitable access to water and sanitation, a national 2018–2020 Action Plan to ensure equitable access to water and sanitation has been officially approved in August 2017 by the State Committee of Water Economy of the Ministry of Energy Infrastructures and Natural Resources of Armenia. This action plan aims to reduce equity gaps by improving access for the 579 rural communities not serviced by centralized water supplies, updating the legislative and institutional framework to ensure alignment with the different dimensions of the human rights to water and sanitation, and operationalizing water and sanitation systems in rural schools, among others.

Source: Ministry of Energy Infrastructures and Natural Resources of Armenia (2017).

9.4

Latin American and the Caribbean

The governments of Latin American and Caribbean countries have long recognized the importance of water supply and sanitation as a vital factor for the preservation and improvement of health (UNECLAC, 1985), but millions of people in the region are still without an adequate source of drinking water, while even more suffer the absence of safe and decent facilities for the disposition of excreta.

In 2015, 65% of the population of Latin America and the Caribbean had access to safely managed drinking water services, but only 22% to safely managed sanitation services. In the same year, 96% used at least a basic water service and 86% at least a basic sanitation service (Figure 9.7) (WHO/UNICEF, 2017a). This means that in the region, there are some 25 million people without access to a basic water service and 222 million without safely managed drinking water services. For sanitation, the situation is far worse: almost 89 million people in the region are without a basic sanitation service, and 495 million without safely managed services (WHO/UNICEF, n.d.). There are large differences between countries (Figure 9.8), but also within countries, as gaps in water and sanitation coverage between the administrative regions within several countries exceed 20 or even 30% (WHO/UNICEF, 2016).

The part of the population that does not have access even to basic water and sanitation services has to adopt alternative solutions (such as, for water supply: individual wells, illegal connections to the water network, water vendors, or taking water directly from rivers, lakes and other water bodies; and for sanitation: latrines and open defecation) (Jouravlev, 2004). Several of these options are expensive per unit of supply and/or do not necessarily guarantee that the water is safe for drinking. Therefore, these 'solutions' are associated with significant health risks, and in the case of sanitation, are one of the principal sources of water pollution.

The majority of people without access to water supply and sanitation services belong to low-income groups and live in rural areas:

- Although unequal income distribution has decreased in the region since the early 2000s, there were still 186 million poor in 2016, representing almost 31% of the population, while 61 million people or 10% of the population were living in extreme poverty (UNECLAC, 2018). Figures 9.9 to 9.12 show the gaps in coverage in different countries by income quintile for water supply and sanitation in urban and rural areas. Gaps in service coverage between income quintiles have slowly decreased over time and are generally larger for sanitation (26% on average) than for water supply (13%). Many people without access to services *"are concentrated in peri-*

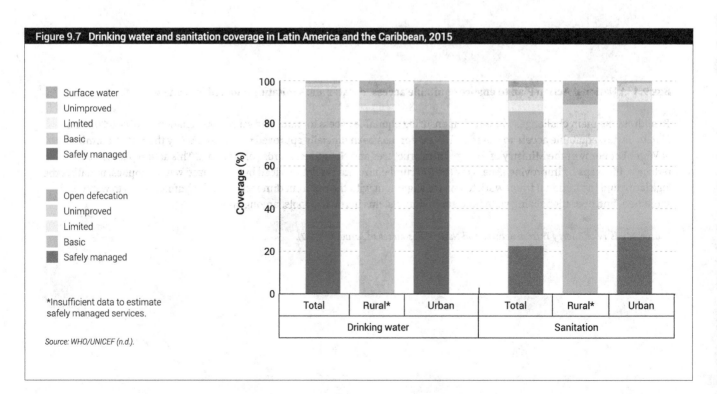

Figure 9.7   Drinking water and sanitation coverage in Latin America and the Caribbean, 2015

Surface water
Unimproved
Limited
Basic
Safely managed

Open defecation
Unimproved
Limited
Basic
Safely managed

*Insufficient data to estimate safely managed services.

Source: WHO/UNICEF (n.d.).

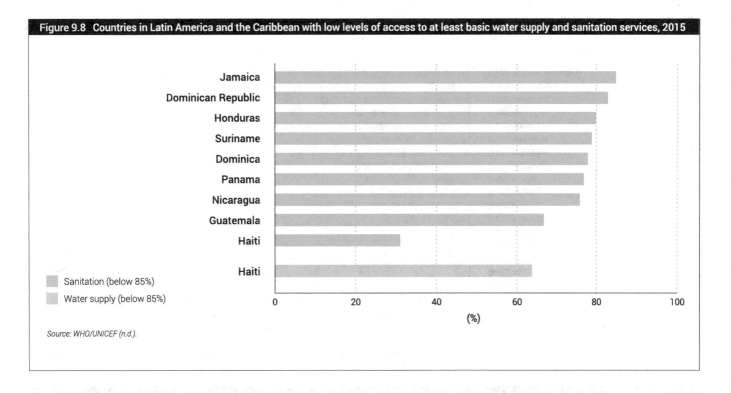

Figure 9.8 Countries in Latin America and the Caribbean with low levels of access to at least basic water supply and sanitation services, 2015

Sanitation (below 85%)

Water supply (below 85%)

Source: WHO/UNICEF (n.d.).

urban areas, mainly in the poverty belts that exist on the periphery of many of the cities in the region. It has proved difficult to provide these marginal areas with services of acceptable quality. The main problems encountered in efforts to expand services to marginal populations have been due, on the one hand, to the high poverty levels and the low payment capacity and culture, and on the other hand, to high construction and operation costs. These populations have often experienced explosive growth and have developed in a disorganized manner, settling in areas far from existing networks and with more difficult topographical conditions." (Jouravlev, 2004, p. 14).

- In the countries of the region, the levels of coverage of water supply and sanitation services are significantly lower in rural areas than in urban areas. In terms of access to at least a basic service, the difference between urban and rural areas is 13% for water supply and 22% for sanitation services (WHO/UNICEF, 2017a). Moreover, the technical solutions used in rural areas (such as wells, septic tanks and latrines) usually do not ensure a level of service quality or functionality that is comparable with those available in cities (mainly household connections) (Jouravlev, 2004). Gaps in service coverage between income quintiles are much larger in rural areas than in cities. Access to water and sanitation also tends to be lower among indigenous peoples (WHO/UNICEF, 2016). Lower levels of coverage in rural areas are explained by several factors, namely: low population densities in rural areas making it difficult to organize service provision in an efficient way and to take advantage of the economies of scale, as well as higher poverty rates and the fact that rural communities tend to have less political influence and visibility than urban populations.

The experience of provision of water supply and sanitation services in Latin America and the Caribbean suggests the following minimum basic principles in order to realize the human rights to water and sanitation, and to achieve SDG 6, so that no one is left behind:

- Efficient service provision is essential for satisfying the human rights to water and sanitation. By lowering the cost of service provision, efficiency leads to better affordability and greater opportunities for use. Conversely, increased costs due to inefficiency on the part of service providers, whether public or private, violate the human rights to water and sanitation. Some of the most common forms of inefficiency include overstaffing, corruption, manipulation of accounting and transfer prices, excessive debts, high transaction costs, loss of economies of scale and scope, and capture by special interest groups (unions, politicians or investors). In short, efficiency and equity are not mutually exclusive, but rather complementary (UNECLAC, 2010).

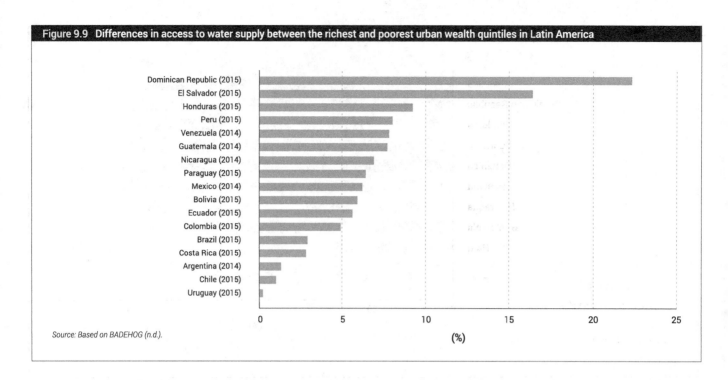

Figure 9.9 Differences in access to water supply between the richest and poorest urban wealth quintiles in Latin America

Source: Based on BADEHOG (n.d.).

(%)

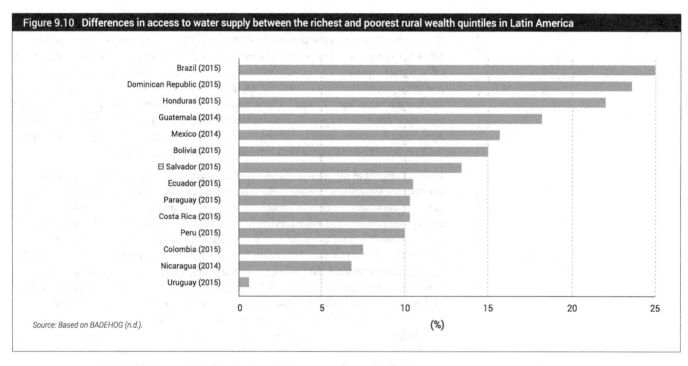

Figure 9.10 Differences in access to water supply between the richest and poorest rural wealth quintiles in Latin America

Source: Based on BADEHOG (n.d.).

(%)

Increased costs due to inefficiency on the part of service providers, whether public or private, violate the human rights to water and sanitation

- Efficiency in this sector is a function of service organization and management. The ability to promote efficiency essentially depends on regulatory frameworks, governance, institutional control, and political culture and will (UNECLAC, 2010). Governments should impose appropriate regulation on both private and municipally or state-owned service providers, based on the notions of fair and reasonable rate-of-return, good faith, due diligence, the duty of efficiency, and the transfer to consumers of the benefits of efficiency. The weight governments assign to the human rights to water and sanitation is reflected in the seriousness and care they show when developing, applying and respecting regulations and institutional frameworks and in their decisions about budgetary allocations (UNECLAC, 2010).

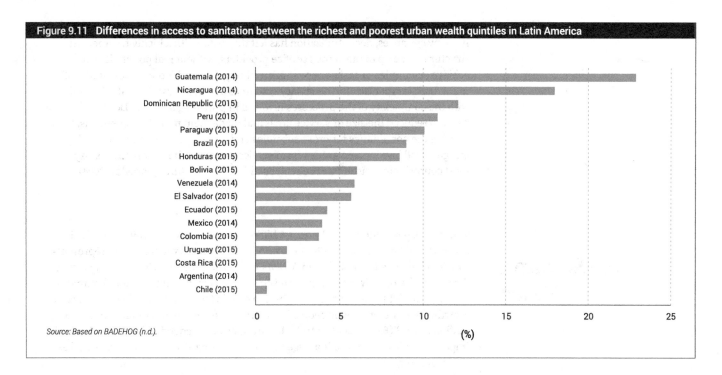

Figure 9.11 Differences in access to sanitation between the richest and poorest urban wealth quintiles in Latin America

Source: Based on BADEHOG (n.d.).

(%)

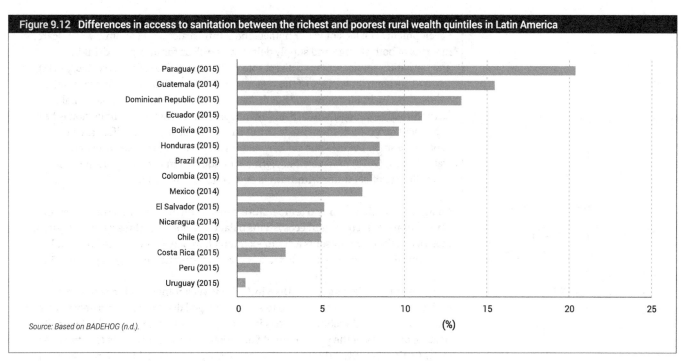

Figure 9.12 Differences in access to sanitation between the richest and poorest rural wealth quintiles in Latin America

Source: Based on BADEHOG (n.d.).

(%)

- These services are expensive to provide and the region has the worst income distribution in the world (UN, 2013). As a result, the poor are not able to exercise their human right to water and sanitation if they do not receive well-organized state support, in the form of both consumption subsidies (to make the water bill more affordable for the poor) and connection subsidies (to facilitate households' connection to the network and the network's expansion). Governments need to recover their traditional role of financing investment in water supply and sanitation, particularly for the purposes of extending coverage to low-income groups. In this respect, political priorities are extremely important. These priorities should be reflected in government budgets, not only in statements to the press (Solanes, 2007).

In many countries, decentralization has left the sector with a highly fragmented structure made up of numerous service providers, without real possibilities to achieve economies of scale or economic viability, and under the responsibility of municipalities that lack the necessary resources and incentives to deal effectively with the complexity of the processes involved in providing services. Decentralization has also reduced the size of service areas and made them more homogeneous, thus limiting the possibilities for cross-subsidies and facilitating the 'cream skimming' that marginalized low-income groups from service provision. It is clearly necessary for most countries to consolidate the sector's industrial structure (Jouravlev, 2004).

9.5
Sub-Saharan Africa

Periodic and chronic water scarcity represents a major challenge to Africa's path to development

The world's population was almost 7.6 billion as of mid-2017, of which 17% live in Africa (1.3 billion) (UNDESA, 2017a). Periodic and chronic water scarcity represents a major challenge to Sub-Saharan Africa's path to development. The poverty rate, as the share of people living on less than US$1.90 a day in 2011 international purchasing power parity (PPP), fell from 57% in 1990 to 43% in 2012. However, due to population growth, the number of poor people has increased from 280 million in 1990 to 330 million in 2012 (Beegle et al., 2016). Moreover, poverty reduction has been slowest in fragile countries, and there is a huge gap between urban and rural areas, as well as across sub-regions.

Periodic and chronic water scarcity represents a major challenge to Africa's path to development. The lack of water management infrastructure (economic water scarcity), in terms of both storage and supply delivery, as well as for improved drinking water and sanitation services, plays a direct role in the persistence of poverty (FAO, 2016). Agriculture contributes 15% of the region's total GDP, with national figures ranging from below 3% in Botswana and South Africa to more than 50% in Chad. Smallholder farms directly employ about 175 million people (OECD/FAO, 2016). Irrigation is heavily dependent on groundwater and evidence suggests that several aquifers are being depleted: a study by the National Aeronautics and Space Administration of the United States (NASA) (2015) reported that eight major aquifers in Africa experienced little to no refilling to offset water withdrawals between 2003 and 2013.

Changes in precipitation and temperature patterns further threaten water availability, agricultural productivity and ecosystems balance. Among the threatened ecosystems in Africa, Lake Chad presents a complex interaction between water security and economic development, which led to a severe humanitarian emergency (Box 9.5).

Achieving the WASH targets of SDG 6 in Africa is yet another challenge that is difficult to overcome, as the access to safely managed drinking water, safely managed sanitation and handwashing facilities is amongst the lowest in the world (Figure 9.13). In 2015, only 24% of the population of Sub-Saharan Africa had access to safe drinking water (WHO/UNICEF, 2017a). However, there is a great variability among countries (Figure 9.14).

In 2015, average access to basic sanitation services in Sub-Saharan Africa was only 28%. People lacking a basic sanitation service either had access to limited sanitation facilities (improved facilities shared by two of more households — 18%), used unimproved facilities such as pit latrines without a slab or platform, hanging latrines or bucket latrines (31%), or practiced open defecation (23%). Only three countries in Sub-Saharan Africa had data to estimate the access to safely managed sanitation: Senegal (24%), Somalia (14%) and Niger (9%) (WHO/UNICEF, 2017a).

In 34 out of 38 African countries with data, less than 50% of the population had basic handwashing facilities in their homes (Figure 9.15). From all Sub-Saharan Africans having basic handwashing facilities, three out of five lived in urban areas (WHO/UNICEF, 2017a).

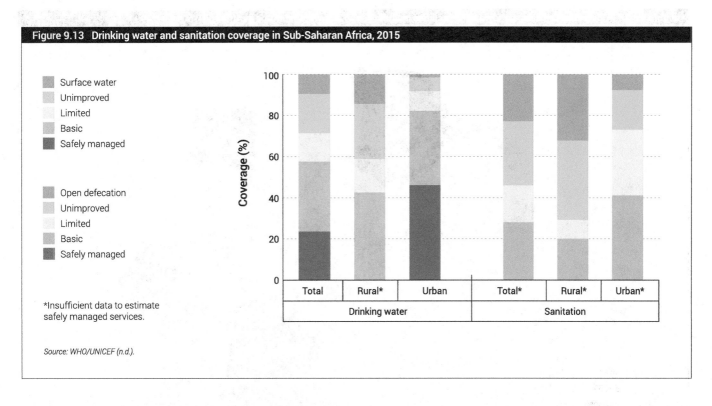

Figure 9.13 Drinking water and sanitation coverage in Sub-Saharan Africa, 2015

*Insufficient data to estimate safely managed services.

Source: WHO/UNICEF (n.d.).

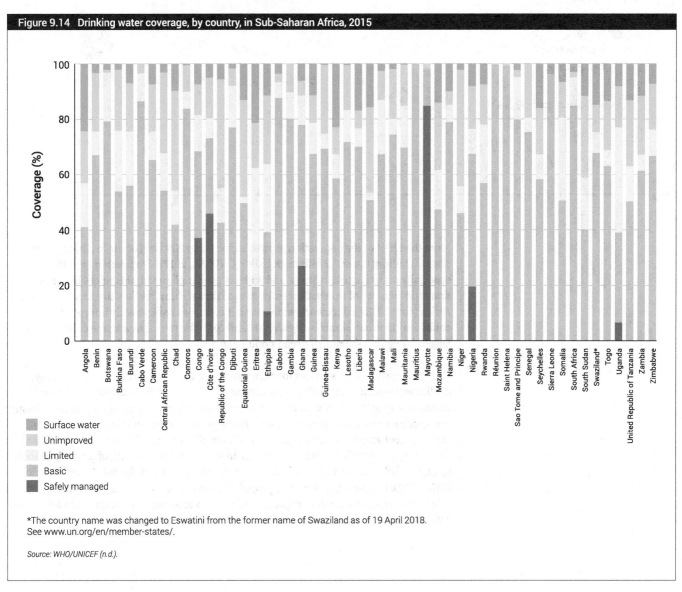

Figure 9.14 Drinking water coverage, by country, in Sub-Saharan Africa, 2015

*The country name was changed to Eswatini from the former name of Swaziland as of 19 April 2018.
See www.un.org/en/member-states/.

Source: WHO/UNICEF (n.d.).

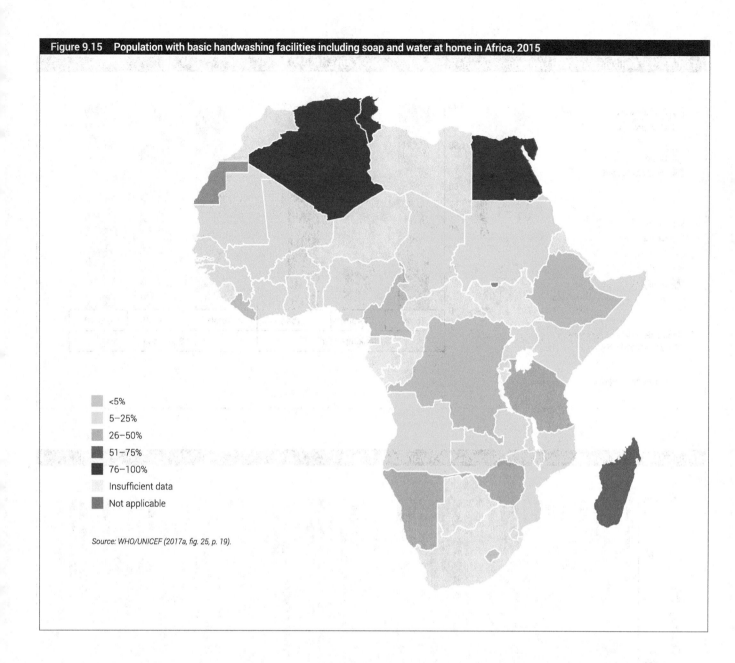

Figure 9.15   Population with basic handwashing facilities including soap and water at home in Africa, 2015

<5%

5–25%

26–50%

51–75%

76–100%

Insufficient data

Not applicable

Source: WHO/UNICEF (2017a, fig. 25, p. 19).

More than half of the population growth expected by 2050 will occur in Africa (more than 1.3 billion, out of 2.2 billion globally) (UNDESA, 2017a). Population growth especially occurs in urban areas, and without proper planning, this might lead to a dramatic increase of slums. Currently, 189 million of slum dwellers live in Sub-Saharan Africa (out of 883 million worldwide). Even if countries have steadily improved living conditions in urban slums between 2000 and 2015, the rate of new home construction lagged far behind the rate of urban population growth (UN, 2018b).

Giving access to WASH services to this growing population, however, is not the only challenge for Africa, as the demands for energy, food, jobs and education will also increase. Population growth can also be seen as an opportunity as 'demographic pressure can spur inventiveness' (Boserup, 1965). However, education remains a challenge in the continent as more than two in five adults are still illiterate (Beegle et al., 2016), and the quality of schooling is often low. While in 2016 an estimated 85% of primary school teachers worldwide were trained, the proportion was only 61% for Sub-Saharan Africa (UN, 2018b). If equal opportunities, proper education and training are guaranteed, the intellectual contribution that might come from this growing population could help Africa get on track for achieving SDG 6.

Box 9.5 BIOsphere and Heritage of Lake Chad (BIOPALT) project: Linking environmental restoration, transboundary resources management and development

Located at the crossroads of Cameroon, the Central African Republic, Chad, Niger and Nigeria, Lake Chad basin provides freshwater and livelihoods to more than 40 million people, while sheltering a high diversity of wildlife (see Figure).

Since the early sixties, the surface of Lake Chad has changed significantly due to variations in rainfall and runoff (urban and agricultural) to the lake and to escalating water use in the region. This caused a significant drop in the water level and a substantial shrinking of the lake surface, by almost 90% from 1963 to 2010 (Gao et al., 2011). In addition to obvious environmental and economic challenges, the shrinkage is seen as one of the reasons for regional insecurity and for the long conflict that has destroyed livelihoods, displaced millions of people and, in general, affected vast portions of the four countries around the lake, already dealing with water insecurity (Nigeria, Niger, Chad and Cameroon) (Okpara et al., 2015).

Figure | Lake Chad: Basin and population

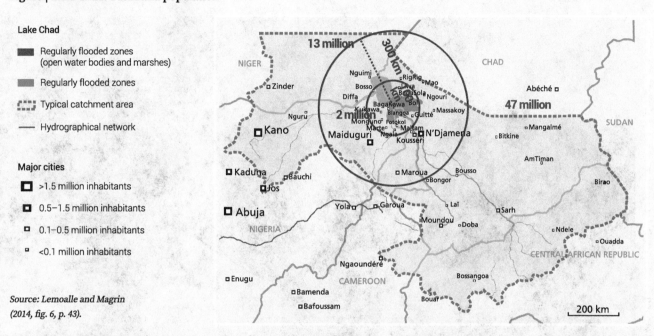

Source: Lemoalle and Magrin
(2014, fig. 6, p. 43).

This led to a humanitarian emergency that is one of the world's most severe. UNOCHA estimated that, in 2018, over 10.7 million people will have needed relief assistance to survive, 72% of which are in Nigeria. The funds needed to address the humanitarian challenges of the people living around the basin have been estimated at US$1.6 billion for 2018. These also include US$90 million for interventions to provide safe and equitable access to water as well as improved facilities to 2.75 million people, many of whom are internally displaced people (IDPs), women and children (UNOCHA, 2018).

Since the beginning of the crisis, governments and humanitarian organizations have developed strategies to work closely with development actors to address the structural causes of the issues that are plaguing Lake Chad. Among these is the Programme to Rehabilitate and Strengthen the Resilience of Lake Chad Basin Systems (PRESIBALT), launched by the Lake Chad Basin Commission and funded by the African Development Bank (LCBC, 2016).

In the PRESIBALT framework, UNESCO is currently implementing the BIOsphere and Heritage of Lake Chad (BIOPALT) project. The project aims to strengthen the capacity of Member States of the Lake Chad Basin Commission (LCBC) to safeguard and sustainably manage the transboundary hydrological, biological and cultural resources of the Lake Chad basin, thereby contributing to reducing poverty and promoting peace (UNESCO, n.d.).

With its focus on joint management of transboundary resources, including water, the project will contribute to addressing the issues of discrimination and inequality in access to water and sanitation. This will be done through a set of actions that will include capacity building for decision makers, experts and local communities on the management of transboundary waters, using UNESCO's methodology From Potential Conflict to Cooperation Potential (PCCP).[1] In particular, the involvement of the community-based organization for the duration of the whole project (not only for the trainings) will help to ensure that local communities, who have often been left behind, will directly shape and benefit from the project outcomes.

---

[1] www.unesco.org/new/en/pccp.

CHAPTER 10

Strategies and response options for inclusive development

World Summit on the Information Society (WSIS) Forum 2017 in Geneva, Switzerland

WWAP | Richard Connor, Stefan Uhlenbrook, Michela Miletto and Engin Koncagül

OHCHR | Rio Hada

With contributions from: Neil Dhot (AquaFed); Tamara Avellán (UNU-FLORES); and Nidhi Nagabhatla (UNU-INWEH)

Taking account of the challenges and opportunities presented throughout this report, this chapter describes a series of strategies and response options that directly address these challenges from technical, economic, knowledge and governance perspectives.

10.1
Introduction

Earlier chapters of this report have examined challenges and opportunities related to achieving universal access to water supply and sanitation — and improving overall water resources management — through technical, social, governance and economic approaches (Chapters 2–5). These challenges have been further elaborated in the context of disadvantaged groups in urban and rural settings (Chapters 6–7), for refugees and forcibly displaced populations (Chapter 8), and across different regions (Chapter 9).

This chapter further builds on these opportunities for improvement and attempts to address several basic questions, namely: *What* needs to be done (and *why* action cannot be avoided), by *whom*, and *how*, in order to 'leave no one behind' with respect to water.

10.2
Enhancing water supply and improving accessibility

Water availability can be seen as a function of two distinct but inseparable features. The first relates to **water *supply***, which corresponds to the volumes of water that can be withdrawn sustainably from surface and sub-surface sources, as well as from unconventional sources. This includes desalination of sea water, water reuse and recycling, and rainwater and fog harvesting. Increasing water use efficiency in all major water use sectors (agriculture, energy, industry and municipal/domestic) can also go a long way toward lowering overall demand and thus freeing up water supplies for other users, including ecosystems. The second relates to ***accessibility***, which involves transporting water from the source and rendering it available to different users in sufficient quantities and appropriate quality for its intended use.

Whereas the need to **improve water resource management** is particularly critical for areas experiencing chronic or recurring water scarcity (where demand exceeds sustainable supplies, or where supplies are compromised by pollution, land degradation or other phenomena), the need to **improve accessibility** exists across all types of hydrological regimes, even in places of relative water abundance. Barriers to improved accessibility are often social and/or economic in nature.[40] Although both supply and accessibility are critical to ensuring water security for all, water accessibility has historically received less media (and arguably political) attention. Yet, from the perspective of 'leaving no one behind' and realizing the human rights to water supply and sanitation, overcoming the challenges of accessibility can be equally — and in many specific cases even more — critical than that of addressing issues of supply and scarcity.

From a technical perspective, the potential responses to addressing the lack of drinking water supply and sanitation services to groups in disadvantaged and marginalized situations can vary significantly from one place to another, depending on **local physical conditions and human and institutional capacities**, among others (see Chapters 2, 3 and 4). Indeed, whereas sizeable high-density urban communities provide opportunities for large-scale centralized water, sanitation and hygiene (WASH) infrastructure and facilities though resource-sharing and economies of scale, less costly decentralized supply and sanitation systems have been shown to be successful solutions in smaller urban settlements (see Chapter 6), including refugee camps (see Chapter 8). For people in low-density rural areas, where shared facilities can offer a more affordable alternative to household-level services, the objective is to bring these facilities closer to people's homes, while ensuring and maintaining their safety and affordability (see Chapter 7).

In terms of selecting the most appropriate WASH technology, the basic principle is therefore not one of 'best practice', but rather one of '**best fit**', based on current and expected future socio-economic circumstances. And, in order to select the 'best fit', it is essential to involve the different user groups during the initial decision-making process as well as throughout the implementation and operational phases.

This does not necessarily imply that each specific case should be addressed without any consideration of broader-scale realities. For example, integrated urban and rural planning can provide exceptional dividends in terms of both water resources management (e.g. source protection) and the provision of WASH and other water services, generating co-benefits related to food and energy security, livelihoods and employment opportunities (WWAP/UN-Water, 2018). Addressing the challenges faced by the rural poor, especially in relation to managing water in the context of climate change, will require increased investment in water infrastructure such as water harvesting or irrigation, improving the advisory services for crop and water management, and planning and implementation of drought preparedness plans. These actions, when coupled with better access to **social protection**, including social security schemes (pensions and insurance) and more targeted social assistance programmes, will improve the economic and productive capacity of poor smallholder farmers and their families (see Chapter 7).

> The need to improve accessibility exists across all types of hydrological regimes, even in places of relative water abundance

10.3
Addressing the investment gap

Evidence suggests that the **return on investment in WASH** can be considerably high, with a global average benefit–cost ratio of 5.5 for improved sanitation and 2.0 for improved drinking water, when broader macroeconomic benefits are taken into account (Hutton and Andrés, 2018). Yet water supply and sanitation remain grossly underfunded. According to one study, a threefold increase in current annual investment levels (to US$114 billion) would be required to meet WASH-related Sustainable Development Goal (SDG) Targets 6.1 and 6.2 (Hutton and Varughese, 2016). Notably, this estimated investment does not include continuous operation and maintenance costs, nor investments needed to achieve the other targets of SDG 6 related to ambient water quality, water use efficiency, ecosystems, integrated water resources management (IWRM) and means of implementation.

---

40 This notion of 'accessibility', or lack thereof, is somewhat synonymous with the concept of 'economic water scarcity', *"whereby access is not limited by resource availability, but by human, institutional and financial constraints over distribution of the resource to different user groups"* (WWAP, 2012, p. 126).

Insufficient funding and lack of effective financing mechanisms have created a barrier to achieving the WASH targets for disadvantaged and marginalized groups. As detailed in Chapter 5, large WASH providers can theoretically resort to **commercial financing**, but in reality, WASH investment only makes up a small portion of private sector financing, which is dominated by transportation and energy infrastructure. Commercial financing can be even more difficult to obtain for smaller service providers and households, who have to rely on other means, such as grants or microfinancing (when available).

A certain proportion of the investment gap could also be overcome through **increased system efficiency**, which uses already available finances more effectively and can significantly reduce overall costs. However, targeted subsidies for vulnerable groups and equitable tariff structures will remain an important source for cost recovery and investments in WASH services.

The support of the **international donor community** will remain critical in the developing world but cannot be the main source of funding. The WASH-related part of official development assistance (ODA) has stabilized at about 5% of total ODA commitments over the last years, and is unlikely to increase dramatically in the future (UN, 2018a). ODA is particularly helpful in mobilizing investments from other sources, such as commercial and blended finance, including the private sector. However, it will be incumbent upon **national governments** to dramatically increase the amounts of public funding made available for the expansion of WASH services. Such increases in domestic public funding also help create an economic environment that facilitates additional investments from other sources, including commercial/repayable finances. Moreover, domestic public funds can be critical to de-risk water infrastructure investments that often require large upfront investments with a relatively long payback time. In many cases this will require reforms to increase the efficiency of the sector and its utilities, and to increase its overall creditworthiness (for instance, by ensuring that utilities are able to function on a cost recovery basis). Necessary **reforms** include technical measures (e.g. distribution systems, reduction of non-revenue water, metering, etc.) as well as non-technical/governance-related measures.

In the water domain, the expression 'privatization' raises a question of terminology, as it is used to designate two quite different notions. The first corresponds to the granting of water licences to commodity companies that use water for products to sell. The second characterizes the process of awarding the operations of a public drinking water or wastewater service, in part or in whole, to an enterprise which operates under the control of the awarding public authority. In both cases, the inclusion of the human rights to water and sanitation must be ensured by private companies and private water operators. In terms of the **privatization of water supply and sanitation services**, good governance (see Chapter 4) is critical to ensure that sovereign responsibilities rest with the designated officials, regardless whether operations are outsourced or not. With or without privatization, weak governance is the root cause of failure of water and sanitation operations, often caused by the lack of financial resources or by failure to prevent corruption. When properly regulated through oversight of the public authority, privatization can provide an additional means to increase overall system efficiency and to bring more water and improved sanitation to more — ideally all — people. Privatization can also enable accountability, services designed for users, appropriate rules that protect human health and the environment, and sufficient investment. However, prior to establishing such a project, the public authority should answer the following questions: i) Is the public utility's operation of existing assets in a difficult situation (e.g. insufficient service, lack of qualified staff, continuous maintenance)? ii) Is the public utility facing important investment programme challenges, such as the extension of infrastructure, or the rehabilitation of existing ones? If so, does this program cover the entire utility or parts thereof? iii) Is the utility facing financial constraints (e.g. difficulty setting economic tariffs or issuing debt)? According to the answers, the public authority will be able to determine if there is scope for a public–private partnership (PPP), and which form of PPP could best accommodate the need (e.g. concession, affermage/lease, build–operate–transfer (BOT), etc.).

Insufficient funding and lack of effective financing mechanisms have created a barrier to achieving the WASH targets for disadvantaged and marginalized groups

However, increasing the amount of funding and investment alone does not necessarily ensure that WASH services will reach all those who are most disadvantaged. Indeed, as described in Chapter 5 and Section 9.4, investments in WASH infrastructure have often failed to reach the poorest people, households and communities. **Subsidies** must therefore be appropriately designed, transparent and targeted, and **tariff structures** must be designed and implemented with the objectives of achieving cost recovery and economic efficiency, while also taking aspects of equity, affordability and the appropriate level of service for each specific targeted population group into account (see Chapter 5).

10.4 Knowledge and capacity development

Scientific research, development and innovation are essential to support informed decision-making. Technical solutions aimed at improving access to WASH services for all, and particularly for groups in vulnerable and disadvantaged situations, require further development. Although some progress has been made in terms of designing equable tariff structures and other ways to improve affordability that benefit — rather than penalize — people in poor and disadvantaged situations, further research and analysis into the economic dimensions of WASH services in support of inclusion would also be beneficial. For example, the tremendous long-term benefits of improved WASH services are well documented (e.g. reduction of childhood diseases, improved education and workforce participation, and benefits in the workplace and in schools, particularly for girls and women), but more research is required to further develop economic models that can robustly assess all benefits at local and even national scales.

Greater **knowledge and information** about the poorest and most disadvantaged groups are required in order to develop effective policies and implement 'best-fit' WASH solutions at the local/community level. Local and traditional knowledge can prove highly valuable in this regard. Unfortunately, people living in informal urban and peri-urban settlements (i.e. slums) are often lacking a recognized status (see Section 6.2), and very poor rural communities are often not appropriately or fairly included in census taking, thus falling 'under the radar'. Citizen- and community-led data collection and documentation can generate new knowledge that helps to better understand needs, resources and capacities, thus empowering local stakeholders to influence governments and openly participate in the design and implementation of the most technically suitable, affordable and socially acceptable WASH solutions.

> **Greater knowledge and information about the poorest and most disadvantaged groups are required in order to develop effective policies and implement 'best-fit' WASH solutions at the local/community level**

It is also critical to recognize the very different realities and challenges afflicting the poor and disadvantaged in rural and urban settings (see Chapters 6 and 7). With the vast majority of population growth expected to occur in both large and smaller cities in developing countries, **accelerated urbanization** poses a great challenge in terms of providing safe, reliable and affordable water supply and sanitation services for the influx of new residents, while maintaining the levels of service already provided to existing users. However, despite sometimes severely restricted financial resources, this rapid urban growth also generates opportunities for implementing locally appropriate WASH solutions — without necessarily replicating the larger, often more investment — and capital-intensive centralized systems that have dominated urban WASH services in most developed countries.

Although sustainable development challenges will be increasingly concentrated in cities, it is essential that rural populations are not 'left behind' in terms of policies and overall support. The **rural poor**, who account for nearly 80% of people living in extreme poverty[41] — the overwhelming majority of whom live in Southern Asia and Sub-Saharan Africa (World Bank, 2016a) — must no longer be overlooked or deliberately ignored in policy-making and planning. The information and capacity-building needs of disadvantaged rural communities are similar to those described above for the urban poor, but also include knowledge related to water resource allocation and the securing of water rights, which they need in order to improve livelihoods and expand their economic base beyond subsistence farming, animal husbandry and/or fishing. Beside the economic status, differences in societal structures and predominant social networks between poor urban and rural communities also need to be considered.

---

[41] The international poverty line for extreme poverty is US$1.90 a day in 2011 Purchasing Power Parity.

Monitoring progress is another important aspect of knowledge and capacity development. Its value goes beyond accessing progress towards SDG Targets 6.1 and 6.2 to also provide valuable information about whether policies and technical solutions adopted to improving WASH services are achieving specified objectives and, if not, what can be done to improve performance. Disaggregated data (with respect to gender, age, income groups, ethnicity, geography, etc.) and social inclusion analyses are key tools in determining which groups are at greatest risk of being 'left behind', and why. Use of information and communication technology (ICT) can greatly facilitate monitoring progress through citizen data collection and improve overall access to knowledge. However, although two-thirds of the global population use the internet, a much smaller proportion has access to it in Africa and South Asia (Poushter, 2016; We are Social and Hootsuite, 2018) (see Prologue, Section 3.viii).

All of these aspects also require improved **institutional capacity** to assist and facilitate policy reforms and citizen participation at the appropriate levels of decision-making and policy implementation on the ground. The development of **human capacity** — through vocational, technical and academic training — needs to be supported, especially at the local and community levels where efforts to achieve progress towards SDG Targets 6.1 and 6.2 are operationalized.

10.5 Governance

> Governance structures need to guarantee fair and equitable allocation of water resources to all

Several chapters of this report highlight the importance of **community-based action** in addressing the root causes of 'leaving people behind' with respect to water and sanitation. As described in Chapter 4, *good governance* seeks to move away from hierarchical power structures while embracing concepts of accountability, transparency, legitimacy, public participation, justice and efficiency — principles that are in line with the human rights-based approach (HRBA). Inclusive, cooperative governance involves the participation of government agencies as well as non-state actors actively engaged in partnerships and dialogue. However, for policy development and (especially) implementation to be truly effective at the community level, central or national governments need to create an enabling institutional environment through which participative governance can take place. This includes institutions with sufficient capacity and authority to monitor and enforce agreed norms, and forums through which stakeholders can provide constructive input or express their opinions. Such institutional transformations are not only possible but are already happening, as exemplified by examples from Armenia (see Box 9.4) and the Lake Chad basin (see Box 9.5).

Governance structures need to guarantee fair and equitable allocation of water resources to all. **Water resource allocation** mechanisms can be established to achieve different socio-economic policy objectives, such as safeguarding food and/or energy security, or for promoting industrial growth, but ensuring that enough water is available (and of suitable quality) to meet everyone's basic human needs (for domestic as well as subsistence purposes) must be a guaranteed priority. As highlighted in Chapters 4 and 7, inequalities in land ownership can translate into unequal access to and benefits from water resources. For example, women's unequal rights to inheritance and land ownership in some countries can directly lead to discrimination with respect to water allocation. Efforts to ensure secure and equal access to water in rural areas will require continued efforts to increase the visibility of small-scale users with regards to water for irrigation, as well as greater recognition of their contribution to national food security.

At the other end of the 'local to global' spectrum, the international community remains heavily committed to the **2030 Agenda for Sustainable Development**. 'Leaving no one behind' with respect to water implies meeting SDG 6, and Targets 6.1 (drinking water) and 6.2 (sanitation) in particular. It is incumbent upon the international community to provide guidance, assistance and support to national and sub-national governments and other actors in implementing policies to provide WASH services to all (and most notably to the poorest and most disadvantaged groups), as well as monitoring and reporting on progress.

Water *conflict* is a term used to describe water disputes resulting from divergent or opposing interests between water users over access to and use of water resources and its services. These can be states, groups or individuals. Although a wide range of water conflicts appear throughout history, rarely have traditional wars been fought primarily over water (Gleick, 1993). Water has more often been a source of tension and a factor in conflicts that began for a range of reasons (see Prologue, Section 1.v). The flipside of the coin is that water, or more specifically the joint management of water resources and systems, can be an opportunity for cooperation between countries, groups or individuals. **Transboundary cooperation** over water can be an important tool for promoting collaboration between countries, which in turn supports peace and stability, economic prosperity and environmental sustainability (Box 10.1).

The linkages between water and **migration** have been attracting increasing attention (Miletto et al., 2017), although they have yet to be fully incorporated into international migration policy (Mach and Richter, 2018).

Forced displacement as a result of either armed conflict or the sudden onset of natural hazards places people in highly vulnerable situations with respect to WASH services. Addressing this challenge would greatly benefit from increased harmonization between developmental assistance (focused on prevention, risk reduction and long-term approaches to avoid crises) and humanitarian aid (which addresses crises as they occur).

The WASH-related challenges faced by **refugees and internally displaced people (IDPs)** require special focused political responsiveness. As described throughout Chapter 8, both contingency planning and crisis response actions are necessary to ensure that refugees and displaced people have access to safely managed WASH services. In the case of service provision in refugee camps, harmonization of service levels with surrounding community/national standards is essential for combatting social discrimination and creating access equality. This should not be seen as an additional burden but as an opportunity, since collective and cooperative efforts to provide WASH to camps can also contribute to improving water infrastructure and services to host communities (see Box 9.1).

> **Forced displacement as a result of either armed conflict or the sudden onset of natural hazards places people in highly vulnerable situations with respect to WASH services**

Box 10.1 Conflict prevention and cooperation over transboundary water resources

The High-Level Panel for Water and Peace demonstrated that transboundary water cooperation can be an important tool for promoting collaboration between countries (Global High-Level Panel on Water and Peace, 2017). Implementing truly integrated water management in transboundary basins, considering all users and uses of water, supports regional integration and can provide benefits far beyond the provision of water services to all members of society. These benefits can include peace and stability, economic prosperity and environmental sustainability. It can also help to address migration crises, when used as an adaptation strategy to cope with asymmetric/unbalanced availability of and access to water and other resources.

The percentage of a transboundary basin's area covered by an operational agreement has been adopted as an indicator to measure the degree of cooperation in place to implement integrated water resources management (IWRM) in a transboundary context (Indicator 6.5.2 of SDG 6; UNECE/UNESCO, 2018). The operational agreements and the joint bodies that oversee its implementation are very diverse. There is no universally applicable solution or 'one model fits all', as solutions should be tailored to specific circumstances. The average percentage of transboundary river and lake basin area covered by operational arrangements across 86 countries amounts to 64%. For aquifers, based on 63 countries, the ratio is 47% (UN, 2018a).

Countries reported several obstacles that were standing in the way of reaching agreements, including *"lack of political will and power asymmetries among riparian countries; fragmented national legal, institutional and administrative frameworks; lack of financial, human and technical capacity; and poor data availability, especially in relation to transboundary aquifers and their boundaries"* (UN, 2018a, pp. 13–14). Achieving Target 6.5 of the Sustainable Development Goals (SDGs), whereby all transboundary basins are covered under an operational agreement by 2030, will therefore require accelerated progress in tackling the relevant challenges.

IWRM remains the central paradigm that underpins good water governance and, as described in Chapter 1, an HRBA can provide a helpful perspective to understanding and implementing IWRM, with emphasis on its accountability, participation and non-discrimination principles. An HRBA to IWRM adds critical elements of equality and non-discrimination, equitable distribution of resources and benefits, and strengthened accountability and remedies. An HRBA seeks to identify groups and individuals who are left behind from development progress, whose rights are being violated or unfulfilled and whose voices are not heard, and to understand the reasons why certain people are unable to claim their rights. An HRBA identifies those who have the responsibility to act, and their obligations as duty-bearers under international law, and works to strengthen the capacity of both duty-bearers to fulfil their obligations and rights-holders to claim and exercise their rights. Private businesses and water service providers also have specific responsibilities to respect all human rights and ensure that their activities do not infringe upon the people's enjoyment of the human rights to water and sanitation.

Women occupy critical roles within water management and conservation, as women possess a unique relationship with water at the household and community levels. One example at the household scale is that women are primary influencers of children. As such, they can instill values of water conservation and sustainable use, thereby supporting future generations in valuing and managing water wisely. Women and girls can also facilitate networking opportunities through participation in the water economy, as tackling rigid gender roles in the water sector is a critical gap, more so in communities living in vulnerable situations (Thompson et al., 2017).

> In order to achieve equality, states have an obligation to prioritize individuals and groups that are particularly vulnerable to discrimination or exclusion

10.6
Roles and responsibilities in realizing the human rights to water and sanitation

All actors involved in the realization of the human rights to water and sanitation on a non-discriminatory and equal basis hold specific obligations and responsibilities.

10.6.1 Obligations of states

Article 2 (1) of the International Covenant on Economic, Social and Cultural Rights (ICESCR) requires states to take steps to progressively realize economic, social and cultural rights, and declares that *"such steps should be deliberate, concrete and targeted as clearly as possible towards meeting the obligations recognized in the Covenant"* (CESCR, 1990, para. 2). Human rights define individuals as rights-holders entitled to water and sanitation, and states as duty-bearers that have to guarantee access to WASH for all, using the maximum of their available resources. According to the ICESCR, State parties must **respect, protect and fulfil** human rights. These obligations are clarified in General Comment No. 15 on the human right to water (CESCR, 2002b):

- **Respect:** States may not prevent people from enjoying their human rights to water and sanitation and may not endorse, perpetuate and reinforce discriminatory and stigmatizing practices.

- **Protect:** States must prevent third parties from interfering with people's enjoyment of their human rights to water and sanitation and foresee remedy infringements.

- **Fulfil:** States are responsible for ensuring that the conditions are in place for everyone to enjoy the human rights to water and sanitation, using the maximum of their available resources.

In order to achieve equality, states have an obligation to prioritize individuals and groups that are particularly vulnerable to discrimination or exclusion. The principles of **non-discrimination and equality** recognize that people face different barriers and have different needs, whether because of inherent characteristics or as a result of discriminatory practices, and therefore require differentiated support or treatment. Human rights law will sometimes require state parties to take affirmative action to diminish or eliminate conditions that cause or perpetuate discrimination.

Under **international human rights law**, states are obliged to respect the enjoyment of the human rights to water and sanitation in other countries, to refrain from actions that interfere with the enjoyment of those rights, and to prevent their own citizens and companies from violating those rights in other countries. Furthermore, states should facilitate the realization of the right to water in other countries, for example through provision of water resources, financial and technical assistance, and necessary aid when required, in a manner that is consistent with the Covenant and other human rights standards, as well as sustainable and culturally appropriate.

10.6.2 Responsibilities of non-state actors

States bear the main responsibility to protect individuals and communities against infringements by non-state actors. However, non-state actors also have human rights responsibilities and may be held accountable for the infringement of human rights (HRC, 2014). For example, the corporate responsibility[42] to respect human rights means that corporations should act with **due diligence** to avoid infringing on the human rights of others, and to identify, prevent and address any harms that do occur (OHCHR, 2011). Non-governmental organizations (NGOs) and international organizations can play an important role in service provision and they need to ensure substantive equality and accountability in such endeavour.

---

[42] As specified in the publication "*Eliminating discrimination and inequalities in access to water and sanitation*" (UN-Water, 2015, p. 26), the term "responsibility" rather than "duty" is meant to indicate that respecting rights is not currently an obligation that international human rights law generally imposes directly on companies, although elements of it may be reflected in domestic laws. It is a global standard of expected conduct acknowledged in virtually every voluntary and soft-law instrument related to corporate responsibility. See: The UN "Protect, Respect and Remedy" Framework for Business and Human Rights (HRC, 2008).

10.6.3 International cooperation

International organizations, such as the United Nations (UN), international trade and financial institutions, and development cooperation partners must ensure that their policies and actions respect human rights. International organizations are called upon to ensure that their assistance is channelled towards the countries or regions that are least able to realize the rights to water and sanitation. Assessments show that at the international level, only half of the development assistance directed towards sanitation and drinking water is targeted at regions where 70% of the global unserved live (WHO, 2012). Moreover, notwithstanding the increasing trend in the overall availability of resources for development cooperation, meeting the world's needs for water and sanitation would require much more targeted and increased investment in these sectors (UNGA, 2016, para. 22). This will also require the incorporation of human rights frameworks in development cooperation partners' funding policies and programme design and implementation (UNGA, 2017, para. 84).

An important element of the human rights-based approach is to strengthen the capacity of states as duty-bearers, as well as the capacity of rights-holders to understand and claim their rights to water and sanitation. When resources are insufficient, states must request external or international assistance (CESCR, 1990) and financial institutions may impose conditions upon assistance for measures that are not compliant with human rights. Promotion of national ownership of development is crucial for the long-term sustainability and accountability of projects sponsored with international support (HRC, 2010). Development partners can support existing national action plans to reduce disparities in access to water and sanitation and build the capacities of duty-bearers to meet their obligations (HRC, 2011c). However, states remain the primary duty-bearer to ensure the progressive realization of the human rights to water and sanitation for all on an equal basis, and have the ultimate obligation to respect, protect and fulfil those rights.

CHAPTER 11

The way forward

Gathering of women and man in a Maasai village in Kenya

WWAP | Richard Connor, Stefan Uhlenbrook and Engin Koncagül

The 2030 Agenda for Sustainable Development, with its Sustainable Development Goals (SDGs), marks a new era of universality. The 193 countries of the United Nations (UN) General Assembly have committed to eradicate poverty and achieve sustainable development in all dimensions within just, equitable, open and inclusive societies in which the water and sanitation-related needs of everyone, especially those in the most vulnerable situations, are met. The fulfilment of the human rights to safe drinking water and sanitation is fundamental to the achievement of all the SDGs.

The links between water and broader decisions regarding food and energy security, humanitarian crises, economic development, and environmental sustainability often remain unrecognized or poorly understood. Yet, in an increasingly globalized world, the impacts of water-related decisions cross borders and affect everyone. The intensification of extreme events, environmental degradation (including decreasing water availability and quality), population growth, rapid urbanization, unsustainable and inequitable patterns of production and consumption (within and between countries), actual and potential conflicts, and unprecedented migratory flows are among the interconnected pressures faced by humanity, hitting those in vulnerable situations often the hardest through their impacts on water. And, as the demand for limited water resources grows and the impacts of climate change become more severe, so does the potential for conflicts over competing uses and between different users of water. However, cooperation and multi-sectoral water interventions can lead to outcomes that are greater than the sum of their parts, for example, where co-benefits along the water–food–energy–environment–poverty nexus outweigh the costs and trade-offs. In this respect, a human rights-based approach to integrated water resources management (IWRM) provides a more holistic people-centred pathway for answering the call to 'leave no one behind'.

Progress towards the 2030 Agenda requires a renegotiation of power relations at all levels, equitable participation and representation of all groups being (or at risk of being) left behind, as well as new partnerships in order to transform the economic, social and political processes that guide water resources management and drive the provision of safe and affordable water supply and sanitation services.

Those 'left behind' need appropriate representation in political and other decision-making processes, either directly or through civil society organizations with a clear mandate from those they represent. This is why public awareness and the empowerment of communities are critical for the realization of the human rights to safe drinking water and sanitation. Providing people in disadvantaged situations with opportunities to actively participate in determining and implementing their own water management solutions can lead to more resilient communities, particularly for those groups farthest from centres of power.

Young Inuits performing during a ceremony in Ottawa, Canada

Good governance — with a focus on accountability for action, integrity and transparency to build trust and empower the most disadvantaged groups — is essential for successful implementation of water policies. Appropriate regulatory and legal frameworks, including a mix of incentives and enforced penalties ('carrots and sticks'), are also critical to achieving progress. Evidence-based knowledge on water resources and water-related issues, continually expanded and analysed, and adequate capacity development for the water sector and beyond are essential in order to guide policy-making and practice. Sufficient financing and the fair and effective management of financial resources form the ultimate expression of political support and are crucial for fulfilling the human rights to safe drinking water and sanitation and realizing the transformative Agenda 2030.

Although each of these responses generally applies to nearly all situations, addressing the inequalities faced by disadvantaged groups will also require tailored solutions that take account of the day-to-day realities of people and communities in vulnerable situations. The challenges and lack of opportunities of people living in extreme poverty can be quite distinct from one group to another. For example, the standard of living that can be achieved for less than US$1.90 per day is likely to be very different for people in urban settlements than for those living in rural communities. Beyond socio-economic and environmental conditions, further distinctions can arise based on the region/country/neighbourhood where they live, what 'groups' they belong to (including gender), and the extent to which they may have (or lack) support from extended family or other social networks, among other factors. Water supply and sanitation policies need to distinguish between different populations and prepare specific actions to address each of them — hence the need for solid, disaggregated data to inform tailored solutions.

Unless exclusion and inequality are explicitly and responsively addressed in both policy and practice, water interventions will continue to fail to reach those most in need and who are likely to benefit most

Overcoming the financial challenges of fulfilling the human rights to water and sanitation is entirely possible, but it is important to identify the most appropriate level of service that is affordable and sustainable for groups in disadvantaged situations. Population density will greatly influence both capital and operational costs of both water supply and sanitation systems in low-income urban areas. For example, the implementation of decentralized wastewater treatment systems (DEWATS) can be appropriate for medium-density peri-urban areas and can enable the eventual use of networked systems once the population density reaches a critical (and economically viable) mass. Given scarce resources, governments should encourage service providers to increase their efficiency, in order to keep costs down and hence to make services more affordable. Improved financial performance can also help attract additional external sources of financing. The recovery of water and useful by-products from treated wastewater can generate supplementary revenue streams for service providers and create new opportunities for local businesses and employment.

Change requires genuinely participatory processes, bringing in and valuing new and diverse voices, so that people — including those 'left behind' — can, as rights-holders, actually influence decisions. This requires shifting deep-seated and unconscious biases and discrimination by changing attitudes and norms within water institutions and at all levels. It also requires a recognition of states as the primary duty-bearers for ensuring that the human rights to safe drinking water and sanitation are realized for all, on a non-discriminatory basis.

Coda

People from different groups are 'left behind' for different reasons. Discrimination, exclusion, marginalization, entrenched power asymmetries and material inequalities are among the main obstacles to achieving the human rights to safe drinking water and sanitation for all and realizing the water-related SDGs of the 2030 Agenda. Poorly designed and inadequately implemented policies, inefficient and improper use of financial resources, as well as policy gaps fuel the persistence of inequalities in access to safe drinking water and sanitation. Unless exclusion and inequality are explicitly and responsively addressed in both policy and practice, water interventions will continue to fail to reach those most in need and who are likely to benefit most.

Improving water resources management and providing access to safe and affordable drinking water and sanitation for all is essential for eradicating poverty, building peaceful and prosperous societies, and ensuring that 'no one is left behind' on the road towards sustainable development. These goals are entirely achievable, provided there is a collective will to do so.

References

Abdulsamed, F. 2011. *Somali Investment in Kenya*. Briefing Paper. London, Chatam House. www.chathamhouse.org/publications/papers/view/109621.

Abbott, K. W. and Snidal, D. 2000. Hard and soft law in international governance. *International Organization*, Vol. 54, No. 3, pp. 421–456.

ADB (Asian Development Bank). 2016. *Asian Water Development Outlook: Strengthening Water Security in Asia and the Pacific*. Manila, ADB. www.adb.org/sites/default/files/publication/189411/awdo-2016.pdf.

Alabaster, G. 2015. *Lake Victoria Water and Sanitation Initiative*. UN-Habitat. Unpublished Progress Report.

Almeida, M., Butler, D. and Friedler, E. 1999. At-source domestic wastewater quality. *Urban Water*, Vol. 1, pp. 49–55. doi.org/10.1016/S1462-0758(99)00008-4.

Altieri, M. and Nicholls, C. 2008. Los impactos del cambio climático sobre las comunidades campesinas y de agricultores tradicionales y sus respuestas adaptativas [Climate change impacts on peasant and traditional farmer communities and their adaptation responses]. *Revista de Agroecología*, (Murcia, Spain), Vol. 3, pp. 7–28. (In Spanish.)

Alvaredo, F., Chancel, L., Piketty, T., Saez, E. and Zucman, G. 2018. *World Inequality Report 2018*. Executive Summary. World Inequality Lab. wir2018.wid.world/files/download/wir2018-full-report-english.pdf.

Amnesty International. 2006. *Israel/Lebanon: Deliberate Destruction or "Collateral Damage"? Israeli Attacks on Civilian Infrastructure*. London, Amnesty International. www.amnesty.org/en/documents/MDE18/007/2006/en/.

Amnesty International/WASH United. 2015. *Recognition of the Human Rights to Water and Sanitation by UN Member States at the International Level: An Overview of Resolutions and Declarations that Recognise the Human Rights to Water and Sanitation*. Amnesty International/WASH United. www.amnesty.org/download/Documents/IOR4013802015english.pdf.

Andrés, L., Biller, D. and Herrera Dappe, M. 2014. *Infrastructure Gap in South Asia: Infrastructure Needs, Prioritization, and Financing*. Policy Research Working Papers Series No. 7032. Washington, DC, World Bank. documents.worldbank.org/curated/en/504061468307152462/pdf/WPS7032.pdf.

Andrés, L. and Fuente, D. 2017. *Scoping Study for Subsidies in Water*. Washington, DC, World Bank. Unpublished.

Andrés, L. and Naithani, S. 2013. *Mechanisms and Approaches in Basic Service Delivery for Access and Affordability*. Washington, DC, World Bank. Unpublished.

Anh, N. V., Ha, T. D., Nhue, T. H., Heinss, U., Morel, A., Moura, M. and Schertenleib, R. 2002. Decentralized wastewater treatment – new concept and technologies for Vietnamese conditions. *5th Specialised Conference on Small Water and Wastewater Treatment Systems*, Istanbul, Turkey, 24–26 September 2002.

APF/OHCHR (Asia Pacific Forum of National Human Rights Institutions/Office of the United Nations High Commissioner for Human Rights). 2013. *The United Nations Declaration on the Rights of Indigenous Peoples: A Manual for National Human Rights Institutions*. Geneva/Sydney, APF/ OHCHR. www.ohchr.org/documents/issues/ipeoples/undripmanualfornhris.pdf.

AQUASTAT. n.d. AQUASTAT website. Food and Agriculture Organization of the United Nations (FAO). www.fao.org/nr/water/aquastat/water_use/index.stm. (Accessed 24 May 2018).

Araujo, M. C., Ferreira, F. H., Lanjouw, P. and Özler, B. 2008. Local inequality and project choice: Theory and evidence from Ecuador. *Journal of Public Economics*, Vol. 92, No 5–6, pp. 1022–1046.

Asano, T. and Levine, A. D. 1996. Wastewater reclamation, recycling and reuse: Past, present, and future. *Water Science and Technology*, Vol. 33, No. 10-11, pp. 1–14. doi.org/10.1016/0273-1223(96)00401-5.

Atashili, J., Poole, C., Ndumbe, P. M., Adimora A. A. and Smith, J. S. 2008. Bacterial vaginosis and HIV acquisition: A meta-analysis of published studies. *AIDS*, Vol. 22, No. 12, pp. 1493–1501. doi.org/10.1097/QAD.0b013e3283021a37.

Bache, I. and Flinders, M. (eds.). 2004. *Multi-level Governance*. Oxford, UK, Oxford University Press.

Bäckstrand, K., Khan, J., Kronsell, A. and Lövbrand, E. 2010. The promise of new modes of environmental governance. K. Bäckstrand, J. Khan, A. Kronsell and E. Lövbrand (eds.), *Environmental Politics and Deliberative Democracy: Examining the Promise of New Modes of Governance*. Cheltenham, UK, Edward Elgar.

BADEHOG (House Survey Data Bank). n.d. Digital Repository, Economic Commission for Latin America and the Caribbean. repositorio.cepal.org/handle/11362/31828.

Baker, K. K., Padhi, B., Torondel, B., Das, P., Dutta, A., Sahoo, K. C., Das, B., Dreibelbis, R., Caruso, B., Freeman, M. C., Sager, L. and Panigrahi, P. 2017. From menarche to menopause: A population-based assessment of water, sanitation, and hygiene risk factors for reproductive tract infection symptoms over life stages in rural girls and women in India. *Plos One*, Vol. 12, No. 12, e0188234. doi.org/10.1371/journal.pone.0188234.

Baker, K. K., Story, W. T., Walser-Kuntz, E., and Zimmerman, M. B. 2018. Impact of social capital, harassment of women and girls, and water and sanitation access on premature birth and low infant birth weight in India. *Plos One*, Vol. 13, No. 10, e0205345. journals.plos.org/plosone/article?id=10.1371/journal.pone.0205345.

Banerjee, P., Chaudhury, S. B. R. and Das, S. K. (eds.). 2005. *Internal Displacement in South Asia: The Relevance of the UN's Guiding Principles*. New Delhi/Thousand Oaks, Calif., Sage Publications.

Barber, M. and Jackson, S. 2014. Autonomy and the intercultural: Interpreting the history of Australian Aboriginal water management in the Roper River Catchment, Northern Territory. *Journal of the Royal Anthropological Institute*, Vol. 20, No. 4, pp. 670–693.

Barnard, S., Routray, P., Majorin, F., Peletz, R., Boisson, S., Sinha, A. and Clasen, T. 2013. Impact of Indian total sanitation campaign on latrine coverage and use: A cross-sectional study in Orissa three years following programme implementation. *Plos One*, Vol. 8, No. 8, e71438. doi.org/10.1371/journal.pone.0071438.

BBS/UNICEF Bangladesh (Bangladesh Bureau of Statistics/United Nations Children's Fund). 2014. *Bangladesh Multiple Indicator Cluster Survey 2012-2013, Progotir Pathey: Final Report*. Dhaka, BBS/UNICEF. microdata.worldbank.org/index.php/catalog/2533.

Beegle, K., Christiaensen, L., Dabalen, A. and Gaddis, I. 2016. *Poverty in a Rising Africa*. Washington, DC, The World Bank. openknowledge. worldbank.org/bitstream/handle/10986/22575/9781464807237.pdf?sequence=10&isAllowed=y.

Betts, A. and Collier, P. 2017. *Refuge: Transforming a Broken Refugee System*. UK, Penguin Books.

Bhattacharya, S., and Banerjee, A. 2015. Water privatization in developing countries: Principles, implementations and socio-economic consequences. *World Scientific News*, No. 4, pp. 17–31. www.worldscientificnews.com/wp-content/uploads/2012/11/WSN-4-2015-17-31.pdf.

Bimbe, N., Brownlee, J., Gregson, J. and Playforth, R. 2015. *Knowledge Sharing and Development in a Digital Age*. IDS Policy Briefing No. 87, Brighton, UK, Institute of Development Studies (IDS).

Blandenier, L. 2015. *Recharge Quantification and Continental Freshwater Lens Dynamics in Arid Regions: Application to the Merti Aquifer (Eastern Kenya)*. PhD Thesis presented at the Centre for Hydrogeology and Geothermics, University of Neuchâtel. Neuchâtel, Switzerland.

Boelens, R. and Zwarteveen, M. 2005. Anomalous water rights and the politics of normalization. D. Roth, R. Boelens and M. Zwarteveen, *Liquid Relations, Contested Water Rights and Legal Complexity*. New Brunswick, NJ, Rutgers University Press.

Bonnet, M., Witt, A. M., Stewart, K. M., Hadjerioua, B. and Mobley, M. 2015. *The Economic Benefits of Multipurpose Reservoirs in the United States-Federal Hydropower Fleet*. Oak Ridge, Tenn., Oak Ridge National Laboratory.

Boserup, E. 1965. *The Conditions of Agricultural Growth: The Economics of Agrarian Change under Population Pressure*. Chicago, Aldine.

Branche, E. 2015. *Multipurpose Water Uses of Hydropower Reservoirs. Sharing the Water Uses of Multipurpose Hydropower Reservoirs: The SHARE Concept*. Le Bourget du Lac Cedex, France, EDF/World Water Council (WWC). www.hydroworld.com/content/dam/hydroworld/online-articles/documents/2015/10/MultipurposeHydroReservoirs-SHAREconcept.pdf.

Brocklehurst, C. and Fuente, D. 2016. Detailed review of a recent publication: Increasing block tariffs perform poorly at targeting subsidies to the poor. *WaSH Policy Research Digest*, Issue No. 5, December 2016: Water tariffs and subsidies, pp. 1–4. Chapel Hill, NC, The Water Institute at the University of North Carolina (UNC).

Bromwich, B. 2015. Nexus meets crisis: A review of conflict, natural resources and the humanitarian response in Darfur with reference to the water–energy–food nexus. *International Journal of Water Resources Development*, Vol. 31, pp. 375–392.

Budhathoki, S. S., Bhattachan, M., Castro-Sánchez, E., Sagtani, R. A., Rayamajhi, R. B., Rai, P. and Sharma, G. 2018. Menstrual hygiene management among women and adolescent girls in the aftermath of the earthquake in Nepal. *BMC Women's Health*. Vol. 1, No. 18. doi.org/10.1186/s12905-018-0527-y.

Burek, P., Satoh, Y., Fischer, G., Kahil, M. T., Scherzer, A., Tramberend, S., Nava, L. F., Wada, Y., Eisner, S., Flörke, M., Hanasaki, N., Magnuszewski, P., Cosgrove, B. and Wiberg, D. 2016. *Water Futures and Solution: Fast Track Initiative (Final Report)*. IIASA Working Paper. Laxenburg, Austria, International Institute for Applied Systems Analysis (IIASA). pure.iiasa.ac.at/13008/.

Burger, C. and Jansen, A. 2014. Increasing block tariff structures as a water subsidy mechanism in South Africa: An exploratory analysis. *Development Southern Africa*, Vol. 31, No. 4, pp. 553–562. doi.org/10.1080/0376835X.2014.906915.

CAP-Net. n.d. *Indigenous People and IWRM*. Training course. campus.cap-net.org/en/course/indigenous-people-and-iwrm/.

Cap-Net/WaterLex/UNDP-SIWI WGF (United Nations Development Programme and Stockholm International Water Institute Water Governance Facility)/Redica. 2017. *Human Rights-Based Approach to Integrated Water Resources Management: Training Manual and Facilitator's Guide*. www.watergovernance.org/resources/human-rights-based-approach-integrated-water-resources-management-training-manual-facilitators-guide/.

Carter, R. C., Harvey, E. and Casey, V. 2010. *User Financing of Rural Handpump Water Services*. IRC Symposium 2010: Pumps, Pipes, and Promises. UK, WaterAid. www.ircwash.org/sites/default/files/Carter-2010-User.pdf.

Castaneda Aguilar, R. A., Doan, D. T. T., Newhouse, D. L., Nguyen, M. C., Uematsu, H., Wagner de Azevedo, J. P. 2016. *Who are the Poor in the Developing World?* Policy Research working paper; no. WPS 7844. Washington, DC, World Bank Group. documents.worldbank.org/curated/en/187011475416542282/Who-are-the-poor-in-the-developing-world.

Castro, J. E. 2013. Water is not (yet) a commodity: Commodification and rationalization revisited. *Human Figurations*, Vol. 2, No. 1.

CEDAW (Convention on the Elimination of All Forms of Discrimination against Women). 1979. www.un.org/womenwatch/daw/cedaw/text/econvention.htm#intro.

CESCR (Committee on Economic, Social and Cultural Rights). 1990. *General Comment No. 3: The Nature of States Parties' Obligations (Art. 2, Para 1, of the Covenant)*. Fifth session, E/1991/23.

_____. 2002a. *General Comment No. 15 (2002). The Right to Water (Arts. 11 and 12 of the International Covenant on Economic, Social and Cultural Rights)*. Twenty-ninth session, E/C.12/2002/11. Economic and Social Council, United Nations.

_____. 2002b. *Substantive Issues Arising in the Implementation of the International Covenant on Economic, Social and Cultural Rights*. Comment No. 15. Twenty-ninth session. E/C.12/2002/11. New York, United Nations. www.undocs.org/e/c.12/2002/11.

_____. 2009. *General Comment No. 20: Non-Discrimination in Economic, Social, and Cultural Rights (Art. 2, Para. 2, of the International Covenant on Economic, Social and Cultural Rights)*. Forty-second session, E/C. 12/GC/20. Economic and Social Council, United Nations. undocs.org/E/C.12/GC/20.

Chen, J., Shi, H., Sivakumar, B. and Peart, M. R. 2016. Population, water, food, energy and dams. *Renewable and Sustainable Energy Reviews*, Vol. 56, pp. 18–28. doi.org/10.1016/j.rser.2015.11.043.

CHR (United Nations Commission on Human Rights). 1998. Report of the Representative of the Secretary-General Mr. Francis M. Deng, submitted pursuant to Commission Resolution 1997/39. Addendum: Guiding Principles on Internal Displacement. E/CN.4/1998/53/Add. www.un-documents.net/gpid.htm.

_____. 2005. Economic, Social and Cultural Rights: Realization of the Right to Drinking Water and Sanitation – Report of the Special Rapporteur, El Hadji Guissé. Fifty-seventh session, E/CN.4/Sub.2/2005/25. Economic and Social Council, United Nations. repository. un.org/handle/11176/362459.

Clementine, M., Pizarro, D. M., Prereira Weiss, L. and Vargas-Ramirez, M. 2016. *How to Provide Sustainable Water Supply and Sanitation to Indigenous Peoples*. The Water Blog, The World Bank. blogs.worldbank.org/water/reaching-last-mile-latin-america-and-caribbean-how-provide-sustainable-water-supply-and-sanitation.

COHRE/AAAS/SDC/UN-Habitat (Centre on Housing Rights and Evictions, Right to Water Programme/American Association for the Advancement of Science/Swiss Agency for Development and Cooperation/United Nations Human Settlements Programme). 2007. *Manual on the Right to Water and Sanitation: A Tool to Assist Policy Makers and Practitioners Develop Strategies for Implementing the Human Right to Water and Sanitation*. Geneva, COHRE. www.worldwatercouncil.org/fileadmin/wwc/Programs/Right_to_Water/ Pdf_doct/RTWP__20Manual_RTWS_Final.pdf.

Comprehensive Assessment of Water Management in Agriculture. 2007. *Water for Food, Water for Life: A Comprehensive Assessment of Water Management in Agriculture*. London/Colombo, Earthscan/International Water Management Institute (IWMI). www.iwmi.cgiar. org/assessment/files_new/synthesis/Summary_SynthesisBook.pdf.

Conseil d'État. 2017a. *Conseil d'État, 31 juillet 2017, Commune de Calais, Ministre d'État, Ministre de l'Intérieur, [Conseil d'État, 31 July 2017, Municipality of Calais, Minister of State, Interior Minister]* Nos. 412125, 412171. www.conseil-etat.fr/Decisions-Avis-Publications/ Decisions/Selection-des-decisions-faisant-l-objet-d-une-communication-particuliere/Conseil-d-Etat-31-juillet-2017-Commune-de-Calais-Ministre-d-Etat-ministre-de-l-Interieur. (In French.)

_____. 2017b. *Conditions d'accueil des migrants à Calais : le Conseil d'État rejette les appels du ministre de l'intérieur et de la commune.* [Conditions of accommodation of migrants in Calais: The Conseil d'État rejects appeals made by the Interior Minister and the municipality] www.conseil-etat.fr/Actualites/Communiques/Conditions-d-accueil-des-migrants-a-Calais. (In French.)

Contzen, N. and Marks, S. 2018. Increasing the regular use of safe water kiosk through collective psychological ownership: A mediation analysis. *Journal of Environmental Psychology*, Vol. 57, pp. 45–52. doi.org/10.1016/j.jenvp.2018.06.008.

Cooke, B. and Kothari, U. E. 2001. *Participation: The New Tyranny?* New York, Zed Books.

Cossio Rojas, V. and Soto Montaño, L. 2011. *Relación entre acceso al agua y nivel de bienestar a nivel de hogares en Tiraque-Bolivia* [Relation between Access to Water and Well-Being at the Household Level in Tiraque, Bolivia]. Reporte de Investigación Nro. 1. Cochabamba, Bolivia, Centro Agua, Universidad Mayor de San Simón. (In Spanish.)

Council of Ministers of Turkey. 2016. Geçici koruma sağlanan yabancıların çalişma izinlerine dair yönetmelik [Regulation on work permits for foreigners under temporary protection]. *Official Gazette* (Ankara), Decision No. 2016/8375, decided by the Council of Ministers on 11 January 2016. www.resmigazete.gov.tr/eskiler/2016/01/20160115-23.pdf. (In Turkish.)

CRED/UNISDR (Centre for Research on the Epidemiology of Disasters/The United Nations Office for Disaster Risk Reduction). 2015. *The Human Cost of Weather-Related Disasters 1995-2015*. Brussels/Geneva, CRED/UNISDR. www.unisdr.org/2015/docs/climatechange/ COP21_WeatherDisastersReport_2015_FINAL.pdf.

Crook, R. C. 2003. Decentralisation and poverty reduction in Africa: The politics of local–central relations. *Public Administration Development*, Vol. 23, No. 1, pp. 77–88. doi.org/10.1002/pad.261.

Crow, B. and Odaba, C. 2009. *Scarce, Costly and Uncertain: Water Access in Kibera, Nairobi*. Santa Cruz, Calif., Center for Global, International and Regional Studies, University of California-Santa Cruz. escholarship.org/uc/item/8c10s316.

Crow-Miller, B., Webber, M. and Molle, F. 2017. The (re)turn to infrastructure for water management? *Water Alternatives*, Vol. 10, No. 2, pp. 195–207.

CRPD (Convention on the Rights of Persons with Disabilities). 2006. www.un.org/development/desa/disabilities/convention-on-the-rights-of-persons-with-disabilities.html.

Cutter, S. L. 2017. The forgotten casualties redux: Women, children, and disaster risk. *Global Environmental Change*, Vol. 42, pp. 117–121. doi.10.1016/j.gloenvcha.2016.12.010.

Danilenko, A., Van den Berg, C., Macheve, B. and Moffitt, L. J. 2014. *The IBNET Water Supply and Sanitation Blue Book 2014: The International Benchmarking Network for Water and Sanitation Utilities Databook*. Washington, DC, World Bank.

Dashora, Y., Dillon, P., Maheshwari, B., Soni, P., Dashora, R., Davande, S., Purohit, R. C. and Mittal, H. K. 2017. A simple method using farmers' measurements applied to estimate check dam recharge in Rajasthan, India. *Sustainable Water Resources Management*, Vol. 4, No. 2, pp. 301–316. doi.org/10.1007/s40899-017-0185-5.

De Albuquerque, C. 2014. *Realising the Human Rights to Water and Sanitation: A Handbook by the UN Special Rapporteur Catarina de Albuquerque*. Portugal, Human Rights to Water and Sanitation UN Special Rapporteur. www.ohchr.org/en/issues/waterandsanitation/ srwater/pages/handbook.aspx.

De la O Campos, A. P., Villani, C., Davis, B. and Takagi, M. 2018. *Ending Extreme Poverty in Rural Areas – Sustaining Livelihoods to Leave no one Behind*. Rome, Food and Agriculture Organization of the United Nations (FAO). www.fao.org/3/CA1908EN/ca1908en.pdf.

De Londras, F. 2010. Dualism, domestic courts, and the rule of international law. M. Sellers and J. Maxeiner (eds.), *Ius Gentium: Comparative Perspectives on Law and Justice*. Dordrecht, The Netherlands, Springer.

Denevan, W. 1995. 2 prehistoric agricultural methods as models for sustainability. *Advances in Plant Pathology*, Vol. 11, pp. 21–43. doi.org/10.1016/S0736-4539(06)80004-8.

Dillon, P. 2005. Future management of aquifer recharge. *Hydrogeology Journal*, Vol. 13, No. 1, pp. 313–316. doi.org/10.1007/s10040-004-0413-6.

Dillon, P., Pavelic, P., Page, D., Beringen, H. and Ward, J. 2009. *Managed Aquifer Recharge: An Introduction*. National Water Commission Waterlines Report Series No. 13. Canberra, Commonwealth Scientific and Industrial Research Organization (CSIRO).

Dodson, L. L. and Bargach, J. 2015. Harvesting fresh water from fog in rural Morocco: Research and impact Dar Si Hmad fogwater project in Aït Baamrane. *Procedia Engineering*, Vol. 107, pp. 186–193. doi.org/10.1016/j.proeng.2015.06.073.

Duarte, J., Jaureguiberry, F. and Racimo, M. 2017. *Sufficiency, Equity and Effectiveness of School Infrastructure in Latin America According to TERCE*. Santiago, Oficina Regional de Educación para América Latina y el Caribe (OREALC/UNESCO Santiago). https://publications. iadb.org/bitstream/handle/11319/8158/Sufficiency-Equity-and-Effectiveness-of-School-Infrastructure-in-Latin-America-according-to-TERCE.PDF?sequence=8.

Eau de Paris/SEDIF/SIAAP/OBUSASS/Ministry of Social Affairs and Health (Eau de Paris/Syndicat des eaux d'Ile-de-France/Syndicat interdépartemental pour l'assainissement de l'agglomération parisienne/OBUSASS/Ministry of Social Affairs and Health). 2013. *Assessing Progress in Achieving Equitable Access to Water and Sanitation. Pilot Project in the Greater Paris Urban Area (France). Report*. www. unece.org/fileadmin/DAM/env/water/activities/Equitable_access/Country_report__Pilot_project_Greater_Paris_urban_area_rev.pdf.

ECHO (European Civil Protection and Humanitarian Aid Operations) Global Solar Water Initiative. 2017. *Humanitarian Reponse: The Future is Solar*. ECHO Global Solar Water Initiative online publication. views-voices.oxfam.org.uk/wp-content/uploads/2017/03/Project-flyer_Solar-blog.pdf.

ECO (Environmental Commissioner of Ontario). 2017. *The 2017 Environmental Protection Report. Good Choices Bad Choices: Environmental Rights and Environmental protection in Ontario*. Toronto, Canada, ECO. eco.on.ca/reports/2017-good-choices-bad-choices/.

Economic and Social Rights Centre. 2016. *State of Water and Sanitation Service Provision Performance in Mombasa County. Community Score Card*. Nairobi, Economic and Social Rights Centre (Hakijamii). www.hakijamii.com/wp-content/uploads/2016/05/Final-Community-Report-Card-Report.pdf.

ECOSOC (Economic and Social Council of the United Nations). 2018. *The Disaster-Related Statistics Framework: Results of the Work of the Expert Group on Disaster-related Statistics in Asia and the Pacific*. Seventy-fourth session of the United Nations Economic and Social Commission of Asia and The Pacific (UNESCAP). www.unescap.org/sites/default/files/E74_24E%5B1%5D_0.pdf.

EcoWatch. 2018. *How Water Scarcity Shapes the World's Refugee Crisis*. www.ecowatch.com/refugee-crisis-water-shortage-2535042186. html.

EESC (European Economic and Social Committee). 2017. *Impact of Digitalisation and the On-Demand Economy on Labour Markets and the Consequences for Employment and Industrial Relations*. Brussels, European Union. www.eesc.europa.eu/resources/docs/qe-02-17-763-en-n.pdf.

Estache, A. and Kouassi, E. 2002. *Sector Organization, Governance, and the Inefficiency of African Water Utilities*. World Bank Policy Research Working Paper No. 2890. Washington, DC, World Bank. https://ssrn.com/abstract=636253.

FAO (Food and Agriculture Organization of the United Nations). 2005. *Voluntary Guidelines to Support the Progressive Realization of the Right to Adequate Food in the Context of National Food Security*. Rome, FAO. www.fao.org/3/a-y7937e.pdf.

_____. 2011. *The State of Food and Agriculture. Women in Agriculture: Closing the Gender Gap for Development*. Rome, FAO. www.fao. org/3/a-i2050e.pdf.

_____. 2014. *The State of Food and Agriculture: Innovations in Family Farming*. Rome, FAO. www.fao.org/3/a-i4040e.pdf.

_____. 2016. *Coping with Water Scarcity in Agriculture: A Global Framework for Action in a Changing Climate*. Rome, FAO. www.fao.org/3/a-i6459e.pdf.

_____. 2017a. *Migration, Agriculture and Climate Change: Reducing Vulnerabilities and Enhancing Resilience*. Rome, FAO. www.fao.org/3/I8297EN/i8297en.pdf.

_____. 2017b. *The State of Food and Agriculture: Leveraging Food Systems for Inclusive Rural Transformation*. Rome, FAO. www.fao.org/3/a-i7658e.pdf.

_____. 2018a. *The State of Food and Agriculture. Migration, Agriculture and Rural Development*. Rome, FAO. www.fao.org/state-of-food-agriculture/en/.

_____. 2018b. *Climate Change Adaptation, Social Protection and Resilience. Cisterns for the Sahel*. Rome, FAO. www.fao.org/3/ca0882en/CA0882EN.pdf.

_____. Forthcoming. *Adapting Irrigation to Climate Change (AICCA) in West and Central Africa*. Project report validated by country counterparts.

_____. n.d. Gender and Land Rights Database. www.fao.org/gender-landrights-database/data-map/statistics/en/?sta_id=1161.

FAO/GWP/Oregon State University (Food and Agriculture Organization of the United Nations/Global Water Partnership/Oregon State University). 2018. *Water Stress and Human Migration: A Global, Georeferenced Review of Empirical Research*. Land and Water Discussion Paper No. 11. Rome, FAO. www.fao.org/3/I8867EN/i8867en.pdf.

FAO/IFAD/UNICEF/WFP/WHO (Food and Agriculture Organization of the United Nations/International Fund for Agricultural Development/United Nation Children's Fund/World Food Programme/World Health Organization). 2017. *The State of Food Security and Nutrition in the World 2017: Building Resilience for Peace and Food Security*. Rome, FAO. www.fao.org/3/a-I7695e.pdf.

_____. 2018. *The State of Food Security and Nutrition in the World 2018: Building Climate Resilience for Food Security and Nutrition.* Rome, FAO. www.fao.org/3/I9553EN/i9553en.pdf.

FAO/IFAD/WFP (Food and Agriculture Organization of the United Nations/International Fund for Agricultural Development/World Food Programme). 2012. *Rural Women and the Millennium Development Goals.* Fact sheet. fao.org/docrep/015/an479e/an479e.pdf.

_____. 2015a. *The State of Food Insecurity in the World. Meeting the 2015 International Hunger Targets: Taking Stock of Uneven Progress.* Rome, FAO. www.fao.org/3/a-i4646e.pdf.

_____. 2015b. *Achieving Zero Hunger: The Critical Role of Investments in Social Protection and Agriculture.* Rome, FAO. www.fao.org/3/a-i4951e.pdf.

FAO/IWMI (Food and Agriculture Organization of the United Nations/International Water Management Institute). 2018. *More People, More Food, Worse Water? A Global Review of Water Pollution from Agriculture.* Rome/Colombo, FAO/IWMI. www.fao.org/3/ca0146en/CA0146EN.pdf.

Faurès, J. M. and Santini, S. (eds.). 2009. *Water and the Rural Poor: Interventions for Improving Livelihoods in Sub-Saharan Africa.* Rome, FAO. www.fao.org/docrep/pdf/010/i0132e/i0132e.pdf.

Ferrant, G., Maria Pesando, L. and Nowacka, K. 2014. *Unpaid Care Work: The Missing Link in the Analysis of Gender Gaps in Labour Outcomes.* OECD Development Centre. www.oecd.org/dev/development-gender/Unpaid_care_work.pdf.

Flint Water Advisory Task Force. 2016. *Flint Water Advisory Task Force: Final Report.* Office of Governor Rick Snyder, State of Michigan. www.michigan.gov/documents/snyder/FWATF_FINAL_REPORT_21March2016_517805_7.pdf.

Foa, R. 2015. *Creating an Inclusive Society: Evidence from Social Indicators and Trends.* Presented at the Expert Group Meeting on "Social Development and Agenda 2030", 23 October 2015, New York. www.un.org/esa/socdev/egms/docs/2015/sd-agenda2030/RobertoFoaPaper.pdf.

Fonseca, C. and Pories, L. 2017. *Financing WASH: How to Increase Funds for the Sector while Reducing Inequalities.* Position paper for the Sanitation and Water for All Finance Ministers Meeting. Briefing Note. The Hague, the Netherlands, IRC/water.org/Ministry of Foreign Affairs/Simavi. www.ircwash.org/resources/financing-wash-how-increase-funds-sector-while-reducing-inequalities-position-paper.

Foster, V. and Briceño-Garmendia, C. (eds.). 2010. *Africa's Infrastructure : A Time for Transformation.* Africa Development Forum. Washington, DC, World Bank. documents.worldbank.org/curated/en/246961468003355256/pdf/521020PUB0EPI1101Official0Use0Only1.pdf.

Franks, T. and Cleaver, F. 2007. Water governance and poverty: A framework for analysis. *Progress in Development Studies,* Vol. 7, No. 4, pp. 291–306. doi.org/10.1177/146499340700700402.

French Parliament. 2013. Loi n° 2013-312 du 15 avril 2013 visant à préparer la transition vers un système énergétique sobre et portant diverses dispositions sur la tarification de l'eau et sur les éoliennes (1) [Law Nr. 2013-312 of 15 April 2013 aiming to prepare the transition towards a lower energy use and setting out several provisions for water and wind energy tariffs (1)]. *Journal Officiel de la République Française* (Paris), Vol. 0089, 16 April 2013, p. 6208. www.legifrance.gouv.fr/eli/loi/2013/4/15/DEVX1234078L/jo/texte. (In French.).

Fuente, D., Gakii Gatua, J., Ikiara, M., Kabubo-Mariara, J., Mwaura, M. and Whittington, D. 2016. Water and sanitation service delivery, pricing, and the poor: An empirical estimate of subsidy incidence in Nairobi, Kenya. *Water Resources Research,* Vol. 52, No. 6, pp. 4845–4862. doi.10.1002/ 2015WR018375.

Funder, M., Bustamante, R., Cossio Rojas, V., Huong, P. T. M., Van Koppen, B., Mweemba, C., Nyambe, I., Phuong, L. T. T. and Skielboe, T. 2012. Strategies of the poorest in local water conflict and cooperation. Evidence from Vietnam, Bolivia and Zambia. *Water Alternatives,* Vol. 5, No. 1, pp. 20–36.

Gao, H., Bohn, T., Podest, E. and McDonald, K. 2011. On the causes of the shrinking of Lake Chad. *Environmental Research Letters,* Vol. 6.

Geere, J.-A. L., Hunter, P. R. and Jagals, P. 2010. Domestic water carrying and its implications for health: A review and mixed methods pilot study in Limpopo Province, South Africa. *Environmental Health,* Vol. 9, No. 1, pp. 1–13. doi.org/10.1186/1476-069X-9-52.

Gikas, P. and Tchobanoglous, G. 2009. The role of satellite and decentralized strategies in water resources management. *Journal of Environmental Management,* Vol. 90, No. 1, pp. 144–152. doi.org/10.1016/j.jenvman.2007.08.016.

Gillot, S., De Clercq, B., Defour, D., Simoens, F., Gernaey, K. and Vanrolleghem, P. A. 1999. *Optimisation of Wastewater Treatment Plant Design and Operation Using Simulation and Cost Analysis.*

Gleick, P. H. 1993. Water and conflict: Freshwater resources and international security. *International Security,* Vol. 18, No. 1, pp. 79–112. doi.10.2307/2539033.

Global High-Level Panel on Water and Peace. 2017. *A Matter of Survival (Report).* Geneva, Geneva Water Hub. www.genevawaterhub.org/resource/matter-survival.

Goksu, A., Trémolet, S., Kolker, J. and Kingdom, B. 2017. *Easing the Transition to Commercial Finance for Sustainable Water and Sanitation.* Working paper. Washington, DC, World Bank. openknowledge.worldbank.org/handle/10986/27948.

Gómez, L. and Ravnborg, H. M. 2011. *Power, Inequality and Water Governance: The Role of Third Party Involvement in Water-Related Conflict and Cooperation.* CGIAR Systemwide Program on Collective Action and Property Rights (CAPRi) Working Paper No. 101. Washington, DC, International Food Policy Research Institute (IFPRI).

Gon, G., Restrepo-Méndez, M. C., Campbell, O. M. R., Barros, A. J. D., Woodd, S., Benova, L. and Graham, W. J. 2016. Who delivers without water? A multi country analysis of water and sanitation in the childbirth environment. *Plos One,* Vol. 11, No. 8, e0160572. doi.org/10.1371/journal.pone.0160572.

Grönwall, J. 2016. Self-supply and accountability: To govern or not to govern groundwater for the (peri-) urban poor in Accra, Ghana. *Environmental Earth Sciences,* Vol. 75, Art. 1163. doi.org/10.1007/s12665-016-5978-6.

Grönwall, J., Mulenga, M. and McGranahan, G. 2010. *Groundwater, Self-Supply and Poor Urban Dwellers: A Review with Case Studies of Bangalore and Lusaka.* Human Settlements Working Paper No.26. London, International Institute for Environment and Development (IIED). pubs.iied.org/10584IIED/.

Gross, M. J., Albinger, O., Jewett, D. G., Logan, B. E., Bales, R. C. and Arnold, R. G. 1995. Measurement of bacterial collision efficiencies in porous media. *Water Research*, Vol. 29, No. 4, pp. 1151–1158. doi.10.1016/0043-1354(94)00235-Y.

Gupta, J. and Van der Zaag, P. 2008. Interbasin water transfers and integrated water resources management: Where engineering, science and politics interlock. *Physics and Chemistry of the Earth*, Parts A/B/C, Vol. 33, No. 1–2, pp. 28–40. doi.org/10.1016/j.pce.2007.04.003.

GWP (Global Water Partnership). 2000. *Integrated Water Resources Management*. GWP Technical Advisory Committee (TAC) Background Paper No. 4. Stockholm, GWP. www.gwp.org/globalassets/global/toolbox/publications/background-papers/04-integrated-water-resources-management-2000-english.pdf.

_____. n.d. *The Need for an Integrated Approach*. GWP website. www.gwp.org/en/About/why/the-need-for-an-integrated-approach/.

Habermas, J. 1975. *Legitimation Crisis*. Boston, USA, Beacon Press.

Hassan, F. 2011. *Water History for our Times, IHP Essays on Water History Vol. 2*. Paris, UNESCO. unesdoc.unesco.org/images/0021/002108/210879e.pdf.

Healy, A., Danert, K., Bristow, G. and Theis, S. 2018. *Perceptions of Trends in the Development of Private Boreholes for Household Water Consumption: Findings from a Survey of Water Professionals in Africa*. RIGSS Working Paper. Cardiff, UK, Cardiff University. www.cardiff.ac.uk/__data/assets/pdf_file/0009/1094769/Perceptions_of_trends_in_the_development_of_private_boreholes_for_household_water_consumption.pdf.

Heffez, A. 2013. How Yemen chewed itself dry: Farming qat, wasting water. *Foreign Affairs*, July 2013. www.foreignaffairs.com/articles/139596/adam-heffez/how-yemen-chewed-itself-dry.

Hejazi, M., Edmonds, J., Chaturvedi, V., Davies, E. and Eom, J. 2013. Scenarios of global municipal water-use demand projections over the 21st century. *Hydrological Sciences Journal*, Vol. 58, No. 3, pp. 519–538. doi.org/10.1080/02626667.2013.772301.

Hellum, A., Kameri-Mbote, P. and Van Koppen, B. (eds.). 2015. *Water is Life: Women's Human Rights in National and Local Water Governance in Southern and Eastern Africa*. Harare, Weaver Press.

Helmreich, B. and Horn, H. 2009. Opportunities in rainwater harvesting. *Desalination*, Vol. 248, No. 1-3, pp. 118–124. doi.10.1016/j.desal.2008.05.046.

Hirschman, A. O. 1970. *Exit, Voice, and Loyalty*. Cambridge, Mass., Harvard University Press.

HLPE (High Level Panel of Experts on Food Security and Nutrition of the Committee on World Food Security). 2013. *Investing in Smallholder Agriculture for Food Security*. Report by the High Level Panel of Experts on Food Security and Nutrition of the Committee on World Food Security. Rome. www.fao.org/fileadmin/user_upload/hlpe/hlpe_documents/HLPE_Reports/HLPE-Report-6_Investing_in_smallholder_agriculture.pdf.

_____. 2015. *Water for Food Security and Nutrition. A Report by the High Level Panel of Experts on Food Security and Nutrition of the Committee on World Food Security*. Rome. www.fao.org/3/a-av045e.pdf.

HLPW (High-Level Panel on Water). 2018. *Making Every Drop Count: An Agenda for Water Action*. Outcome Document. sustainabledevelopment.un.org/content/documents/17825HLPW_Outcome.pdf.

Hodgson, S. 2004. *Land and Water – The Rights Interface*. FAO Legislative Study No. 84. Rome, Food and Agriculture Organization of the United Nations (FAO). www.fao.org/3/a-y5692e.pdf.

_____. 2016. *Exploring the Concept of Water Tenure*. FAO Land and Water Discussion Paper No. 10. Rome, Food and Agriculture Organization or the United Nations (FAO). www.fao.org/3/a-i5435e.pdf.

House, S., Cavill, S. and Ferron, S. 2017. Equality and non-discrimination (EQND) in sanitation programmes at scale, Part 1 of 2. *Frontiers of CLTS: Innovations and Insights*, No. 10, Brighton, UK, Institute of Development Studies (IDS).

House, S., Ferron, S., Sommer, M. and Cavill, S. 2014. *Violence, Gender and WASH: A Practitioner's Toolkit – Making Water, Sanitation and Hygiene Safer through Improved Programming and Services*. London, WaterAid/SHARE.

HRC (Human Rights Council). 2008. *Promotion and Protection of All Human Rights, Civil, Political, Economic, Social and Cultural Rights, Including the Right to Development. Protect, Respect and Remedy: A Framework for Business and Human Rights*. Report of the Special Representative of the Secretary-General on the issue of human rights and transnational corporations and other business enterprises, John Ruggie. Eight session, 7 April 2008, A/HRC/8/5. www2.ohchr.org/english/bodies/hrcouncil/docs/8session/A-HRC-8-5.doc.

_____. 2009. *Promotion and Protection of all Human Rights, Civil, Political, Economic, Social and Cultural Rights, including the Right to Development*. Report of the independent expert on the issue of human rights obligations related to access to safe drinking water and sanitation, Catarina de Albuquerque. Twelfth session, 1 July 2009, A/HRC/12/24. https://documents-dds-ny.un.org/doc/UNDOC/GEN/G09/144/37/PDF/G0914437.pdf?OpenElement.

_____. 2010. *Joint Report of the Independent Expert on the Question of Human Rights and Extreme Poverty, Magdalena Sepúlveda Cardona, and the Independent Expert on the Issue of Human Rights Obligations related to Access to Safe Drinking Water and Sanitation, Catarina de Albuquerque*. Fifteenth session, 22 July 2010, A/HRC/15/55. https://documents-dds-ny.un.org/doc/UNDOC/GEN/G10/154/51/PDF/G1015451.pdf?OpenElement.

_____. 2011a. *Guiding Principles on Business and Human Rights: Implementing the United Nations "Protect, Respect and Remedy" Framework*. Report of the Special Representative of the Secretary General on the issue of human rights and transnational corporations and other business enterprises, John Ruggie. Seventeenth session. 21 March 2011, A/HRC/17/31, www.ohchr.org/Documents/Issues/Business/A-HRC-17-31_AEV.pdf.

_____. 2011b. *Human Rights and Transnational Corporations and Other Business Enterprises*. Seventeenth session, 6 July 2011, A/HRC/RES/17/4, https://documents-dds-ny.un.org/doc/RESOLUTION/GEN/G11/144/71/PDF/G1114471.pdf?OpenElement.

_____. 2011c. *Report of the Special Rapporteur on the Human Right to Safe Drinking Water and Sanitation, Catarina de Albuquerque*. Eighteenth session, 4 July 2011, A/HRC/18/33. www2.ohchr.org/english/bodies/hrcouncil/docs/18session/A-HRC-18-33_en.pdf.

____. 2013. *Report of the Special Rapporteur on the Human Right to Safe Drinking Water and Sanitation, Catarina de Albuquerque*. Twenty-fourth session, 11 July 2013, A/HRC/24/44. www.ohchr.org/EN/HRBodies/HRC/RegularSessions/Session24/Documents/A-HRC-24-44_en.pdf.

____. 2014. *Common Violations of the Human Rights to Water and Sanitation*. Report of the Special Rapporteur on the human right to safe drinking water and sanitation, Catarina de Albuquerque. Twenty-seventh session, 30 June 2014, A/HRC/27/55. www.ohchr.org/en/hrbodies/hrc/regularsessions/session27/documents/a_hrc_27_55_eng.doc.

____. 2015. *Report of the Special Rapporteur on the Human Right to Safe Drinking Water and Sanitation*. Thirtieth Session, 5 August 2015. A/HRC/30/39. undocs.org/A/HRC/30/39.

____. 2016a. *The Human Rights to Safe Drinking Water and Sanitation*. Resolution adopted by the Human Rights Council on 29 September 2016, Thirty-third session, A/HRC/RES/33/10. https://digitallibrary.un.org/record/850266?ln=en.

____. 2016b. *Report of the Special Rapporteur on the Human Right of Safe Drinking Water and Sanitation*. Thirty-third Session, 27 July 2016, A/HRC/33/49. ap.ohchr.org/documents/dpage_e.aspx?si=A/HRC/33/49.

____. 2018a. *Report of the Special Rapporteur on the Human Right to Safe Drinking Water and Sanitation on his Mission to Mongolia*. Thirty-ninth Session, 18 July 2018. A/HRC/39/55/Add.2. undocs.org/A/HRC/39/55/Add.2.

____. 2018b. *Report of the Special Rapporteur on the Issue of Human Rights Obligations relating to the Enjoyment of a Safe, Clean, Healthy and Sustainable Environment*. Thirty-seventh Session, 3 August 2018, A/HRC/37/59. undocs.org/A/HRC/39/55.

HRI (International Human Rights Instruments). 1994. *Compilation of General Comments and General Recommendations adopted by Human Rights Treaty Bodies. General Comment No. 18: Non-Discrimination*. Thirty-seventh session, 29 July 1994, HRI/GEN/1/Rev. 1. undocs.org/HRI/GEN/1/Rev.1.

Huong, P. T. M., Phuong, L. T. T., Skielboe, T. and Ravnborg, H. M. 2011. *Poverty and Access to Water and Water Governance Institutions in Con Cuong District, Nghe An Province, Vietnam – Report on the Results from a Household Questionnaire Survey*. DIIS Working Paper 2011, No. 04. Copenhagen, Danish Institute for International Studies (DIIS). www.diis.dk/en/research/poverty-and-access-to-water-and-water-governance-institutions-in-con-cuong-district-nghe-an.

Hutton, G. 2012a. *Global Costs and Benefits of Drinking-Water Supply and Sanitation Interventions to Reach the MDG Target and Universal Coverage*. WHO/HSE/WSH/12.01. Geneva, World Health Organization (WHO). www.who.int/water_sanitation_health/publications/2012/globalcosts.pdf.

____. 2012b. *Monitoring 'Affordability' of Water and Sanitation Services after 2015: Review of Global Indicator Options*. Working paper. Submitted to the United Nations Office of the High Commissioner for Human Rights, Geneva. https://washdata.org/file/425/download.

Hutton, G. and Andrés, L. 2018. *Counting the Costs and Benefits of Equitable WASH Service Provision*. Working paper. Washington, DC, World Bank.

Hutton, G., Rodriguez, U-P., Winara, A., Nguyen, V. A., Phyrum, K., Chuan, L., Blackett, I. and Weitz, A. 2014. Economic efficiency of sanitation interventions in Southeast Asia. *Water Sanitation and Hygiene for Development*, Vol. 4, No. 1, pp. 23–36. doi.org/10.2166/washdev.2013.158.

Hutton, G. and Varughese, M. 2016. *The Costs of Meeting the 2030 Sustainable Development Goal Targets on Drinking Water, Sanitation and Hygiene*. Water and Sanitation Program (WSP): Technical Paper. Washington, DC, The World Bank. www.worldbank.org/en/topic/water/publication/the-costs-of-meeting-the-2030-sustainable-development-goal-targets-on-drinking-water-sanitation-and-hygiene.

IAWJ (International Association of Women Judges). 2012. *Stopping the Abuse of Power through Sexual Exploitation: Naming, Shaming, and Ending Sextortion*. Washington, DC, IAWJ. www.iawj.org/wp-content/uploads/2017/04/Corruption-and-Sextortion-Resource-1.pdf.

ICCPR (International Covenant on Civil and Political Rights). 1966. www.ohchr.org/en/professionalinterest/pages/ccpr.aspx.

ICID (International Commission on Irrigation and Drainage). 2005. *Experiences in Interbasin Water Transfers for Irrigation, Drainage or Flood Management (3rd Draft 15 August 2005)*. Unpublished report.

ICOLD (International Commission on Large Dams). n.d. *World Register of Dams. General Synthesis*. www.icold-cigb.net/GB/world_register/general_synthesis.asp.

ICESCR (International Covenant on Economic, Social and Cultural Rights). 1967. treaties.un.org/doc/Treaties/1976/01/19760103%2009-57%20PM/Ch_IV_03.pdf.

ICRC (International Committee of the Red Cross). 2017. *Yemen: ICRC President Visits Country; 600,000 Cholera Cases Expected by End 2017*. Press Release, 23 July 2017. intercrossblog.icrc.org/blog/peter-maurer-visits-yemen-cholera.

ICWE (International Conference on Water and the Environment). 1992. *The Dublin Statement on Water and Sustainable Development*. Adopted on 31 January 1992. Dublin. www.un-documents.net/h2o-dub.htm.

IDB (Inter-American Development Bank). 1999. *Spilled Water. Institutional Commitment in the Provision of Water Services*. Washington, DC, IDB. publications.iadb.org/handle/11319/331.

IDMC (Internal Displacement Monitoring Centre). 2017. *Global Report on Internal Displacement (GRID) 2017*. Geneva, IDMC. www.internal-displacement.org/global-report/grid2017/.

____. 2018. *Global Report on Internal Displacement (GRID) 2018*. Geneva, IDMC. www.internal-displacement.org/global-report/grid2018/.

IEA (International Energy Agency). 2016. *Water Energy Nexus: Excerpt from the World Energy Outlook 2016*. Paris, IEA Publications. www.iea.org/publications/freepublications/publication/WorldEnergyOutlook2016ExcerptWaterEnergyNexus.pdf.

____. 2017. *Energy Access Outlook 2017: From Poverty to Prosperity*. Paris, IEA Publications. www.iea.org/publications/freepublications/publication/WEO2017SpecialReport_EnergyAccessOutlook.pdf.

IFAD (International Fund for Agricultural Development). 2015. *Land Tenure Security and Poverty Reduction.* Rome, IFAD. www.ifad.org/documents/38714170/39148759/Land+tenure+security+and+poverty+reduction.pdf/c9d0982d-40e4-4e1e-b490-17ea8fef0775.

_____. 2017. *Sending Money Home: Contributing to the SDGs, One Family at a Time.* Rome, IFAD. www.ifad.org/documents/38714170/39135645/Sending+Money+Home+-+Contributing+to+the+SDGs%2C+one+family+at+a+time.pdf/c207b5f1-9fef-4877-9315-75463fccfaa7.

IIPFWH (International Indigenous Peoples' Forum on World Heritage). n.d. *Indigenous Peoples' Involvement in World Heritage.* IIPFWH website. iipfwh.org/indigenous-involvement-in-world-heritage/.

Ikeda, J. and Arney, H. 2015. *Financing Water and Sanitation for the Poor: The Role of Microfinance in Addressing the Water and Sanitation Gap.* Learning Note. Washington, DC, Water and Sanitation Program (WSP), World Bank. www.findevgateway.org/library/financing-water-and-sanitation-poor-role-microfinance-institutions-addressing-water-and.

ILO (International Labour Organization). 1957. *Indigenous and Tribal Populations Convention (No. 107).* Geneva, ILO. www.ilo.org/dyn/normlex/en/f?p=NORMLEXPUB:12100:0::NO:12100:P12100_INSTRUMENT_ID:312252:NO.

_____. 1989. *Indigenous and Tribal Populations Convention (No. 169).* Geneva, ILO. www.ilo.org/dyn/normlex/en/f?p=NORMLEXPUB:12100:0::NO::P12100_ILO_CODE:C169.

_____. 2015. *The Future of Work Centenary Initiative.* ILC 104/2015, Report I. Geneva, ILO. www.ilo.org/ilc/ILCSessions/104/reports/reports-to-the-conference/WCMS_369026/lang--en/index.htm.

_____. 2016. *Sustainable Development Goals: Indigenous Peoples in Focus.* Geneva, ILO. www.ilo.org/wcmsp5/groups/public/---ed_emp/---ifp_skills/documents/publication/wcms_503715.pdf.

_____. 2017a. *Labour Force Estimates and Projections (LFEP) 2017: Key Trends.* LFEP Brief. Geneva, ILO. www.ilo.org/ilostat-files/Documents/LFEPbrief.pdf.

_____. 2017b. *Indigenous Peoples and Climate Change: From Victims to Change Agents through Decent Work.* Geneva, ILO. www.ilo.org/wcmsp5/groups/public/---dgreports/---gender/documents/publication/wcms_551189.pdf.

_____. 2017c. *WASH@Work: A Self-Training Handbook.* Geneva, ILO. www.ilo.org/wcmsp5/groups/public/---ed_dialogue/---sector/documents/publication/wcms_535058.pdf.

_____. 2017d. *Understanding the Drivers of Rural Vulnerability: Towards Building Resilience, Promoting Socio-Economic Empowerment and Enhancing the Socio-Economic Inclusion of Vulnerable, Disadvantaged and Marginalized Populations for an Effective Promotion of Decent Work in Rural Economies.* Employment Working Paper No. 214. Geneva, ILO. www.ilo.org/employment/Whatwedo/Publications/working-papers/WCMS_568736/lang--en/index.htm.

_____. 2018a. *Employment Intensive Investment Programme (EIIP): Creating Jobs through Public Investment.* Geneva, ILO. www.ilo.org/wcmsp5/groups/public/---ed_emp/---emp_policy/---invest/documents/publication/wcms_619821.pdf.

_____. 2018b. *Market Systems Analysis for Refugee Livelihoods in Jigjiga, Ethiopia.* Geneva, ILO. www.ilo.org/empent/Projects/refugee-livelihoods/market-assessments/WCMS_630984/lang--en/index.htm.

INEC (Instituto Nacional de Estadística y Censos). n.d. *Medición de los indicadores ODS de Agua, Saneamiento e Higiene (ASH) en el Ecuador* [Measuring SDG Indicators on Water, Sanitation and Hygiene (WASH) in Ecuador]. www.ecuadorencifras.gob.ec/documentos/web-inec/EMPLEO/2017/Indicadores%20ODS%20Agua,%20Saneamiento%20e%20Higiene/Presentacion_Agua_2017_05.pdf. (In Spanish.)

IPCC (Intergovernmental Panel on Climate Change). 2014. *Climate Change 2014. Synthesis Report.* Contribution of Working Groups I, II and III to the Fifth Assessment Report to the Intergovernmental Panel on Climate Change. Geneva, IPCC. www.ipcc.ch/report/ar5/syr/.

IWA (International Water Association). 2014. *Specific Water Consumption for Households for Capitals Cities in Liters/Capita/Day in 2010–2014.* IWA website. waterstatistics.iwa-network.org/graph/19.

IWA/UN-Habitat (International Water Association/United Nations Human Settlements Programme). 2011. *Water Operators Partnerships: Building WOPs for Sustainable Development in Water and Sanitation.* London/Nairobi, IWA/UN-Habitat. mirror.unhabitat.org/pmss/(X(1)S(0ksnuwnk52i4kekhnol4zmy0))/getElectronicVersion.aspx?nr=2851&alt=1.

Jackson, S., Tan, P. L., Mooney, C., Hoverman, S. and White, I. 2012. Principles and guidelines for good practice in Indigenous engagement in water planning. *Journal of Hydrology,* Vol. 474, pp. 57–65. doi.org/10.1016/j.jhydrol.2011.12.015.

Jeuland, M. A., Fuente, D. E., Ozdemir, S., Allaire, M. C. and Whittington, D. 2013. The long-term dynamics of mortality benefits from improved water and sanitation in less developed countries. *Plos One,* Vol. 8, No. 10, pp. e74804. doi.org/10.1371/journal.pone.0074804.

Jewett, D. G., Logan, B. E., Arnold, R. G. and Bales, R. C. 1999. Transport of *Pseudomonas fluorescens* strain P17 through quartz sand columns as a function of water content. *Journal of Contaminant Hydrology,* Vol. 36, No. 1–2, pp. 73–89. doi.org/10.1016/S0169-7722(98)00143-0.

Jiménez, A., Cortobius, M. and Kjellén, M. 2014. *Working with Indigenous Peoples in Rural Water and Sanitation: Recommendations for an Intercultural Approach.* Stockholm, Stockholm International Water Institute (SIWI). www.watergovernance.org/wp-content/uploads/2015/06/2014-Recomendations-report-web.pdf.

Jiménez, A., Molina, M. F. and Le Deunff, H. 2015. Indigenous peoples and industry water users: Mapping the conflicts worldwide. *Aquatic Procedia,* Vol. 5, pp. 69–80. doi.org/10.1016/j.aqpro.2015.10.009.

Jiménez, A. and Pérez-Foguet, A. 2010. Building the role of local government authorities towards the achievement of the right to water in rural Tanzania. *Natural Resources Forum,* Vol. 34, No. 2, pp. 93–105. doi.org/10.1111/j.1477-8947.2010.01296.x.

Jiménez Fernández de Palencia, A. and Pérez-Foguet, A. 2011. Implementing pro-poor policies in a decentralized context: The case of the rural water supply and sanitation program in Tanzania. *Sustainability Science,* Vol. 6, No. 1, pp. 37–49.

Johnson, B. R., Hiwasaki, L., Klaver, I. J., Ramos-Castillo, A. and Strang, V. (eds.). 2012. *Water, Cultural Diversity and Global Environmental Change: Emerging Trends, Sustainable Futures?* UNESCO/Springer SBM, Jakarta/Dordrecht, Netherlands. unesdoc.unesco.org/images/0021/002151/215119e.pdf.

Jones, H., Parker, K. J. and Reed, R. 2002. *Water Supply and Sanitation Access and Use by Physically Disabled People: A Literature Review.* Loughborough, UK, Water, Engineering and Development Centre, Loughborough University. wedc-knowledge.lboro.ac.uk/docs/research/WEJY3/Literature_review.pdf.

Jouravlev, A. 2004. *Drinking Water Supply and Sanitation Services on the Threshold of the XXI Century.* Serie Recursos Naturales e Infraestructura No.74. Santiago, United Nations Economic Commission for Latin America and the Caribbean (UNECLAC). repositorio.cepal.org/handle/11362/6454.

Khandker, S., Khalily, B. and Khan, Z. 1995. *Grameen Bank: Performance and Sustainability.* World Bank Discussion Paper No. 306. Washington, DC, World Bank. documents.worldbank.org/curated/en/893101468741588109/Grameen-Bank-performance-and-sustainability.

Kodamaya, S. 2009. *Recent Changes in Small-scale Irrigation in Zambia: The Case of a Village in Chibombo District.* Project report for 2008 of the Vulnerability and Resilience of Social-Ecological Systems. Tokyo, Research Institute for Humanity and Nature. www.chikyu.ac.jp/resilience/files/ReportFY2008/ResilienceProject_Report2009_10.pdf.

Kolsky, P. J., Perez, E. and Tremolet, S. C. M. 2010. *Financing On-Site Sanitation for the Poor: A Six Country Comparative Review and Analysis.* Water and Sanitation Program Working Paper. Washington, DC, World Bank. documents.worldbank.org/curated/en/165231468341112439/Financing-on-site-sanitation-for-the-poor-a-six-country-comparative-review-and-analysis.

Komives, K., Foster, V., Halpern, J. and Wodon, Q. 2005. *Water, Electricity, and the Poor: Who Benefits from Utility Subsidies?* Washington, DC, World Bank. documents.worldbank.org/curated/en/606521468136796984/Water-electricity-and-the-poor-who-benefits-from-utility-subsidies.

Kwame, Y. F. 2018. *Youth for Growth: Transforming Economies through Agriculture.* Chicago, Ill., The Chicago Council on Global Affairs. www.thechicagocouncil.org/publication/youth-growth-transforming-economies-through-agriculture.

LCBC (Lake Chad Basin Commission). 2016. *Programme for the Rehabilitation and Strengthening of the Resilience of Socio-ecologic Systems of the Lake Chad Basin (PRESIBALT): National Coordination of Cameroon Commissioned!* Press Release, 28 October 2016. www.cblt.org/en/news/programme-rehabilitation-and-strengthening-resilience-socio-ecologic-systems-lake-chad-basin.

Lemoalle J. and Magrin G. 2014. *Le développement du lac Tchad : Situation actuelle et futurs possibles* [The Development of Lake Chad : Current Situation and Possible Futures]. Marseille, France, Institut de Recherche pour le Développement (IRD). www.documentation.ird.fr/hor/fdi:010063402. (In French.)

Libralato, G., Volpi Ghirardini, A. and Avezzù, F. 2012. To centralise or to decentralise: An overview of the most recent trends in wastewater treatment management. *Journal of Environmental Management,* Vol. 94, No. 1, pp. 61–68. doi.org/10.1016/j.jenvman.2011.07.010.

Lienert, J. and Larsen, T. A. 2006. Considering user attitude in early development of environmentally friendly technology: A case study of NoMix toilets. *Environmental Science & Technology,* Vol. 40, No. 16, pp. 4838–4844. doi.org/10.1021/es060075o.

Lim, S. S., Vos, T., Flaxman, A. D., Danaei, G., Shibuya, K. et al. 2012. A comparative risk assessment of burden of disease and injury attributable to 67 risk factors and risk factor clusters in 21 regions, 1990–2010: A systematic analysis for the Global Burden of Disease Study 2010. *The Lancet,* Vol. 380, No. 9859, pp. 2224–2260. doi.org/10.1016/S0140-6736(12)61766-8.

Mach, E. 2017. *Water and Migration: How Far would you go for Water?* Caritas in Veritate Foundation. www.environmentalmigration.iom.int/sites/default/files/Paper_in%20print.pdf.

Mach, E. and Richter, C. 2018. *Water and Migration: Implications for Policy Makers.* The 2018 High-level Political Forum Blog. sustainabledevelopment.un.org/hlpf/2018/blog#20mar.

Maheshwari, B., Varua, M., Ward, J., Packham, R., Chinnasamy, P., Dashora, Y., Dave, S., Soni, P., Dillon, P., Purohit, R., Hakimuddin, Shah, T., Oza, S., Singh, P., Prathapar, S., Patel, A., Jadeja, Y., Thaker, B., Kookana, R., Grewal, H., Yadav, K., Mittal, H., Chew, M. and Rao, R. 2014. The role of transdisciplinary approach and community participation in village scale groundwater management: Insights from Gujarat and Rajasthan, India. *Water,* Vol. 6, No. 11, pp. 3386–3408. doi.org/10.3390/w6113386.

Manuel, M., King, M. and McKechnie, A. 2011. *Getting Better Results from Assistance to Fragile States.* ODI Briefing Papers. London, Overseas Development Institute (ODI). www.odi.org/sites/odi.org.uk/files/odi-assets/publications-opinion-files/7297.pdf.

Mara, D. D. and Alabaster, G. 2008. A new paradigm for low-cost urban water supplies and sanitation in developing countries. *Water Policy,* Vol. 10, No. 2, pp. 119–129.

Massoud, M. A., Tarhini, A. and Nasr, J. A. 2009. Decentralized approaches to wastewater treatment and management: Applicability in developing countries. *Journal of Environmental Management,* Vol. 90, No. 1, pp. 652–659. doi.org/10.1016/j.jenvman.2008.07.001.

Mata-Lima, H., Alvino-Borba, A., Pinheiro, A., Mata-Lima, A. and Almeida, J. A. 2013. *Impactos dos desastres naturais nos sistemas ambiental e socioeconômico: O que faz a diferença?* [Impacts of Natural Disasters on Environmental and Socio-Economic Systems: What Makes the Difference?] *Ambiente & Sociedade* (São Paulo, Brazil), Vol.16, No. 3. dx.doi.org/10.1590/S1414-753X2013000300004. (In Portuguese.)

Mayntz, R. 1998. *New Challenges to Governance Theory.* Jean Monnet Chair Papers. Florence, Italy, European University Institute (EUI).

MCRC (Michigan Civil Rights Commission). 2018. *The Flint Water Crisis: Systemic Racism Through the Lens of Flint. One Year Later: An Update on the Recommendations of the Michigan Civil Rights Commission.* (March 26, 2018). MCRC. www.michigan.gov/documents/mdcr/Flint_Water_Update_620973_7.pdf.

_____. n.d. *MCRC Executive Summary – Flint Water Crisis Report.* www.michigan.gov/documents/mdcr/MCRC_EXECUTIVE_SUMMARY_RECOMMENDATIONS_031617_554730_7.pdf.

MDHHS (Michigan Department of Health and Human Services). 2018. *Blood Lead Level Test Results for Selected Flint Zip Codes, Genesee County, and the State of Michigan*. Executive Summary. MDHHS. www.michigan.gov/documents/flintwater/2018-08-29_Monthly_Executive_Blood_Lead_Report_Final_637980_7.pdf.

Mekonnen, M. M. and Hoekstra, A. Y. 2016. Four billion people facing severe water scarcity. *Science Advances*, Vol. 2, No. 2. doi.org/10.1126/sciadv.1500323.

Ménard, C., Jiménez, A. and Tropp, H. 2018. Addressing the policy-implementation gaps in water services: The key role of meso-institutions. *Water International*, Vol. 43, No. 1, pp. 13–33. doi.org/10.1080/02508060.2017.1405696.

Menocal, A. R., Taxell, N., Stenberg Johnsøn, J., Schmaljohann, M., Guillan Montero, A., De Simone, F., Dupuy, K. and Tobias, J. 2015. *Why Corruption Matters: Understanding Causes, Effects and How to Address them*. Evidence paper on corruption. London, UK Department for International Development (DFID) and UKAid. assets.publishing.service.gov.uk/government/uploads/system/uploads/attachment_data/file/406346/corruption-evidence-paper-why-corruption-matters.pdf.

Mercandalli, S. and Losch, B. (eds.). 2017. *Rural Africa in Motion. Dynamics and Drivers of Migration South of the Sahara*. Rome, Food and Agriculture Organization of the United Nations/Centre de Coopération Internationale en Recherche Agronomique pour le Développement (FAO/CIRAD).

Mercy Corps. 2014. *Tapped Out: Water Scarcity and Refugee Pressures in Jordan*. Portland, Oreg., Mercy Corps. www.mercycorps.org/sites/default/files/MercyCorps_TappedOut_JordanWaterReport_March204.pdf.

Metcalfe, C., Murray, C., Collins, L. and Furgal, C. 2011. Water quality and human health in indigenous communities in Canada. *Global Bioethics*, Vol. 24, No. 1–4, pp. 91–94. doi.org/10.1080/11287462.2011.10800705.

Migiro, K. and Mis, M. 2014. *Feature – Kenyan Women Pay the Price for Slum Water "Mafias"*. Online article. Reuters. in.reuters.com/article/women-cities-kenya-water/feature-kenyan-women-pay-the-price-for-slum-water-mafias-idINKCN0JA0P620141126.

Miletto, M., Caretta, M. A., Burchi, F. M. and Zanlucchi, G. 2017. *Migration and its Interdependencies with Water Scarcity, Gender and Youth Employment*. WWAP. Paris, UNESCO. unesdoc.unesco.org/images/0025/002589/258968E.pdf.

Ministry of Energy Infrastructures and Natural Resources of Armenia. 2017. *Development of an Action Plan for the Provision of Equitable Access to Water Supply and Sanitation in Armenia Country Report*. www.unece.org/fileadmin/DAM/env/water/activities/Equitable_access/Country_Report___Final_Action_Plan__29_05.2017_FINAL.pdf.

Ministry of Interior of Turkey. 2018. *Migration Statistics, Temporary Protection*. Website. Directorate General of Migration Management, Ministry of Interior, Republic of Turkey. www.goc.gov.tr/icerik6/temporary-protection_915_1024_4748_icerik.

Ministry of Solidarities and Health/Ministry of Ecological Transition and Solidarities of France. n.d. Santé Environnement : 3e Plan National 2015 > 2019 [Health Environment: 3rd National Plan 2015 > 2019]. Paris, French Republic. solidarites-sante.gouv.fr/IMG/pdf/pnse3_v_finale.pdf. (In French.)

Ministry of Water and Irrigation of Jordan. 2015. *National Water Strategy 2016–2025*. Ministry of Water and Irrigation, Hashemite Kingdom of Jordan. www.mwi.gov.jo/sites/en-us/Hot%20Issues/Strategic%20Documents%20of%20%20The%20Water%20Sector/National%20Water%20Strategy(%202016-2025)-25.2.2016.pdf.

Molle, F., Mollinga, P. and Wester, P. 2009. Hydraulic bureaucracies and the hydraulic mission: Flows of water, flows of power. *Water Alternatives*, Vol. 2, No. 3, pp. 328–349.

Munoz Boudet, A. M., Buitrago, P., Leroy De La Briere, B., Newhouse, D. L., Rubiano Matulevich, E. C., Scott, K., Suarez Becerra, P. 2018. *Gender Differences in Poverty and Household Composition through the Life-Cycle: A Global Perspective*. Policy Research Working Paper; No. WPS 8360. Washington, DC, World Bank Group. documents.worldbank.org/curated/en/135731520343670750/Gender-differences-in-poverty-and-household-composition-through-the-life-cycle-a-global-perspective.

Mweemba, C. E., Funder, M., Nyambe, I. and Van Koppen, B. 2011. *Poverty and Access to Water in Namwala District, Zambia – Report on the Results from a Household Questionnaire Survey*. DIIS Working Paper 2011, No. 19. Copenhagen, Danish Institute for International Studies (DIIS). doi.10.13140/RG.2.1.4078.2880.

Nagabhatla, N and Metcalfe, C. M. (eds.). 2018. *Multifunctional Wetlands: Pollution Abatement and Other Ecological Services from Natural and Constructed Wetlands*. Springer International Publishing.

NASA (National Aeronautics and Space Administration). 2015. *Global Groundwater Basins in Distress*. NASA Earth Observatory website. earthobservatory.nasa.gov/images/86263/global-groundwater-basins-in-distress.

National Institute of Public Health of Republic of Macedonia/Journalists for Human Rights. 2016. *Achieving the Human Right to Water and Sanitation: Introduction, Availability, Methodology of Work*. www.unece.org/fileadmin/DAM/env/water/activities/Equitable_access/PDF_ACHIEVING_THE_HUMAN_RIGHT_TO_WATER_AND_SANITATION__1_.pdf.

Navaneethan, U., Al Mohajer, M. and Shata, M. T. 2008. Hepatitis E and pregnancy: Understanding the pathogenesis. *Liver International*, Vol. 28, No. 9. doi.org/10.1111/j.1478-3231.2008.01840.x.

Ng'ethe, V. 2018. *Nairobi's Water Supply: 2 Claims about Losses & High Prices in Slums Evaluated*. Africa Check. africacheck.org/reports/nairobis-water-2-claims-losses-high-cost-slums-evaluated/.

Niasse, M. 2017. *Coordinating Land and Water Governance for Food Security and Gender Equality*. Global Water Partnership Technical Committee (TEC) Background Papers No. 24. Stockholm, Global Water Partnership (GWP).

Oakley, S. M., Gold, A. J. and Oczkowski, A. J. 2010. Nitrogen control through decentralized wastewater treatment: Process performance and alternative management strategies. *Ecological Engineering*, Vol. 36, No. 11, pp. 1520–1531. doi.10.1016/j.ecoleng.2010.04.030.

OECD (Organisation for Economic Co-operation and Development). 2011. *Water Governance in OECD Countries: A Multi-Level Approach*. OECD Studies on Water. Paris, OECD. www.oecd-ilibrary.org/environment/water-governance-in-oecd-countries_9789264119284-en.

_____. 2012. *OECD Environmental Outlook to 2050: The Consequences of Inaction*. Paris, OECD Publishing. doi.org/10.1787/9789264122246-en.

____. 2015. *OECD Principles on Water Governance*. Paris, OECD. www.oecd.org/governance/oecd-principles-on-water-governance.htm.

____. 2016. *Mitigating Droughts and Floods in Agriculture: Policy Lessons and Approaches, OECD Studies on Water*. OECD Publishing, Paris. dx.doi.org/10.1787/9789264246744-en.

____. n.d. OECD Data. data.oecd.org/.

OECD/FAO (Organisation for Economic Co-operation and Development/Food and Agriculture Organization of the United Nations). 2016. *OECD–FAO Agricultural Outlook 2016–2025*. Paris, OECD Publishing. www.fao.org/3/a-i5778e.pdf.

OHCHR (Office of the High Commissioner for Human Rights). 2011. *Guiding Principles on Business and Human Rights: Implementing the United Nations "Project, Respect and Remedy" Framework*. New York, United Nations. www.ohchr.org/Documents/Publications/GuidingPrinciplesBusinessHR_EN.pdf.

____. 2017a. *France must provide Safe Drinking Water and Sanitation for Migrants in the "Calais Jungle", say UN Rights Experts*. Geneva, United Nations. ohchr.org/en/NewsEvents/Pages/DisplayNews.aspx?NewsID=22240&LangID=E.

____. 2017b. *Mandates of the Special Rapporteur on the Right of Everyone to the Enjoyment of the Highest Attainable Standard of Physical and Mental Health and the Special Rapporteur on the Human Rights to Safe Drinking Water and Sanitation*. Geneva, United Nations.

____. 2018. *France urged by UN Experts to take Effective Measures to bring Water and Sanitation Services to Migrants*. Press release, 4 April 2018. Geneva, United Nations. www.ohchr.org/en/NewsEvents/Pages/DisplayNews.aspx?NewsID=22917&LangID=E.

____. n.d. Special Rapporteur on the human rights to safe drinking water and sanitation. Resolutions. www.ohchr.org/EN/Issues/WaterAndSanitation/SRWater/Pages/Resolutions.aspx.

OHCHR/CESR (Office of the High Commissioner for Human Rights/Center for Economic and Social Rights). 2013. *Who will be Accountable? Human Rights and the Post-2015 Development Agenda*. Geneva/New York, OHCHR/CESR. www.ohchr.org/Documents/Publications/WhoWillBeAccountable.pdf.

OHCHR/UN-Habitat/WHO (Office of the High Commissioner for Human Rights/United Nations Human Settlements Programme/World Health Organization). 2010. *The Right to Water*. Fact Sheet No. 35. Geneva, OHCHR. www.ohchr.org/Documents/Publications/FactSheet35en.pdf.

Ojwang, R. O., Dietrich, J., Anebagilu, P. K., Beyer, M. and Rottensteiner, F. 2017. Rooftop rainwater harvesting for Mombasa: Scenario development with image classification and water resources simulation. *Water*, Vol. 9, No. 5, Art. 359. doi.10.3390/w9050359.

Okpara, U. T., Stringer, L. C., Dougill, A. J. and Bila, M. D. 2015. Conflicts about water in Lake Chad: Are environmental, vulnerability and security issues linked? *Progress in Development Studies*, Vol. 15, No. 4, pp. 308–325. doi.org/10.1177/1464993415592738.

Ostry, J. D., Berg, A. and Tsangarides, C. G. 2014. *Redistribution, Inequality, and Growth*. Discussion Note. International Monetary Fund (IMF). Research Department. www.imf.org/external/pubs/ft/sdn/2014/sdn1402.pdf.

Otterpohl, R., Braun, U. and Oldenburg, M. 2004. Innovative technologies for decentralised water-, wastewater and biowaste management in urban and peri-urban areas. *Water Science and Technology*, Vol. 48, No. 11–12, pp. 23–32. doi.10.2166/wst.2004.0795.

Oweis, T. Y. and Hachum, A. Y. 2003. Improving water productivity in the dry areas of West Asia and North Africa. J. W. Kijne, R. Barker and D. J. Molden (eds.), *Water Productivity in Agriculture: Limits and Opportunities for Improvement*. Comprehensive Assessment of Water Management in Agriculture Series, No. 1. Wallingford, UK, CAB International.

Pacific Institute. n.d. *Water Conflict*. Pacific Institute website. www.worldwater.org/water-conflict/.

Pahl-Wostl, C., Gupta, J. and Petry, D. 2008. Governance and the global water system: A theoretical exploration. *Global Governance*, Vol. 14, No. 4, pp. 419–435.

Pani Haq Samiti Vs. Brihan Mumbai Municipal Corporation. 2012. *Public Interest Litigation No. 10 of 2012*. Mumbai, India, Bombay High Court. www.ielrc.org/content/e1407.pdf.

Parliament of Kenya. 2016. The Community Land Act. *Kenya Gazette Supplement No. 148 (Acts No. 27)*. Republic of Kenya.

Patel, S. and Baptist, C. 2012. Editorial: Documenting by the undocumented. *Environment and Urbanization*, Vol. 24, No. 1, pp. 3–12. doi.org/10.1177/0956247812438364.

Patwardhan, A. 2017. *This Incredible Innovation is lifting a Huge Weight off Women's Shoulders in Maharashtra's Villages*. The Better India, 2 June 2017. www.thebetterindia.com/103278/incredible-innovation-lifting-huge-weight-off-womens-shoulders-maharashtras-villages/.

Paydar, Z., Cook, F., Xevi, E. and Bristow, K. 2010. An overview of irrigation mosaics. *Irrigation and Drainage*, Vol. 60, No. 4, pp. 454–463. doi.org/10.1002/ird.600.

Paz Mena, T., Gómez, L., Rivas Hermann, R. and Ravnborg, H. M. 2011. *Pobreza y acceso al agua e instituciones para la gobernanza del agua en el municipio de Condega, Nicaragua – Informe sobre los resultados de una encuesta a hogares* [Poverty, Access to Water and Water Governance Institutions in the Municipality of Condega, Nicaragua – Report on the Results of a Household-Level Survey]. DIIS Working Paper 2011, No. 2. Copenhagen, Danish Institute for International Studies (DIIS). www.diis.dk/files/media/documents/publications/nicaragua_final_diis_wp_2011_02.pdf. (In Spanish.)

PBL Netherlands Environmental Assessment Agency. 2018. The Geography of Future Water Challenges. The Hague, BPL Netherlands Environmental Assessment Agency. www.pbl.nl/node/64678.

Pedersen, C. A. and Ravnborg, H. M. 2006. *Water Reform – Implications for Rural Poor People's Access to Water*. DIIS Brief. Copenhagen, Danish Institute for International Studies (DIIS).

Peter-Varbanets, M., Zurbrügg, C., Swartz, C. and Pronk, W. 2009. Decentralized systems for potable water and the potential of membrane technology. *Water Research*, Vol. 43, No. 2, pp. 245–265. doi.10.1016/j.watres.2008.10.030.

Piattoni, S. 2010. *The Theory of Multi-Level Governance: Conceptual, Empirical, and Normative Challenges*. Oxford, UK, Oxford University Press.

Picciotto, R. 2013. Involuntary resettlement in infrastructure projects: A development perspective. G. K. Ingram and K. L. Brandt (eds.), *Infrastructure and Land Policies*. Cambridge, Mass., Lincoln Institute of Land Policy. www.lincolninst.edu/sites/default/files/pubfiles/involuntary-resettlement-in-infrastructure-projects_0.pdf.

Pierre, J. (ed.). 2000. *Debating Governance: Authority, Steering, and Democracy*. Oxford, UK, Oxford University Press.

Poushter, J. 2016. *Smartphone Ownership and Internet Usage Continues to Climb in Emerging Economies. But Advanced Economies still have Higher Rates of Technology Use*. Pew Research Center. assets.pewresearch.org/wp-content/uploads/sites/2/2016/02/pew_research_center_global_technology_report_final_february_22__2016.pdf.

Prüss-Ustün, A., Wolf, J., Corvalán, C., Bos, R. and Neira, M. 2016. *Preventing Disease through Healthy Environments: A Global Assessment of the Burden of Disease from Environmental Risks*. Geneva, World Health Organization (WHO). www.who.int/quantifying_ehimpacts/publications/preventing-disease/en/.

Purushothaman, S., Tobin, T., Vissa, S., Pillai, P., Silliman, S. and Pinheiro, C. 2012. *Seeing Beyond the State: Grassroots Women's Perspectives on Corruption and Anti-Corruption*. New York, United Nations Development Programme (UNDP). www.undp.org/content/dam/undp/library/Democratic%20Governance/Anti-corruption/Grassroots%20women%20and%20anti-corruption.pdf.

Qadir, M., Jiménez, G. C., Farnum, R. L., Dodson, L. L. and Smakhtin, V. 2018. Fog water collection: Challenges beyond technology. *Water*, Vol. 10, No. 4, pp. 372. doi.org/10.3390/w10040372.

Qadir, M., Sharma, B. R., Bruggeman, A., Choukr-Allah, R. and Karajeh, F. 2007. Non-conventional water resources and opportunities for water augmentation to achieve food security in water scarce countries. *Agricultural Water Management*, Vol. 87, No. 1, pp. 2–22. doi.org/10.1016/j.agwat.2006.03.018.

Rapsomanikis, G. 2015. *The Economic Lives of Smallholder Farmers: An Analysis based on Household Data from Nine Countries*. Rome, Food and Agriculture Organization of the United Nations (FAO). www.fao.org/3/a-i5251e.pdf.

Ravnborg, H. M. 2013. *Pesticides and International Environmental Governance*. DIIS Policy Brief. Copenhagen, Danish Institute or International Studies (DIIS). www.diis.dk/files/media/publications/import/extra/pb2013_pesticides-international-governance_hmr_web.pdf.

_____. 2015. Water competition, water governance and food security. I. Christoplos and A. Pain (eds.), *New Challenges to Food Security: From Climate Change to Fragile States*. London and New York, Routledge.

_____. 2016. Water governance reform in the context of inequality: Securing rights or legitimizing dispossession? *Water International*, Vol. 41, No. 6, pp. 928–943. doi.org/10.1080/02508060.2016.1214895.

Ravnborg, H. M. and Jensen, K. M. 2012. The water governance challenge: The discrepancy between what is and what should be. *Water Science and Technology: Water Supply*, Vol. 12, No. 6, pp. 799–809. dx.doi.org/10.2166/ws.2012.056.

Razzaque, J. 2002. *Human Rights and the Environment: Developments at the National Level, South Asia and Africa*. Background Paper No. 4, presented at Joint UNEP-OHCHR Expert Seminar on Human Rights and the Environment, 14–16 January 2002, Geneva.

Rheingans, R., Kukla, M., Faruque, A. S., Sur, D., Zaidi, A. K., Nasrin, D., Farag, T. H., Levine, M. M. and Kotloff, K. L. 2012. Determinants of household costs associated with childhood diarrhea in 3 South Asian settings. *Clinical Infectious Diseases*, Vol. 55, Supplement 4, S327–S335. doi.10.1093/cid/cis764.

Ribot, J. C., Agrawal, A. and Larson, A. M. 2006. Recentralizing while decentralizing: How national governments reappropriate forest resources. *World Development*, Vol. 34, No. 11, pp. 1864–1886. doi.org/10.1016/j.worlddev.2005.11.020

Rigaud, K. K., De Sherbinin, A., Jones, B., Bergmann, J., Clement, V., Ober, K., Schewe, J., Adamo, S., McCusker, B., Heuser, S. and Midgley, A. 2018. *Groundswell: Preparing for Internal Climate Migration*. Washington, DC, World Bank. www.worldbank.org/en/news/infographic/2018/03/19/groundswell---preparing-for-internal-climate-migration.

Rights and Resources Initiative. 2017. *Securing Community Land Rights: Priorities and Opportunities to Advance Climate & Sustainable Development Goals*. Washington, DC, Rights and Resources Initiative. rightsandresources.org/wp-content/uploads/2017/09/Stockholm-Priorities-and-Opportunities-Brief-Factsheet.pdf.

Rockström, J., Habitu, N., Oweis, T. Y. and Wani, S. 2007. Managing water in rainfed agriculture. Comprehensive Assessment of Water Management in Agriculture, *Water for Food, Water for Life: A Comprehensive Assessment of Water Management in Agriculture*. London/Colombo, EarthScan/International Water Management Institute (IWMI).

Ronayne, M. 2005. *The Cultural and Environmental Impact of Large Dams in Southeast Turkey*. Fact-Finding Mission Report. Galway, Ireland/London, National University of Ireland/the Kurdish Human Rights Project (KHRP).

Roser, M. and Ortiz-Ospina, E. 2018. *Global Extreme Poverty*. Our World in Data. ourworldindata.org/extreme-poverty.

Ryan, C. and Elsner, P. 2016. The potential for sand dams to increase the adaptive capacity of East African drylands to climate change. *Regional Environmental Change*, Volume 16, No. 7, pp. 208–2096. doi.org/10.1007/s10113-016-0938-y.

Satterthwaite, D. 2012. What happens when slum dwellers put themselves on the map. Editorial note. *Environment and Urbanization*, Vol. 24, No. 1. www.iied.org/what-happens-when-slum-dwellers-put-themselves-map.

SEI (Stockholm Environment Institute). 2013. *Sanitation Policy and Practice in Rwanda: Tackling the Disconnect*. Policy Brief. Stockholm, SEI.

Shah. T. 2005. Groundwater and human development: Challenges and opportunities in livelihoods and environment. *Water, Science & Technology*, Vol. 51, No. 8, pp. 27–37.

Smets, H. 2009. Access to drinking water at an affordable price in developing countries. M. El Moujabber, L. Mandi, G. Trisorio-Liuzzi, I. Martín, A. Rabi and R. Rodríguez (eds.), *Technological Perspectives for Rational Use of Water Resources in the Mediterranean Region*. Bari, Italy, Mediterranean Agronomic Institute (CIHEAM), pp. 57–68. (Options Méditerranéennes: Série A. Séminaires Méditerranéennes; n. 88).

_____. 2012. Quantifying the affordability standard. M. Langford and A. F. S. Russell (eds.), *The Human Right to Water: Theory, Practice and Prospects*. Cambridge, UK, Cambridge University Press, pp. 225–275.

Sobrevila, C. 2008. *The Role of Indigenous Peoples in Biodiversity Conservation: The Natural but often forgotten Partners*. Washington, DC, World Bank. documents.worldbank.org/curated/en/995271468177530126/The-role-of-indigenous-peoples-in-biodiversity-conservation-the-natural-but-often-forgotten-partners.

SOIL (Sustainable Organic Integrated Livelihoods). n.d. *About SOIL*. www.oursoil.org/who-we-are/about-soil/.

Solanes, M. 2007. Fifteen years of experience. *Circular of the Network for Cooperation in Integrated Water Resource Management for Sustainable Development in Latin America and the Caribbean*, No. 26. repositorio.cepal.org/handle/11362/39396.

Solón, P. 2007. Diversidad cultural y privatización del agua [Cultural diversity and water privatization]. R. Boelens, M. Chiba, D. Nakashima and V. Retana (eds.), *El agua y los pueblos indígenas* [Water and Indigenous Peoples]. Conocimientos de la Naturaleza 2. Paris, UNESCO. unesdoc.unesco.org/images/0014/001453/145353so.pdf. (in Spanish.)

Sosa, M. and Zwarteveen, M. 2016. Questioning the effectiveness of planned conflict resolution strategies in water disputes between rural communities and mining companies in Peru. *Water International*, Vol. 41, No. 3, pp. 483–500. doi.org/10.1080/02508060.2016.1141463.

Søreide, T. 2016. *Corruption and Criminal Justice. Bridging Economic and Legal Perspectives*. Cheltenham, UK/Northampton, Mass., Edward Elgar.

Stapleton, S. O., Nadin, R., Watson, C. and Kellett, J. 2017. *Climate Change, Migration and Displacement: The Need for a Risk-Informed nd Coherent Approach*. London/New York, Overseas Development Institute (ODI)/United Nations Development Programme (UNDP). www.odi.org/publications/10977-climate-change-migration-and-displacement-need-risk-informed-and-coherent-approach.

Subbaraman, R. and Murthy, S. L. 2015. The rights to water in the slums of Mumbai, India. *Bulletin of the World Health Organization*, Vol. 93, pp. 815–816. www.who.int/bulletin/volumes/93/11/15-155473/en/.

Sumpter, C. and Torondel, B. 2013. A systematic review of the health and social effects of menstrual hygiene management. *Plos One*, Vol. 8, No. 4. doi.org/10.1371/journal.pone.0062004.

Switzer, D. and Teodoro, M. P. 2017. Class, race, ethnicity, and justice in safe drinking water compliance. *Social Science Quarterly*, Vol. 99, No. 2, pp. 524–535. doi.org/10.1111/ssqu.12397.

Tallis, H., Kareiva, P., Marvier, M. and Chang, A. 2008. An ecosystem services framework to support both practical conservation and economic development. *Proceedings of the National Academy of Sciences of the United States of America (PNAS)*, Vol. 105, No. 28, pp. 9457–64. doi.org/10.1073/pnas.0705797105.

Thompson, K., O'Dell, K., Syed, S. and Kemp, H. 2017. Thirsty for change: The untapped potential of women in urban water management. *Deloitte Insights*, 23 January 2017. www2.deloitte.com/insights/us/en/deloitte-review/issue-20/women-in-water-management.html.

Tropp, H. 2007. Water governance: Trends and needs for new capacity development. *Water Policy*, Vol. 9 (Supplement 2), pp. 19–30.

Tsagarakis, K. P., Mara, D. D. and Angelakis, A. N. 2001. Wastewater management in Greece: Experience and lessons for developing countries. *Water Science and Technology*, Vol. 44, No. 6, pp. 163–172.

Turral, H., Burke, J. and Faurès, J. 2011. *Climate Change, Water and Food Security*. FAO Water Reports No. 36. Rome, Food and Agriculture Organization of the United Nations (FAO). www.fao.org/docrep/014/i2096e/i2096e.pdf.

Ulrich, A., Reuter, S. and Gutterer, B. (eds.). 2009. *Decentralised Wastewater Treatment Systems (DEWATS) and Sanitation in Developing Countries: A Practical Guide*. UK/Germany, Water, Engineering and Development Centre, Loughborough University/Bremen Overseas Research and Development Association (WEDC/BORDA).

UN (United Nations). 1951. *Convention relating to the Status of Refugees*. www.refworld.org/docid/3be01b964.html.

_____. 1967. *Protocol relating to the Status of Refugees*. www.refworld.org/docid/3ae6b3ae4.html.

_____. 1992. *United Nations Conference on Environment & Development: Agenda 21*. sustainabledevelopment.un.org/content/documents/Agenda21.pdf.

_____. 1997. *Convention of the Law of the Non-navigational Uses of International Watercourses*. legal.un.org/ilc/texts/instruments/english/conventions/8_3_1997.pdf.

_____. 2008. *United Nations Declaration on the Rights of Indigenous Peoples*. www.un.org/esa/socdev/unpfii/documents/DRIPS_en.pdf.

_____. 2011. *Report of the Secretary-General's Panel of Experts on Accountability in Sri Lanka*. www.un.org/News/dh/infocus/Sri_Lanka/POE_Report_Full.pdf.

_____. 2013. *Sustainable Development in Latin America and the Caribbean: Follow-up to the United Nations Development Agenda beyond 2015 and to Rio+20. Preliminary version*. United Nations. www.cepal.org/rio20/noticias/paginas/8/43798/2013-273_Rev.1_Sustainable_Development_in_Latin_America_and_the_Caribbean_WEB.pdf.

_____. 2017. *Sustainable Development Goals Report 2017*. New York, United Nations. www.un.org/development/desa/publications/sdg-report-2017.html.

_____. 2018a. *Sustainable Development Goal 6: Synthesis Report 2018 on Water and Sanitation*. New York, United Nations. www.unwater.org/app/uploads/2018/07/SDG6_SR2018_web_v5.pdf.

_____. 2018b. *The Sustainable Development Goals Report 2018*. New York, United Nations. unstats.un.org/sdgs/report/2018.

UNDESA (United Nations Department of Economic and Social Affairs). 2004. *A Gender Perspective on Water Resources and Sanitation.* Background Paper No. 2. New York, United Nations. www.unwater.org/publications/gender-perspective-water-resources-sanitation/.

_____. 2007. *Providing Water to the Urban Poor in Developing Countries: The Role of Tariffs and Subsidies.* Sustainable Development Innovation Briefs No. 4. United Nations. sustainabledevelopment.un.org/content/documents/no4.pdf.

_____. 2009. *State of the World's Indigenous Peoples.* New York, United Nations. www.un.org/esa/socdev/unpfii/documents/SOWIP/en/ SOWIP_web.pdf.

_____. 2015. *The World's Women 2015: Trends and Statistics.* New York. United Nations. unstats.un.org/unsd/gender/worldswomen.html.

_____. 2017a. *World Population Prospects: The 2017 Revision, Key Findings and Advance Tables.* Working Paper No. ESA/P/WP/248. New York, United Nations. esa.un.org/unpd/wpp/publications/

_____. 2017b. *International Migration Report 2017: Highlights.* New York, United Nations. www.un.org/development/desa/publications/ international-migration-report-2017.html.

_____. 2018. *World Urbanization Prospects 2018. Maps.* esa.un.org/unpd/wup/Maps/.

UNDG (United Nations Development Group). 2003. *The Human Rights Based Approach to Development Cooperation towards a Common Understanding among UN Agencies.* UNDG. undg.org/document/the-human-rights-based-approach-to-development-cooperation-towards-a-common-understanding-among-un-agencies/.

UNDP (United Nations Development Programme). 2006. *Human Development Report 2006. Beyond Scarcity: Power, Poverty and the Global Water Crisis.* New York, Palgrave Macmillan. hdr.undp.org/sites/default/files/reports/267/hdr06-complete.pdf.

_____. 2009. *Human Development Report 2009. Overcoming Barriers: Human Mobility and Development.* New York, UNDP. hdr.undp.org/ sites/default/files/reports/269/hdr_2009_en_complete.pdf.

_____. 2011a. *Small-Scale Water Providers in Kenya: Pioneers or Predators?* New York, UNDP. www.undp.org/content/dam/undp/library/ Poverty%20Reduction/Inclusive%20development/Kenya%20paper(web).pdf.

_____. 2011b. *Chemicals and Gender.* Energy & Environment Practice Gender Mainstreaming Guidance Series. Chemicals Management. www.undp.org/content/dam/aplaws/publication/en/publications/environment-energy/www-ee-library/chemicals-management/ chemicals-and-gender/2011%20Chemical&Gender.pdf.

_____. 2016. *Overview. Human Development Report 2016: Human Development for Everyone.* New York, UNDP. hdr.undp.org/sites/default/ files/HDR2016_EN_Overview_Web.pdf.

UNDP-SIWI WGF (United Nations Development Programme-Stockholm International Water Institute Water Governance Facility). 2017. *Women and Corruption in the Water Sector: Theories and Experiences from Johannesburg and Bogotá.* WGF Report No. 8. Stockholm, SIWI. watergovernance.org/resources/wgf-report-8-women-corruption-water-sector-theories-experiences-johannesburg-bogota/.

UNDP-SIWI WGF/UNICEF (United Nations Development Programme-Stockholm International Water Institute Water Governance Facility/ United Nations International Children's Emergency Fund). 2015. *WASH and Accountability: Explaining the Concept.* Accountability for Sustainability Partnership. Stockholm/New York, UNDP-SIWI WGF/UNICEF. www.unicef.org/wash/files/Accountability_in_WASH_ Explaining_the_Concept.pdf.

UNECE (United Nations Economic Commission for Europe). 1992. *Convention on the Protection and Use of Transboundary Watercourses and International Lakes.* Helsinki. www.unece.org/fileadmin/DAM/env/water/publications/WAT_Text/ECE_MP.WAT_41.pdf.

_____. n.d.a. *Countries are Committed to Address Inequities in Access to Water and Sanitation Services under the Protocol on Water and Health.* www.unece.org/info/media/news/environment/2018/countries-are-committed-to-address-inequities-in-access-to-water-and-sanitation-services-under-the-protocol-on-water-and-health/doc.html.

_____. n.d.b. *Equitable Access to Water and Sanitation.* www.unece.org/env/water/pwh_work/equitable_access.html.

UNECE/UNESCO (United Nations Economic Commission for Europe/United Nations Educational, Scientific and Cultural Organization). 2018. *Progress on Transboundary Water Cooperation: Global Baseline for SDG Indicator 6.5.2.* Paris, United Nations and UNESCO. www.unwater.org/app/uploads/2018/11/SDG6_Indicator_Report_652_High_Quality_2018.pdf.

UNECE/WHO Europe (United Nations Economic Commission for Europe/World Health Organization Regional Office for Europe). 1999. *Protocol on Water and Health to the 1992 Convention on the Protection and Use of Transboundary Watercourses and International Lakes.* United Nations. treaties.un.org/doc/source/RecentTexts/27-5a-eng.htm.

_____. 2012. *No One Left Behind: Good Practices to ensure Equitable Access to Water and Sanitation in the Pan-European Region.* New York and Geneva, United Nations. www.unece.org/env/water/publications/ece_mp.wh_6.html.

_____. 2013. *The Equitable Access Score-Card: Supporting Policy Processes to achieve the Human Right to Water and Sanitation.* United Nations. www.unece.org/index.php?id=34032.

_____. 2016. *Guidance Note on the Development of Action Plans to ensure Equitable Access to Water and Sanitation.* New York and Geneva, United Nations. www.unece.org/index.php?id=44284.

UNECLAC (United Nations Economic Commission for Latin America and the Caribbean). 1985. *The Water Resources of Latin America and the Caribbean and their Utilization: A Report on Progress in the Application of the Mar del Plata Action Plan.* Santiago, United Nations. repositorio.cepal.org/bitstream/handle/11362/8494/S8500065_en.pdf.

_____. 2010. Editorial remarks. *Circular of the Network for Cooperation in Integrated Water Resource Management for Sustainable Development in Latin America and the Caribbean,* No. 31. repositorio.cepal.org/handle/11362/39406.

_____. 2018. *Social Panorama of Latin America 2017.* Santiago, United Nations. repositorio.cepal.org//handle/11362/42717.

UNESCAP (United Nations Economic and Social Commission for Asia and the Pacific). 2010. *Statistical Yearbook for Asia and the Pacific 2009.* Bangkok, UNESCAP. www.unisdr.org/files/13373_ESCAPSYB2009.pdf.

_____. 2016. *Asia-Pacific Countries with Special Needs. Development Report 2016 on Adapting the 2030 Agenda for Sustainable Development at National Level.* Bangkok, UNESCAP. www.unescap.org/publications/asia-pacific-countries-special-needs-development-report-2016-adapting-2030-agenda.

_____. 2017. *Statistical Yearbook for Asia and the Pacific 2016: SDG Baseline Report.* Bangkok, UNESCAP. www.unescap.org/sites/default/files/ESCAP_SYB2016_SDG_baseline_report.pdf.

_____. 2018. *Leave No One Behind: Disaster Resilience for Sustainable Development. Asia-Pacific Disaster Report 2017.* Bangkok, UNESCAP. www.unescap.org/publications/asia-pacific-disaster-report-2017-leave-no-one-behind.

UNESCAP/UNESCO/ILO/UN Environment/FAO/UN-Water (United Nations Economic and Social Commission for Asia and the Pacific/United Nations Educational, Scientific and Cultural Organization/International Labour Organization/United Nations Environment/Food and Agricultural Organization of the United Nations/United Nations Water). 2018. *Clean Water and Sanitation: Ensure Availability and Sustainable Management of Water and Sanitation for All.* SDG 6 Goal Profile. www.unescap.org/resources/sdg6-goal-profile.

UNESCO (United Nations Educational, Scientific and Cultural Organization). 2016. *Global Education Monitoring Report 2016. Place: Inclusive and Sustainable Cities.* Paris, UNESCO. unesdoc.unesco.org/images/0024/002462/246230E.pdf.

_____. 2017a. *Global Education Monitoring Report Summary 2017/8: Accountability in Education: Meeting our Commitments.* Paris, UNESCO. unesdoc.unesco.org/images/0025/002593/259338e.pdf.

_____. 2017b. *Literacy Rates continue to rise from one Generation to the Next.* Fact Sheet No. 45. Paris, UNESCO. uis.unesco.org/sites/default/files/documents/fs45-literacy-rates-continue-rise-generation-to-next-en-2017_0.pdf.

_____. 2017c. *Education for Sustainable Developments Goals: Learning Objectives.* Paris, UNESCO. unesdoc.unesco.org/images/0024/002474/247444e.pdf.

_____. 2018a. *Culture for the 2030 Agenda.* Paris, UNESCO. unesdoc.unesco.org/images/0026/002646/264687e.pdf.

_____. 2018b. *UNESCO Policy on engaging with Indigenous Peoples.* Paris, UNESCO. unesdoc.unesco.org/images/0026/002627/262748e.pdf.

_____. n.d. *BIOsphere and Heritage of Lake Chad (BIOPALT) Project.* UNESCO website. en.unesco.org/biopalt?language=en.

UNESCO-IHP (United Nations Educational, Scientific and Cultural Organization-International Hydrological Programme). n.d. *Recovering the Ancestral Water System of Los Paltas with Ecohydrological Approach to supply Water to the City of Catacocha in Southern Ecuador.* Ecohydrology Web Platform. ecohydrology-ihp.org/demosites/view/1046.

UNESCO (United Nations Educational, Scientific and Cultural Organization) Living Heritage. n.d. *Traditional System of Corongo's Water Judges.* UNESCO website. ich.unesco.org/en/RL/traditional-system-of-corongos-water-judges-01155.

UNESCO (United Nations Educational, Scientific and Cultural Organization) World Heritage Centre. n.d. Cultural Landscape of Bali Province: The Subak System as a Manifestation of the Tri Hita Karana Philosophy. UNESCO website. whc.unesco.org/en/list/1194.

UNESCWA (United Nations Economic and Social Commission for Western Asia). 2011. *Water for Cities: Responding to the Urban Challenge in the ESCWA Region.* Technical Paper No. 1. Beirut, UNESCWA. www.unescwa.org/sites/www.unescwa.org/files/publications/files/e_escwa_sdpd_11_technical_paper-1_e.pdf.

_____. 2013. *Population and Development Report Issue No. 6: Development Policy Implications of Age-Structural Transitions in Arab Countries.* New York, United Nations. www.unescwa.org/sites/www.unescwa.org/files/publications/files/e_escwa_sdd_13_2_e.pdf.

UNESCWA/IOM (United Nations Economic and Social Commission for Western Asia/International Organization for Migration). 2015. *2015 Situation Report on International Migration: Migration, Displacement and Development in a Changing Arab Region.* Beirut, UNESCWA. https://publications.iom.int/system/files/pdf/sit_rep_en.pdf.

_____. 2017. *2017 Situation Report on International Migration: Migration in the Arab Region and the 2030 Agenda for Sustainable Development.* Beirut, UNESCWA. www.unescwa.org/sites/www.unescwa.org/files/publications/files/2017-situation-report-international-migration-english.pdf.

UNFPA (United Nations Population Fund). 2014. *State of World Population 2014. The Power of 1.8 Billion: Adolescents, Youth and the Transformation of the Future.* New York, UNFPA. unfpa.org/swop-2014.

UNGA (United Nations General Assembly). 1948. *Universal Declaration of Human Rights.* Resolution adopted by the General Assembly, Third session, A/RES/3/217 A. www.un-documents.net/a3r217a.htm.

_____. 1986. *Declaration on the Right to Development.* Ninety-seventh plenary meeting. www.un.org/documents/ga/res/41/a41r128.htm.

_____. 2010. *The Human Right to Water and Sanitation.* Resolution adopted by the General Assembly on 28 July 2010, Sixty-fourth session, A/RES/64/292. www.un.org/ga/search/view_doc.asp?symbol=A/RES/64/292.

_____. 2013. *Human Right to Safe Drinking Water and Sanitation.* Note by the Secretary-General. Sixty-eight session, A/68/264. undocs.org/A/68/264.

_____. 2015a. *Transforming our World: The 2030 Agenda for Sustainable Development.* Resolution adopted by the General Assembly on 25 September 2015. Seventieth session, A/RES/70/1. www.un.org/en/development/desa/population/migration/generalassembly/docs/globalcompact/A_RES_70_1_E.pdf.

_____. 2015b. *The Human Rights to Safe Drinking Water and Sanitation.* Resolution adopted by the General Assembly on 17 December 2015, Seventieth session, A/RES/70/169. undocs.org/A/RES/70/169.

_____. 2016. *Human Rights to Safe Drinking Water and Sanitation.* Note by the Secretary-General. Seventy-first session. A/71/302. undocs.org/A/71/302.

_____. 2017. *Human Rights to Safe Drinking Water and Sanitation.* Note by the Secretary-General. Seventy-second session. A/72/127. undocs.org/A/72/127.

UN-Habitat (United Nations Human Settlements Programme). 2003. *The Challenge of Slums: Global Report on Human Settlements 2003.* London/Sterling, Va., Earthscan Publications.

_____. 2005. *Urbanization Challenges in Sub-Saharan Africa.* Nairobi, UN-Habitat. unhabitat.org/books/urbanization-challenges-in-sub-saharan-africa/.

_____. 2006. *Urban Inequities Survey.* Manual. UN-Habitat. mirror.unhabitat.org/downloads/docs/Urban-Inequities-Survey-Manual.pdf.

_____. 2011. *Enhanced Partnerships between the Development Banks and UN-Habitat.* Prepared as a background paper for GC 23 side-meeting on Investments in Sustainable Urban Development, 12th April 2011. Unpublished report.

_____. 2013. *State of the Worlds Cities Report 2012/2013: Prosperity of Cities.* Nairobi, UN-Habitat. sustainabledevelopment.un.org/content/documents/745habitat.pdf.

_____. 2014. *Kibera: Integrated Water Sanitation and Waste Management Project – Progress and Promise: Innovations in Slum Upgrading.* Post-Project Intervention Assessment Report. Nairobi, UN-Habitat. unhabitat.org/books/kibera-integrated-water-sanitation-and-waste-management-project/.

_____. n.d. World Urban Campaign. *Delegated Management Model for Improving Access to Water in Urban Informal Settlements in Kenya.* World Urban Campaign website. www.worldurbancampaign.org/delegated-management-model-improving-access-water-urban-informal-settlements-kenya.

UN-Habitat/IHS-Erasmus University Rotterdam (United Nations Human Settlements Programme/Institute for Housing and Urban Development Studies-Erasmus University Rotterdam). 2018. *The State of African Cities 2018 – The Geography of African Investment.* Nairobi, UN-Habitat. unhabitat.org/books/the-state-of-african-cities-2018-the-geography-of-african-investment/.

UNHCR (United Nations High Commissioner for Refugees). 2004. Protracted Refugee Situations. Thirtieth meeting of the Standing Committee. www.unhcr.org/excom/standcom/40c982172/protracted-refugee-situations.html.

_____. 2017. *ReHoPE – Refugee and Host Population Empowerment. Strategic Framework – Uganda.*

_____. 2018a. *Global Trends: Forced Displacement in 2017.* UNHCR website. www.unhcr.org/globaltrends2017/.

_____. 2018b. *ACNUR felicita al Gobierno de Colombia por haber registrado más de 440 mil venezolanos en dos meses* [UNHCR congratulates the Government of Colombia for having registered over 440,000 Venezuelans in Two Months Time]. UNHCR website. www.acnur.org/noticias/press/2018/6/5b27e1644/acnur-felicita-al-gobierno-de-colombia-por-haber-registrado-mas-de-440.html. (In Spanish.)

_____. 2018c. *Monitoring Reports.* UNHCR internal monitoring reports. Unpublished.

_____. 2018d. *Urban WASH Planning Guidance Note.* UNHCR. wash.unhcr.org/download/urban-wash-planning-guidance-and-case-studies/.

_____. 2018e. *UNHCR Turkey: Key Facts and Figures.* UNHCR. reliefweb.int/sites/reliefweb.int/files/resources/66218.pdf.

_____. 2018f. *The Global Compact on Refugees: UNHCR Quick Guide.* www.unhcr.org/5b6d574a7.

_____. n.d. High Alert List for Emergency Preparedness (HALEP). UNHCR website. emergency.unhcr.org/entry/190378/high-alert-list-for-emergency-preparedness-halep.

UNICEF (United Nations Children's Fund). 2014. *25 Years of The Convention on The Rights of the Child. Is the World a Better Place for Children? A Statistical Analysis of Progress since the Adoption of the Convention of the Rights of the Child.* New York, UNICEF. www.unicef.org/crc/files/02_CRC_25_Years_UNICEF.pdf.

_____. 2016. *UNICEF: Collecting Water is often a Colossal Waste of Time for Women and Girls.* Press release. www.unicef.org/media/media_92690.html.

_____. 2017. *Country Urbanization Profiles: A Review of National Health or Immunization Policies and Immunization Strategies.* New York, UNICEF. www.unicef.org/health/files/Urban_profile_discussion_paper_vJune28.pdf.

UNICEF/World Bank. 2016. *Ending Extreme Poverty: A Focus on Children.* Briefing Note. www.unicef.org/publications/index_92826.html.

UNISDR/UNECE (United Nations Office for Disaster Risk Reduction/United Nations Economic Commission for Europe). 2018. *Words into Action Guide: Implementation Guide for addressing Water-Related Disasters and Transboundary Cooperation. Integrating Disaster Risk Management with Water Management and Climate Change Adaptation.* New York/Geneva, United Nations.

United Nations Security Council. 2004. *The Rule of Law and Transitional Justice in Conflict and Post-Conflict Societies.* Report of the Secretary General. www.un.org/en/ga/search/view_doc.asp?symbol=S/2004/616.

UN News. 2016. *UN inaugurates Water Project in Haiti benefiting 60,000 People as Part of Fight against Cholera.* United Nations. news.un.org/en/story/2016/12/547652-un-inaugurates-water-project-haiti-benefiting-60000-people-part-fight-against.

UNOCHA (United Nations Office for the Coordination of Humanitarian Affairs). 2018. *Humanitarian Needs and Requirement Overview 2018: Lake Chad Basin Emergency.* UNOCHA. reliefweb.int/report/nigeria/lake-chad-basin-emergency-2018-humanitarian-needs-and-requirement-overview-february.

UNPFII (United Nations Permanent Forum on Indigenous Issues). 2016. *Substantive Inputs to the 2016 High Level Political Forum, Thematic Review of the 2030 Agenda for Sustainable Development.* United Nations. www.un.org/esa/socdev/unpfii/documents/2016/Docs-updates/INPUTS_2016_HLPF_eng.pdf.

_____. n.d. *Who are Indigenous Peoples? Indigenous Peoples, Indigenous Voices: Factsheet.* www.un.org/esa/socdev/unpfii/documents/5session_factsheet1.pdf.

UNSD (United Nations Statistic Division). n.d. *Goal 7: Ensure Access to Affordable, Reliable, Sustainable and Modern Energy for All - SDG Indicators.* UNSD website. unstats.un.org/sdgs/report/2016/goal-07/.

UNU-INWEH (United Nations University-Institute for Water Environment and Health). n.d. *Uncover Resources: Alleviating Global Water Scarcity through Unconventional Water Resources and Technologies*. Project Flyer. inweh.unu.edu/wp-content/uploads/2016/09/Unconventional-Water-Resources_Flyer.pdf.

UN-Water. 2015. *Eliminating Discrimination and Inequalities in Access to Water and Sanitation*. UN-Water. www.unwater.org/publications/eliminating-discrimination-inequalities-access-water-sanitation/.

UN-Water DPAC/WSSCC (UN-Water Decade Programme on Advocacy and Communications/Water Supply and Sanitation Collaborative Council). n.d. *The Human Right to Water and Sanitation*. Media brief. www.un.org/waterforlifedecade/pdf/human_right_to_water_and_sanitation_media_brief.pdf.

UN Women. 2017. *Making the SDGs count for Women and Girls with Disabilities*. Issue brief. UN Women. www.unwomen.org/en/digital-library/publications/2017/6/issue-brief-making-the-sdgs-count-for-women-and-girls-with-disabilities.

_____. 2018. *Turning Promises into Action: Gender Equality in the 2030 Agenda for Sustainable Development*. UN Women. www.unwomen.org/en/digital-library/publications/2018/2/gender-equality-in-the-2030-agenda-for-sustainable-development-2018.

Van Eeden, A., Mehta, L. and Van Koppen, B. 2016. Whose waters? Large-scale agricultural development and water grabbing in the Wami-Ruvu River Basin, Tanzania. *Water Alternatives*, Vol. 9, No. 3, pp. 608–626.

Van Koppen, B., Giordano, M. and Butterworth, J. A. 2007. *Community-Based Water Law and Water Resource Management Reform in Developing Countries*. Comprehensive Assessment of Water Management in Agriculture Series. Wallingford, UK, CABI International.

Van Koppen, B., Sokile, C. S., Hatibu, N., Lankford, B. A., Mahoo, H. and Yanda, P. Z. 2004. *Formal Water Rights in Rural Tanzania: Deepening the Dichotomy?* Working Paper No. 71. Colombo, International Water Management Institute (IWMI).

Van Koppen, B., Van der Zaag, P., Manzungu, E. and Tapela, B. 2014. Roman water law in rural Africa: The unfinished business of colonial dispossession. *Water International*, Vol. 39, No. 1, pp. 49–62. doi.org/10.1080/02508060.2013.863636.

Vickers, A., 2006. New directions in lawn and landscape water conservation. *Journal of the American Water Works Association*, Vol. 98, No. 2, pp. 56–156. doi.org/10.1002/j.1551-8833.2006.tb07586.x.

Vilane, B. R. T. and Dlamini, T. L. 2016. An assessment of groundwater pollution from on-site sanitation in Malkerns, Swaziland. *Journal of Agricultural Science and Engineering*, Vol. 2, No. 2, pp. 11–17.

WaterAid. 2016. *Water at what Cost? The State of the World's Water 2016*. Briefing Report. https://washmatters.wateraid.org/sites/g/files/jkxoof256/files/Water%20%20At%20What%20Cost%20%20The%20State%20of%20the%20Worlds%20Water%202016.pdf.

Water Boards/WETUM (Water Employees Trade Union of Malawi). 2014. *Collective Bargaining Agreement between Water Boards and Water Employees Trade Union of Malawi*. mywage.com/labour-law/collective-agreements-database-malawi/collective-bargaining-agreement-between-water-boards-and-water-employees-trade-union-of-malawi---2014.

WaterCanada. 2017. *First Nations Water and Wastewater Under-Resourced in Federal Budget*. WaterCanada. www.watercanada.net/pbo-budget-sufficiency-first-nations-water-wastewater/.

WaterLex. 2014. *Integrating the Human Right to Water and Sanitation in Development Practice*. www.waterlex.org/waterlex-toolkit/how-to-articulate-the-human-right-to-water-and-sanitation-and-integrated-water-resources-management/.

WaterLex/WASH United. 2014. *The Human Rights to Water and Sanitation in Courts Worldwide: A Selection of National, Regional and International Case Law*. Geneva, WaterLex and WASH United. www.waterlex.org/new/wp-content/uploads/2015/01/Case-Law-Compilation.pdf.

Water.org. 2018. *Programmatic Impact Update: Second Quarter Report* (January 2018–March 2018).

We are Social and Hootsuite. 2018. *2018 Digital Yearbook - Internet, Social Media, And Mobile Data for 239 Countries Around the World*.

White, S., Kuper, H., Itimu-Phiri, A., Holm, R. and Biran, A. 2016. A qualitative study of barriers to accessing water, sanitation and hygiene for disabled people in Malawi. *Plos One*, Vol. 11, No. 5, pp. e0155043. doi.10.1371/journal.pone.0155043.

Whittington, D., Jeuland, M., Barker, K. and Yuen, Y. 2012. Setting priorities, targeting subsidies among water, sanitation, and preventive health interventions in developing countries. *World Development*, Vol. 40, No. 8, pp. 1546–1568. doi.org/10.1016/j.worlddev.2012.03.004.

WHO (World Health Organization). 2011. *World Report on Disability*. Geneva, Switzerland. www.who.int/disabilities/world_report/2011/report.pdf.

_____. 2012. *UN-Water Global Analysis and Assessment of Sanitation and Drinking-Water (GLAAS) 2012 Report: The Challenge of Extending and Sustaining Services*. Geneva, WHO. www.who.int/water_sanitation_health/publications/glaas_report_2012/en/.

_____. 2015. *WHO Global Disability Action Plan 2014–2021. Better Health for all People with Disability*. Geneva, WHO. www.who.int/disabilities/actionplan/en/.

_____. 2016a. *World Health Statistics 2016: Monitoring Health for the SDGs*. Geneva, WHO. www.who.int/gho/publications/world_health_statistics/2016/en/.

_____. 2016b. *Health Statistics and Information Services. Disease Burden and Mortality Estimates*. WHO website. www.who.int/healthinfo/global_burden_disease/estimates/en/index1.html.

_____. 2017a. *Guidelines for Drinking-Water Quality, Fourth Edition, incorporating the First Addendum*. Geneva, WHO. www.who.int/water_sanitation_health/publications/drinking-water-quality-guidelines-4-including-1st-addendum/en/.

_____. 2017b. *UN-Water Global Analysis and Assessment of Sanitation and Drinking-Water (GLAAS) 2017 Report: Financing Universal Water, Sanitation and Hygiene under the Sustainable Development Goals*. Geneva, WHO. www.who.int/water_sanitation_health/publications/glaas-report-2017/en/.

_____. 2018. *WHO Fact Sheet: Obesity and Overweight*. WHO website. www.who.int/news-room/fact-sheets/detail/obesity-and-overweight. (accessed July 27, 2018).

_____. n.d. *TrackFin: Tracking Financing to Sanitation, Hygiene and Drinking-Water*. WHO website. www.who.int/water_sanitation_health/ monitoring/investments/trackfin/en/.

WHO/UNICEF (World Health Organization/United Nations Children's Fund). 2010. *Progress on Sanitation and Drinking Water: 2010 Update*. Geneva, WHO. www.who.int/water_sanitation_health/publications/9789241563956/en/.

_____. 2012. *Progress on Drinking Water and Sanitation: 2012 Update*. New York, UNICEF. www.unicef.org/publications/files/ JMPreport2012(1).pdf.

_____. 2013. *Post-2015 WASH Targets and Indicators*. www.unicef.org/wash/files/4_WSSCC_JMP_Fact_Sheets_4_UK_LoRes.pdf.

_____. 2015a. *Water, Sanitation and Hygiene in Health Care Facilities: Status in Low- and Middle-Income Countries and a Way Forward*. WASH in Health Care Facilities for Better Health Care Services. Geneva, WHO. apps.who.int/iris/bitstream/ handle/10665/154588/9789241508476_eng.pdf;jsessionid=58AC04B658866F927CD12D167D8A77AC?sequence=1.

_____. 2015b. *Progress on Drinking Water and Sanitation: 2015 Update and MDG Assessment*. Geneva, WHO. files.unicef.org/publications/ files/Progress_on_Sanitation_and_Drinking_Water_2015_Update_.pdf.

_____. 2016. *Inequalities in Sanitation and Drinking Water in Latin America and the Caribbean: A Regional Perspective based on Data from the WHO/UNICEF Joint Monitoring Programme (JMP) for Water Supply and Sanitation and an Inequality Analysis using Recent National Household Surveys and Censuses*. washdata.org/file/410/download.

_____. 2017a. *Progress on Drinking Water, Sanitation and Hygiene: 2017 Update and SDG Baselines*. Geneva, WHO/UNICEF. washdata.org/ sites/default/files/documents/reports/2018-01/JMP-2017-report-final.pdf.

_____. 2017b. *Safely Managed Drinking Water – Thematic Report on Drinking Water 2017*. Geneva, WHO. https://data.unicef.org/wp-content/uploads/2017/03/safely-managed-drinking-water-JMP-2017-1.pdf.

_____. 2018a. *Drinking Water, Sanitation and Hygiene in Schools: Global Baseline Report 2018*. New York, WHO/UNICEF. https://washdata. org/sites/default/files/documents/reports/2018-11/JMP%20WASH%20in%20Schools%20WEB%20final.pdf.

_____. 2018b. *A Snapshot of Drinking Water, Sanitation and Hygiene in the Arab Region: 2017 Update and SDG Baselines*. WHO/UNICEF Joint Monitoring Programme for Water Supply, Sanitation and Hygiene (JMP). www.unescwa.org/sites/www.unescwa.org/files/events/ files/jmp_arab_region_snapshot_20march2018_0.pdf.

_____. n.d. *Data*. WHO/UNICEF Joint Monitoring Programme for Water Supply, Sanitation and Hygiene (JMP). washdata.org/data.

WHO/WEDC (World Health Organization/Water, Engineering and Development Centre). 2011. *Delivering Safe Water by Tanker*. Technical Notes on Drinking-Water, Sanitation and Hygiene in Emergencies. Geneva/Loughborough, UK, WHO/WEDC. www.unicef.org/cholera/ Annexes/Supporting_Resources/Annex_9/WHO-tn12_safe_water_tanker_en.pdf.

Wilbur, J. 2010. *Principles and Practices for the Inclusion of Disabled People in Access to Safe Sanitation: A Case Study from Ethiopia*. WaterAid Briefing Note. UK, WaterAid. www.communityledtotalsanitation.org/sites/communityledtotalsanitation.org/files/media/ principles_practices_inclusive_sanitation.pdf.

Wilder, M. and H. Ingram. 2018. Knowing equity when we see it: Water equity in contemporary global contexts. K. Conca and E. Weinthal (eds.). *The Oxford Handbook of Water Politics and Policy*. New York, Oxford University Press. doi.org/10.1093/ oxfordhb/9780199335084.013.11.

Wong, S. and Guggenheim, S. 2018. *Community-Driven Development: Myths and Realities*. Policy Research Working Paper No. 8435. Washington, DC, World Bank. documents.worldbank.org/curated/en/677351525887961626/pdf/WPS8435.pdf.

World Bank. 2002. *Water Tariffs & Subsidies in South Asia: Understanding the Basics*. Working paper no. 1. Washington, DC, World Bank/ Water and Sanitation Program. documents.worldbank.org/curated/en/466651468776100746/pdf/265380PAPER0WSP0Water0tariffs0no-01. pdf.

_____. 2003. *Implementation of Operational Directive 4.20 on Indigenous Peoples: An Independent Desk Review*, Washington, DC, World Bank. documents.worldbank.org/curated/en/570331468761746572/pdf/multi0page.pdf.

_____. 2011. *Economic Assessment of Sanitation Interventions in the Philippines*. Technical paper. Washington, DC, World Bank/Water and Sanitation Program (WSP). documents.worldbank.org/curated/en/511481468094767464/pdf/724180WSP0Box30sessment0Philippines.pdf.

_____. 2012. *World Development Report 2012: Gender Equality and Development*. Washington, DC, World Bank. https://siteresources. worldbank.org/INTWDR2012/Resources/7778105-1299699968583/7786210-1315936222006/Complete-Report.pdf.

_____. 2013. *Investment Project Financing: Economic Analysis Guidance Note*. siteresources.worldbank.org/PROJECTS/ Resources/40940-1365611011935/Guidance_Note_Economic_Analysis.pdf.

_____. 2016a. *Poverty and Shared Prosperity 2016: Taking on Inequality*. Washington, DC, World Bank Group. https://openknowledge. worldbank.org/bitstream/handle/10986/25078/9781464809583.pdf.

_____. 2016b. *Science of Delivery for Quality Infrastructure and SDGs: Water Sector Experience of Output-Based Aid*. Working paper. Washington, DC, World Bank. documents.worldbank.org/curated/en/655991468143364878/pdf/Water-Sector-Study.pdf.

_____. 2016c. *5 Ways Public–Private Partnerships can promote Gender Equality*. Infrastructure & Public-Private Partnerships Blog, World Bank Group. https://blogs.worldbank.org/ppps/5-ways-public-private-partnerships-can-promote-gender-equality.

_____. 2017a. *Reducing Inequalities in Water Supply, Sanitation, and Hygiene in the Era of the Sustainable Development Goals: Synthesis Report of the WASH Poverty Diagnostic Initiative*. WASH Synthesis Report. Washington, DC, World Bank Group. openknowledge. worldbank.org/bitstream/handle/10986/27831/W17076ov.pdf?sequence=6.

_____. 2017b. *WASH Inequalities in the Era of the Sustainable Development Goals: Rising to the Challenge.* Global Synthesis Report of the Water Supply, Sanitation, and Hygiene (WASH) Poverty Diagnostic Initiative. Washington, DC, World Bank.

_____. 2018. *Kenya: Using Private Financing to Improve Water Services.* MFD briefs 05/2018. Washington, DC, World Bank. www.worldbank.org/en/about/partners/brief/kenya-using-private-financing-to-improve-water-services.

_____. n.d. *Harmonized List of Fragile Situations.* World Bank website. www.worldbank.org/en/topic/fragilityconflictviolence/brief/harmonized-list-of-fragile-situations.

World Bank/UNICEF (United Nations Children's Fund). 2017. *Sanitation and Water for All: How can the Financing Gap be Filled?* A Discussion Paper. Washington, DC, World Bank. https://openknowledge.worldbank.org/bitstream/handle/10986/26458/114545-WP-P157523-PUBLIC-SWA-Country-Preparatory-Process-Discussion-Paper-8-Mar-17.pdf?sequence=1&isAllowed=y.

WWAP (United Nations World Water Assessment Programme). 2006. *Water: A Shared Responsibility. The United Nations World Water Development Report 2.* Paris, UNESCO. unesdoc.unesco.org/images/0014/001454/145405E.pdf.

_____. 2012. *The United Nations World Water Development Report 4: Managing Water under Uncertainty and Risk.* Paris, UNESCO. www.unesco.org/new/fileadmin/MULTIMEDIA/HQ/SC/pdf/WWDR4%20Volume%201-Managing%20Water%20under%20Uncertainty%20and%20Risk.pdf.

_____. 2014. *The United Nations World Water Development Report 2014: Water and Energy.* Paris, UNESCO. unesdoc.unesco.org/images/0022/002257/225741E.pdf.

_____. 2015. *The WWAP Water and Gender Toolkit for Sex-Disaggregated Water Assessment, Monitoring and Reporting.* Gender and Water Series. UNESCO. www.unesco.org/new/en/natural-sciences/environment/water/wwap/water-and-gender/water-and-gender-toolkit/.

_____. 2016. *The United Nations World Water Development Report 2016: Water and Jobs.* Paris, UNESCO. unesdoc.unesco.org/images/0024/002439/243938e.pdf.

_____. 2017. *The United Nations World Water Development Report 2017: Wastewater – The Untapped Resource.* Paris, UNESCO. unesdoc.unesco.org/images/0024/002471/247153e.pdf.

WWAP/UN-Water (United Nations World Water Assessment Programme/United Nations Water). 2018. *The United Nations World Water Development Report 2018: Nature-Based Solutions for Water.* Paris, UNESCO. unesdoc.unesco.org/images/0026/002614/261424e.pdf.

Yeboah K. F. 2018. *Youth for Growth: Transforming Economies through Agriculture.* Chicago, Ill., The Chicago Council on Global Affairs. www.thechicagocouncil.org/publication/youth-growth-transforming-economies-through-agriculture.

Zahir, Y. 2009. *Water Balance Study for Kharaz Camp, Ras Al Aara and al-Madarba District, Lahj Governate, Yemen.* Research study prepared for UNHCR. Unpublished report.

Zarfl, C., Lumsdon, A. E., Berklekamp, J., Tydecks, L. and Tockner, K. 2015. A global boom in hydropower dam construction. *Aquatic Sciences,* Vol. 77, No. 1, pp. 161–170.

Zetter, R. and Ruaudel, H. 2016. *Refugees' Right to Work and Access to Labour Markets – An Assessment. Part 1: Synthesis.* Working Paper. Global Knowledge Platform on Migration and Development (KNOMAD). www.knomad.org/sites/default/files/2017-12/KNOMAD%20Study%201-%20Part%20II-%20Refugees%20Right%20to%20Work%20-%20An%20Assessment.pdf.

Abbreviations
and acronyms

AECID	Agencia Española de Cooperación Internacional para el Desarrollo – Spanish Agency for International Cooperation and Development
AIDS	Acquired Immune Deficiency Syndrome
ANDA	Autoridades de la Administración Nacional de Acueductos y Alcantarillados – National Water and Sewerage Administration of El Salvador
BIOPALT	BIOsphère et Patrimoine du Lac Tchad - BIOsphere and Heritage of Lake Chad
BOT	Build–operate–transfer
CDD	Community-driven development
DALYs	Disability-adjusted life years
DDT	Dichlorodiphenyltrichloroethane
DEWATS	Decentralized wastewater treatment systems
ECHO	European Civil Protection and Humanitarian Aid Operations
Eco-DRR	Nature-based solutions for disaster risk reduction
ESD	Education for sustainable development
EWS	Early warning systems
FAO	Food and Agriculture Organization of the United Nations
FESPAD	Fundación de Estudios para la Aplicación del Derecho – Foundation for Studies on the Application of Law in El Salvador
GDP	Gross domestic product
GEM	Global Education Monitoring
GLAAS	Global Analysis and Assessment of Sanitation and Drinking-Water
GPOBA	Global Partnership on Output-Based Aid
HALEP	High Alert List for Emergency Preparedness
HDI	Human Development Index
HICs	High-income countries
HIV	Human Immunodeficiency Virus
HRBA	Human rights-based approach
IBT	Inter-basin transfer (Chapter 2)
IBT	Increasing block tariff (Chapter 5)
ICESCR	International Covenant on Economic, Social and Cultural Rights
ICRC	International Committee of the Red Cross
ICT	Information and communication technology
IDPs	Internally displaced people
IFAD	International Fund for Agricultural Development
ILO	International Labour Organization
IPCC	Intergovernmental Panel on Climate Change

IWRM	Integrated water resources management
JMP	Joint Monitoring Programme
LDCs	Least Developed Countries
LMICs	Low- and middle-income countries
MAR	Managed aquifer recharge
MDGs	Millennium Development Goals
MHM	Menstrual health management
MICS	Multiple Indicator Cluster Survey
NGO	Non-governmental organization
ODA	Official development assistance
OHCHR	Office of the United Nations High Commissioner for Human Rights
OECD	Organisation for Economic Cooperation and Development
O&M	Operations and maintenance
POE	Point of entry
POU	Point of use
PPP	Purchasing power parity (Prologue, Chapters 7 and 9)
PPP	Public–private partnership (Chapters 5 and 10)
PRESIBALT	Programme de Réhabilitation et de Renforcement de la Résilience des Systèmes Socio-Ecologiques du Bassin du Lac Tchad - Programme to Rehabilitate and Strengthen the Resilience of Lake Chad Basin Systems
SDGs	Sustainable Development Goals
SMEs	Small- and medium-sized enterprises
SOIL	Sustainable Organic Integrated Livelihoods
SSS	Small-scale system
SUEN	Türkiye Su Enstitüsü – Turkish Water Institute
UIS	Urban Inequities Survey
UK	United Kingdom
UN	United Nations
UNDESA	United Nations Department of Economic and Social Affairs
UNESCAP	United Nations Economic and Social Commission for Asia and the Pacific
UNESCO	United Nations Educational, Scientific and Cultural Organization
UNHCR	United Nations High Commissioner for Refugees
UNICEF	United Nations International Children's Emergency Fund
USA	United States of America
USAID	United States Agency for International Development
UTI	Urinary tract infection
WASH	Water, Sanitation and Hygiene
WETUM	Water Employees Trade Union of Malawi
WGF	Water Governance Facility
WHO	World Health Organization
WSSCC	Water Supply and Sanitation Collaborative Council

Boxes, figures and tables

Boxes

Figures

Tables

Photo credits

THE UNITED NATIONS WORLD WATER DEVELOPMENT REPORT

ISBN 978-92-3-100264-9
© UNESCO 2018
156 pages
Price: EUR 45.00

WWDR 2018 Full colour, with boxes, figures, maps, tables, notes, photographs, references, and list of abbreviations and acronyms, as well as Forewords by UNESCO Director-General Audrey Azoulay and UN-Water Chair and IFAD President Gilbert F. Houngbo

ISBN 978-92-3-100309-7
© UNESCO 2019
202 pages
Price: EUR 45.00

WWDR 2019 Full colour, with boxes, figures, maps, tables, notes, photographs, references, and list of abbreviations and acronyms, as well as Forewords by UNESCO Director-General Audrey Azoulay and UN-Water Chair and IFAD President Gilbert F. Houngbo

To purchase a printed copy of the book, please visit: publishing.unesco.org

To request a CD-ROM containing the report and associated publications, please write to: wwap@unesco.org

To download the PDF format of the report and associated publications, WWDR previous editions and media material, please visit: www.unesco.org/water/wwap

USB key content: WWDR 2019, Executive Summary in nine languages, Facts and Figures in five languages and WWDR previous editions

ASSOCIATED PUBLICATIONS

Executive Summary of
the WWDR 2018

12 pages

Available in Arabic, Chinese, English, French, German, Hindi, Italian, Portuguese, Russian and Spanish

Facts and Figures from
the WWDR 2018

12 pages

Available in English, French, Italian, Portuguese and Spanish

Executive Summary of
the WWDR 2019

12 pages

Available in Arabic, Chinese, English, French, German, Hindi, Italian, Korean, Portuguese, Russian and Spanish

Facts and Figures from
the WWDR 2019

12 pages

Available in English, French, Italian, Portuguese and Spanish

To download these documents, please visit: www.unesco.org/water/wwap

United Nations
Educational, Scientific and
Cultural Organization

World Water
Assessment
Programme

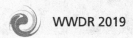
WWDR 2019

UN-Water coordinates the efforts of United Nations entities and international organizations working on water and sanitation issues. By doing so, UN-Water seeks to increase the effectiveness of the support provided to Member States in their efforts towards achieving international agreements on water and sanitation. UN-Water publications draw on the experience and expertise of UN-Water's Members and Partners.

Sustainable Development Goal 6 Synthesis Report 2018 on Water and Sanitation

The SDG 6 Synthesis Report 2018 on Water and Sanitation was published in June 2018 ahead of the High-level Political Forum on Sustainable Development where Member States reviewed SDG 6 in-depth. Representing a joint position from the United Nations family, the report offers guidance to understanding global progress on SDG 6 and its interdependencies with other goals and targets. It also provides insight into how countries can plan and act to ensure that no one is left behind when implementing the 2030 Agenda for Sustainable Development.

Sustainable Development Goal 6 Indicator Reports

This series of reports shows the progress towards targets set out in SDG 6 using the SDG global indicators. The reports are based on country data, compiled and verified by the United Nations agencies serving as custodians of each indicator. The reports show progress on drinking water, sanitation and hygiene (WHO/UNICEF Joint Monitoring Programme for Water Supply, Sanitation and Hygiene for targets 6.1 and 6.2), wastewater treatment and ambient water quality (UN Environment, UN-Habitat and WHO for target 6.3), water use efficiency and level of water stress (FAO for target 6.4), integrated water resources management and transboundary cooperation (UN Environment, UNECE and UNESCO for target 6.5), ecosystems (UN Environment for target 6.6) and means for implementing SDG 6 (UN-Water Global Analysis and Assessment of Sanitation and Drinking-Water for targets 6.a and 6.b).

World Water Development Report

This annual report, coordinated and published by UNESCO on behalf of UN-Water, represents the coherent and integrated response of the United Nations system to freshwater-related issues and emerging challenges. The theme of the report is harmonized with the theme of World Water Day (22 March) and changes annually.

Policy and Analytical Briefs

UN-Water's Policy Briefs provide short and informative policy guidance on the most pressing freshwater-related issues that draw upon the combined expertise of the United Nations system. Analytical Briefs provide an analysis of emerging issues and may serve as basis for further research, discussion and future policy guidance.

UN-WATER PLANNED PUBLICATIONS 2019

- Update of UN-Water Policy Brief on Water and Climate Change
- UN-Water Policy Brief on the Water Conventions
- UN-Water Analytical Brief on Water Efficiency